School Leadership for the 21st Century

The last few years have seen the reform and restructuring of education, not only in the UK but also in many other countries across the world. As a result of this, it is now more important than ever that school leaders and school managers develop the skills which will enable them to manage their new responsibilities effectively.

The success of reforms is determined not only by the nature of the reforms themselves, and how they are implemented, but also by a secondary wave of reform – changes in the leadership and management behaviour of individual school leaders. The key to full realisation of effective schooling in a reformed and restructured education system depends on the capability of the leaders and staff at the school level. Effective leaders need to have a clear conceptualisation of the changing context of education and the changing nature of self-managing schools. They also need to have a clear understanding of their own leadership and management skills within that environment. Only through this combination can they undertake successfully the key tasks of leading and managing a school. It is upon these leadership and management perspectives that this book focuses.

The book takes a competency and knowledge approach. It provides a clear framework which will enable school leaders to develop and reflect upon their own skills, and thus improve the effectiveness of their schools. All school managers will find that this book gives them a much needed insight into how to lead schools into the twenty-first century. It will be of particular value to those on HEADLAMP, the National Professional Qualification for Headteachers and other competency-based schemes.

Brent Davies is Professor and Director of Educational Leadership and Management at Lincoln University campus. **Linda Ellison** is Principal Lecturer in Education Management at Leeds Metropolitan University. Both have published very widely in the field.

School Leadership for the 21st Century

A competency and knowledge approach

Brent Davies and Linda Ellison

London and New York

First published 1997
by Routledge
11 New Fetter Lane, London EC4P 4EE

Simultaneously published in the USA and Canada
by Routledge
29 West 35th Street, New York, NY 10001

Selection and editorial material © 1997 Brent Davies and
Linda Ellison; individual chapters © their authors

Typeset in Palatino by Florencetype Ltd, Stoodleigh, Devon

Printed and bound in Great Britain by
Clays Ltd, St. Ives PLC

British Library Cataloguing in Publication Data
A catalogue record for this book is available from the British Library

Library of Congress Cataloging in Publication Data
School leadership for the 21st century : a competency and knowledge
    approach / Brent Davies and Linda Ellison.
        p.   cm.
    Includes bibliographical references and index.
    1. Educational leadership–Great Britain.   2. School management
and organization – Great Britain.   I. Davies, Brent, 1949–
II. Ellison, Linda.
LB2831.626.G7S36 1997
371.2'00941–dc20   96–21561
CIP

ISBN 0–415–13366–1

This book is dedicated to Brian Caldwell. For many years we have taken and used his ideas and they have proved a constant inspiration for our work. We are now delighted to integrate Brian's work into a book which we have written.

Contents

Figures

Tables

1 Introduction

Brent Davies

The reform and restructuring of education that has taken place in the United Kingdom and in many other countries initially encouraged those in schools and those responsible for schools to place a premium on developing skills that would enable them to manage effectively their new responsibilities. Significant in these new skills were those that were associated with self-managing or self-governing schools in the form of budgetary management and associated fields such as planning and marketing. Ten years after the 1988 Education Reform Act (DES 1988), the reforms it introduced can be seen to have had a profound effect on the education sector and have led to considerable reflection on the nature of effective reform. It is our contention that there are two waves of reform that occur in education systems. The first is the changes to the structure and framework of the system. In the case of the UK the National Curriculum, national testing and examination frameworks and school-based financial management allied to parental choice and new inspection and reporting systems can be seen to have been a radical reform and restructuring of the education system. The effectiveness of such reforms is of course partly determined by the nature of the reforms themselves and their implementation strategy but also in our view by the effectiveness of the second wave of the reform movement. This consists of the changes in the leadership and management behaviour of the individuals who are leading and managing the individual schools themselves. Just as the old saying that 'you can take a horse to water but you cannot make it drink' is true, so giving individual leaders and managers in schools new responsibilities and accountability relationships does not, in itself, make them innovative and educationally entrepreneurial when their previous experience was in directive risk-averse bureaucratic structures. The key to full realisation of effective schooling in a reformed and restructured education system depends on the capability of the leaders and the staff at the school level. We contend that having a clear understanding of the changing context in which education is now operating and of the constantly changing nature of self-managing schools, allied to a clear understanding by the educational leader of her/his own leadership and management skills to operate effectively in that environment, are pre-requisites to undertaking successfully the key tasks in leading and managing a school. These under-standings and skills enable the second wave of reform at school level, that of creating effective schools in this new environment, to take place. These leadership and management perspectives form the central thrust of this book.

THE NATURE AND FOCUS OF THE BOOK

This book provides a senior executive perspective on strategic leadership in self-managing schools for those seeking insights for leading and managing schools as they move into the twenty-first century. It draws on leading writers in the field to give all those engaged in senior manage-ment in schools a clear view of the key issues that face them and it outlines specific management strategies and approaches to competency development which should enable readers to deal better with those issues. The book is aimed at senior leaders and managers and governors in primary and secondary schools. It is of particular value to those on the HEADLAMP (Headteachers' Leadership and Management Programme) and National Professional Qualification for Headteachers schemes as it combines a similar competency and content approach. It is also focused on the increasing number of teachers undertaking higher degrees in edu-cational leadership and management.

There has been an explosion of interest and work in the development of management competence and competency approaches for leaders and managers in the education sector and we see this as the major thrust of leadership and management development work in the future. Our aim is to develop an innovative way of merging traditional knowledge approaches with competency approaches. In addition, while this book focuses on the present, it aims significantly to deliver a 'leading edge' and 'futures' perspective to educational leadership and management for the year 2000 and beyond. It is a 'theory into practice' book that aims to provide a framework to enable the development of visionary educa-tional leaders.

THE FRAMEWORK OF THE BOOK

The book is organised in three parts. These parts provide a conceptual framework for the reader to use as follows:

- Rethinking, reconceptualising and reassessing – the educational context, the school and personal leadership and management competencies.

- Reviewing key leadership and management areas.
- Envisaging the future.

Initially, by using a reengineering approach Part I seeks to develop a fundamental rethinking and reconceptualisation of three areas: the changing context in which the education sector is set, the nature of self-managing schools and the leadership and management competencies required of individuals working in this changing environment. This part provides a framework for analysing the individual and organisational competency needs that flow from the leadership and management knowledge content areas that are outlined in the following part.

Part II consists of nine key educational leadership and management knowledge areas to which the reader can review and apply the competency framework established in the first part. These knowledge areas are grouped into three sections: developing a broad strategic perspective, core leadership and management functions and facilitating the leadership and management process.

Part III takes a futures perspective on global educational trends that determine the nature of leadership and management in self-managing schools in the twenty-first century.

The chapters are grouped as follows:

Part I

Rethinking and reconceptualising

2   Rethinking the educational context: a reengineering
     approach
3   Reconceptualising the nature of self-managing schools

Reassessing leadership and management competencies

4   Understanding competence and competency
5   Determining and developing competencies in schools
6   Establishing a development framework for this book

Part II

Developing a broad strategic perspective

7   Developing a strategic perspective
8   Managing change
9   Leading and managing for quality

THE CONTRIBUTORS AND THEIR CHAPTERS

My co-editor Linda Ellison and I have brought together a number of leading figures in the educational leadership and management field to provide a strategic and futures orientation to the various chapters in this book. Chapters 1 and 2 emerge out of the work I have undertaken with Gib Hentschke at the University of Southern California. Gib was a reengineer before the term was brought into popular use in the early 1990s. His notion that we should stop doing 'dumb things' and should fundamentally rethink the nature of what we are doing, allied to applying a business paradigm, has been a major contribution to my thinking. Those readers with an English language or Classics education will no doubt be concerned with the lack of a hyphen in the word 'reengineer'. The original American usage is to leave it out – the total quality management movement would probably say that it did not add value! More recent UK versions of reengineering have split between inserting the hyphen and not. We will stay with my earlier USA version of the spelling. While in these chapters we use concepts imported from the business world, they are just that; Gib remains committed to the core educational values associated with educating the next generation of our respective nations' children. While critics of much modern management writing decry it as 'pop management' we believe that it is irrelevant where the ideas come from as long as they help us to develop our own frameworks for making sense of schools and their contexts and to develop strategies for effective leadership. Using a reengineering approach, these early chapters examine the radical changes about to impact on the education world and set out basic questions to ask about the nature and development of self-managing schools. While the chapters give a definition of reengineering (see p. 14), we consider it equally important to reengineer mind-sets as well as processes within organisations.

The work that I have undertaken with Alan Trotter has led to a fundamental rethinking in my understanding of the role of competencies in leadership and management development. Alan's work with the Coverdale organisation together with his work in schools, as shown in his excellent book *Better Self-Management: A Handbook for Education Staff* (Trotter 1993), has enabled him to bring business perspectives on competency to the educational world. Linda and I were able to experience the pioneering work done in the UK by the National Educational Assessment Centre (NEAC). This excellent process did a great deal to enhance our understanding of the field. Alan Trotter's work, initially with Linda and me but also latterly with John West-Burnham and Fergus O'Sullivan, has significantly helped us to form our own view of competency development. Chapters 4, 5 and 6 take the perspective that while the technical competency to undertake a specific task is important, of greater significance are the generic competencies that individuals bring to a variety of situations. These chapters also operate from the standpoint that, while undergoing some kind of external test or competency assessment may yield interesting results, there is a danger of limited ownership and empowerment if the participants of such a process see it as something done *to* them and not as a development process that they undertake. Our stance in the book therefore is one which rests on the leader or manager undertaking a series of self-directed activities individually and with peers to build her/his own competency development map. We believe that this builds greater participation in and ownership of the competency development process as well as greater commitment to implementing the development strategies emanating from it. There is a fundamental difference between being tested and developing one's own assessment framework. That difference we believe is ownership and commitment. In establishing a self-development framework, these chapters end with Chapter 6 outlining a framework that can be applied at the close of each of the chapters in Part II.

Part II reviews a number of key leadership and management areas. In Chapter 7 Linda and I build on the work that we first started and reported in *School Development Planning* (Davies and Ellison 1992). While the operational side of planning has more effectively incorporated the financial resource management elements, the major shift in planning work in schools has been to adopt a more strategic and 'futures' orientation. This chapter articulates a three stage model of 'futures thinking' (five to fifteen years), strategic planning (three to five years) and school development planning (one to three years) as one which is worthy of consideration by the strategic leader in the school. Following the establishment of a planning framework in this chapter, the task of managing the necessary transitions in a time of rapid and turbulent change is the focus of Viv Garrett's contribution in Chapter 8. Viv has worked extensively with senior managers nationally and internationally on adopting effective change strategies. This experience is reflected in a comprehensive and perceptive account of managing change. With effective leadership, strategy and change can be integrated into an organisation's culture, thus enabling the organisation to shift from rigid planning and sudden changes to one that is constantly adjusting and feeding back environmental changes into its pattern of organisation. Central to a strategic perspective is to integrate the concept of quality into all aspects of schooling. John West-Burnham's work on quality approaches to education has gained him a well-deserved national and international reputation in this field. Having written extensively in the field, since his book *Managing Quality in Schools* (West-Burnham 1992), John faced the difficult task of writing a new and insightful interpretation of the application of quality approaches. He has risen outstandingly to the task and the chapter, I am sure, will become a much quoted work in the field. Chapter 9 provides a very appropriate drawing together of the first section of Part II of the book.

The way that strategy, change and the quality organisation are managed and developed is obviously a key function of the people involved. Central to this is the role of the leader. John West-Burnham has worked on leadership development in the UK and overseas. His incisive analysis, in Chapter 10, of the key aspects of leadership provides a very thoughtful framework for readers to review their own leadership approaches. However, leadership should be considered as part of a wider involvement of staff in school management. Max Sawatzki undertakes a significant analysis of strategies and approaches to leading and managing staff for high performance in Chapter 11. Max has developed an international portfolio of clients in the business and education world with whom he works on developing strategic leadership and high performance management teams. His work with Brian Caldwell has made a major contribution to the thinking about self-managing schools on an international basis. Following consideration of the people dimension, Chapter 12 considers the core activity of a school, the management of learning and teaching. Tony Tuckwell and Mike Billingham are two outstanding headteachers and educational leaders with whom Linda and I have worked. Their strategic grasp of managing this process draws on a critical understanding of the literature and a wealth of professional experience.

In putting together the three chapters that facilitate the leadership and management process in schools we were fortunate in obtaining the contributions of two nationally recognised experts in the field, Peter Downes and John Warwick. I first came across Peter Downes' work on self-managing schools when I invited him to become a keynote speaker on school finance at a national conference in the mid-1980s. His reputation in the field was further enhanced by his book *Local Financial Management in Schools* (Downes 1988) and the intervening years have witnessed a prodigious output in addresses and articles together with his work for the Secondary Heads Association and, in particular, its work on funding formulae based on activity led staffing as reported in *A Better Cake: Towards a Rational Approach to Funding* (West *et al.* 1994). In Chapter 13 Peter puts forward a leading example of effective financial management in schools. John Warwick, who is an Associate Director of SIMS Ltd, has been working at the leading edge of the development of information technology for school management for well over a decade. When much of the debate on technology concentrates on the operational level of what system or what machinery to buy, John's chapter (15) focuses on the major strategic questions that face leaders and managers in schools in understanding the strategic dimensions of information flows in organisations. He concludes the chapter with a very perceptive review of current and future developments in technology and their impact on schools. These understandings provide a vital part of the competencies that leaders and managers require. In between these two chapters Linda and I have been able to extend our earlier work on marketing (see Davies and Ellison 1991) by making a significant shift to developing a more strategic view of markets and the marketing process. One of the dangers of marketing is that schools get involved too rapidly in the individual processes and do not stand back and assess the strategic cycle and importance. Chapter 14 develops that strategic perspective for the leader of a school.

Brian Caldwell's work on self-managing schools has probably made him *the* international expert in the field. His ground-breaking books with Jim Spinks *The Self-Managing School* (Caldwell and Spinks 1988) and *Leading the Self-Managing School* (Caldwell and Spinks 1992), have become not only international best-sellers but also the key works in the field. When Linda and I needed an author to set the scene for the future of self-managing schools, Brian was the natural choice for Part III. In the event, even our very high expectations for the final chapter were outstandingly exceeded. Brian wrote two chapters which provide international 'leading edge' insights into the nature of leading and managing schools in the next millennium. They provide the launchpad for visionary leadership in schools in the twenty-first century.

Linda and I, in putting this book together, aimed to produce a volume that would be seen not as a collection of individual chapters but as an integrated approach which would enable readers to form their own understandings and, most importantly, in using the competency development framework, to build their own development maps. To this end we wish you well as you travel through the book!

REFERENCES

Caldwell, B. J. and Spinks, J. M. (1988) *The Self-Managing School*, London: Falmer.
Caldwell, B. J. and Spinks, J. M. (1992) *Leading the Self-Managing School*, London: Falmer.
Davies, B. and Ellison, L. (1991) *Marketing the Secondary School*, Harlow: Longman.
Davies, B. and Ellison, L. (1992) *School Development Planning*, Harlow: Longman.
Department of Education and Science (1988) *Education Reform Act*, London: HMSO.
Downes, P. (1988) *Local Financial Management in Schools*, Oxford: Blackwell.
Trotter, A. (1993) *Better Self-Management: A Handbook for Education Staff*, Harlow: Longman.
West, A., West, R. and Pennell, A. (1994) *A Better Cake: Towards a Rational Approach for Financing Education*, report commissioned by the Secondary Heads Association, London: Centre for Educational Research, London School of Economics and Political Science.
West-Burnham, J. (1992) *Managing Quality in Schools*, Harlow: Longman.

Part I

Rethinking and reconceptualising

Reassessing leadership and management competencies

2 Rethinking the educational context
A reengineering approach

Brent Davies

Leaders and managers in schools are faced with the challenge of operating in a rapidly changing world. In this world the globalisation of economic systems, technological advance and the increased expectations that society has of its education system have replaced past certainties with new and uncertain frameworks. Dynamic change has become the order of the day. How do leaders and managers meet this challenge and develop approaches in order to operate successfully in this new environment? We would suggest that, faced with the increasing complexities of the modern world, school leaders need to understand three key perspectives, each of which is itself operating at three different levels, namely that of the wider global environment, that of the organisation and that of the individual.

The first perspective to understand is the changing nature of the wider society in which schools are set. This involves not only understanding the globalisation of economic, societal and technological trends and how they manifest themselves today but also involves assessing how they are likely to impact on schools in the future. An interesting combination of forces – the reengineering movement (called business process reengineering) from the business world and the reform and restructuring movement in education – is providing a useful framework to rethink radically the context in which we work. That is the focus of this chapter.

The second perspective involves a more complex analysis of the self-managing schools themselves and the possible future trends in autonomy that may develop. School-site management has been implemented in several countries, but delegation to schools has often been in the context of administrative devolution of powers rather than freeing up schools to have extensive control of their own affairs. In a sense, there is now a second wave of devolution, where concepts of extensive devolution *within schools* as well as more extensive autonomy *for schools* are being considered to replace the existing forms of administrative devolution. Chapter 3 focuses on reconceptualising the nature of self-managing schools in the future.

The third perspective concerns the need for the individual leaders and managers in schools to understand clearly the nature and extent of their own leadership and management competencies and their management knowledge. Each leader needs a realistic assessment of her/his own current abilities so that the gap between those and the leadership skills likely to be needed in the future can be filled. This involves setting out a personal development map and action plan based on an assessment process of competence and competency. This is the focus of Chapters 4, 5 and 6.

RETHINKING THE EDUCATIONAL CONTEXT

A child starting school at the age of five in the year 2000 has a long educational journey to the completion of a university or a vocational education and will probably not start work until the year 2015 or later. That same child will be in the labour force in the year 2050 and beyond. What is more, that child could be working with technologies that have not yet been invented in an organisation that has yet to be created. While it is necessary that those with strategic responsibilities in schools must have the management skills to operate in today's educational environment, it is also very important that they develop the educational leadership capacity to challenge today's orthodoxy and to envision what the future educational and societal framework will be. It is one of the roles of leaders of educational organisations to interpret and make sense of future realities for members of their organisations. We are very good at looking backwards but not so effective at looking forward to the same extent. This paradox can be illustrated by the work of Beare and Slaughter (1993: 145) who use the concept of the 'extended present' as in Figure 2.1.

While most families can trace back, through oral history provided by their parents and grandparents, events of fifty or eighty years ago they find it more difficult to envisage some of the trends that will shape the future even in ten or fifteen years' time. This illustrates a fundamental flaw in both our personal lives and our professional lives; we need to have a view not only of our current situation and how we have arrived there but also of the longer-term future if we are to set our leadership and management actions in the appropriate context.

The problem that faces the educational leader in the school is that incremental patterns of management behaviour and of thinking predominate. One of the major contributory factors to this is the budgetary process. Annual budgets encourage, by their very nature, a year-on-year pattern of development. Managers in schools see the flexibility and framework for action in terms of whether there will be a marginal increase or decrease in funding in the next year. As a result, managers

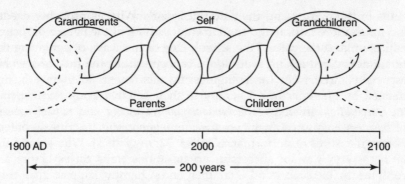

Figure 2.1 The extended present: the family chain

often see themselves as reacting to a series of short-term financial time horizons rather than being able to take the longer view. This encourages traditional incremental thinking to spill over into other areas such as curriculum and the nature of teaching and learning.

One of the means of adjusting to new ways of thinking has been to adopt ideas from the Total Quality Management movement. Certainly, concepts of focusing on the customer, setting benchmarks, defining fitness for purpose and aiming for continuous improvement are valuable ways of thinking in establishing effective management practices. These four ideas can be seen to be working themselves through certain parts of the education system. There is now a greater focus on the customer, for example by listening and taking into account the views of parents and children, both in the formal mechanisms of school choice and in the approaches to management within the school. Setting up benchmarks and defining fitness for purpose took a significant step forward during the first half of the 1990s. Indeed in the UK the Office for Standards in Education (OFSTED) can be considered to be establishing criteria for 'fitness for purpose' in its standards of assessment. The emergence, in many countries, of state curriculum and testing frameworks has put a floor under standards by providing benchmarks against which to assess progress. As well as this 'control and accountability culture', it is also evident that there has been the development of an 'improvement culture'. This is demonstrated by the increased emphasis on school planning as witnessed by the School Development Planning initiative in the UK and the School Charter initiative in Australia as means of school improvement.

However, as Davies (1994) points out in 'TQM: an idea whose time has come and gone', incremental improvement, while beneficial, will not be enough to cope with the changes facing schools in the future. Incremental change may not be sufficient for dealing with the fundamental shifts in technology and the pattern of work. What is probably needed is a much more radical and fundamental rethink of the nature of society, education and the role of the school. One of the ways of achieving this fundamental rethinking is to adopt concepts from the business world, especially those from the reengineering movement. Reengineering, as defined by Hammer and Champy in their seminal book *Reengineering the Corporation*, involves 'the *fundamental rethinking* and *radical redesign* of *business processes* to achieve *dramatic improvement* in critical contemporary measures of performance' (1993: 32; my italics). Why should this be necessary? Cannot successful organisations carry on as before and continue to be successful? Hammer and Champy suggest that three forces are driving companies into a new and unfamiliar operational context. Those forces are *customers*, *competition*, and *change*.

Customers

The mass market developed in the 1950s, 1960s and 1970s. During this time customers were glad to receive any product but this situation has now changed to one of a 'quality product' approach aimed at individual customers. The following factors can be seen to have emerged during the 1980s and 1990s in Western economies:

- Customers have experienced quality and good service and expect more and better quality in the future.
- Customers are better informed, having more data on which to make their decisions.
- Customers know their legal rights in cases of dispute.
- Customers are less deferential.
- Customers dictate what they want, when they want it and how they want to pay for it.
- Customers want to be seen as individuals and to receive a customised product.
- Customers are aware that there is a plentiful supply and that they can pick and choose.

The parallel trends in the education sector in general, and the school sector in particular, are almost identical. State curriculum and testing frameworks are providing benchmarks to help parents to measure the quality of education received and the achievement made by their children. The culture in which the school knew best and parents were kept at arm's length has been replaced by a move to a more equal home/school relationship. Selection of school through open enrolment legislation has, in several countries, increased choice and given more power to the parent as customer. However a fundamental problem has emerged in that, while customers expect and receive 100 per cent quality when they buy consumer goods, there is less satisfaction with the products and services from the public sector, including the education service. OFSTED inspection reports highlight that 20 per cent of lessons at Key Stage 3 (age 11-14) are less than satisfactory (OFSTED 1996). This divergence between increasing quality standards in the material goods markets, where consumers expect high quality all the time, and the public sector, where serious quality problems remain, produces comparisons which cause friction between the consumers and producers of education services.

Competition

The increasing importance of the customer is evident in markets where there is increasing competition. Chapter 13 considers that the establishment of quasi-markets in education has brought competitive forces into play within the education sector. What is happening in the global goods and services market in terms of competition? Hammer and Champy (1993) see competitive pressures as producing a situation where:

> Good performers drive out the inferior, because the lowest price, the highest quality, the best service available from any one of them soon becomes the standard for all competitors. Adequate is no longer good enough. If a company can't stand shoulder to shoulder with the world's best in a competitive category, it soon has no place to stand at all.
>
> (Hammer and Champy 1993: 21)

What are the features of the intensified competition in the global economy that are affecting companies and forcing them to reassess their position? The following highlight some of these:

- Low wage economies of the Far East and China are allying themselves to high technology to threaten traditional firms and there are more recent forms of competition from Eastern Europe and the old Soviet Empire.
- Technological leaders are emerging with new firms starting up without the 'baggage' that traditional firms have in terms of structures and costs and they are driving the traditional firms out of business.
- Niche targeting of specific markets means that entrepreneurial firms are establishing bridgeheads in markets previously dominated by large corporations.

Does any of this apply to education? Is education not somehow different from the business world? While it may be different, education is not isolated from the pressures and trends that are making themselves increasingly evident. Global competition has a profound impact on the future of our children. Unless they develop high quality thinking, problem-solving and technological skills to compete with the best in the world, they will be competing for the low wage/low skill jobs. Also, competition among existing suppliers of education (schools), while in itself increasing, is being joined by competition from non-traditional sources including technology. Access to high quality education via satellite and Internet sources may challenge our traditional perception of how individuals obtain education; schools may no longer be the prime source. Chapter 14 explores the changes that schools are having to make by adopting marketing strategies to respond to competition. While a competitive environment forces organisations to be able to change in response to changes in that environment, it is also necessary to understand the nature of change itself.

Change

Constant change, and increasingly rapid change, can be seen to be the norm. Indeed we may be undergoing a very fundamental change, as described by Peter Drucker (1993):

> Every few hundred years in Western history there occurs a sharp transformation ... Within a few short decades, society rearranges itself ... its world view; its basic values; its social and political structures ...We are currently living through such a transformation.
>
> (Drucker 1993: 1)

Drucker goes on to state 'knowledge is fast becoming the sole factor of production, sidelining both capital and labor' (1993: 33). For those of us employed in the knowledge industry the implications are profound. The key points to consider are:

- Change has become pervasive, persistent and normal.
- There is an accelerating rate of technological advance.
- The business cycle and the economic cycle are no longer predictable.

Thus,

- The nature of work, the economy and employment in the future are also uncertain.
- All products have shorter life-cycles, reducing from years to months.

One of the big myths in education is that the changes initiated in the 1980s have worked their way through the system and that we are now in a stable pattern for the next few years. It would seem that the expectations of customers, the nature of competition and the ongoing rate of change itself are unlikely to leave education in a backwater. Education should be at the forefront of society's attempts to come to terms with this new reality. It is difficult to imagine that education, and the nature of schooling, will not itself have to change radically. The nature of change is considered in detail in Chapter 8.

FUNDAMENTAL RETHINKING AND RADICAL REDESIGN

The most significant concept in reengineering as explained in Hammer and Champy (1993) and subsequently reinforced in Hammer and Stanton's excellent book *The Reengineering Revolution: A Handbook* (1995) is that:

> The verb 'to reengineer' takes as its object a business process and nothing else. We reengineer how work is done, how outputs are created from inputs. We cannot and do not reengineer organizational units.
>
> (Hammer and Champy 1993: 17)

This places the emphasis away from traditional attempts at restructuring which have resulted, for example, at the secondary stage of education in restructuring efforts in changing from department to faculty structures with little impact on the learning and teaching practices. Reengineering would involve focusing on core processes such as the coherence and progression of the learning processes experienced by children and how they can be improved. This links to the well-known strategic management maxim that 'structure follows strategy'. In reengineering it is necessary to focus on processes not on structures. Typically a process crosses a number of organisational boundaries. The primary/ secondary transfer stage presents an interesting example. In the primary school one teacher is responsible for a whole class, teaching a range of subjects and ensuring a holistic view of the child's learning development. In the secondary school the child, a month or so later, can have eight or ten teachers teaching up to forty time slots. How is the coherence of the holistic learning process being managed? There has been a restructuring into a number of organisational units called departments but what consideration is given to the coherence of the learning process? Some secondary schools have rethought this abrupt change to a child's learning processes and grouped pupils in larger time blocks with a smaller team of teachers to preserve the coherence of the learning process. This is a good example of a process-orientated approach. At a more simple administrative level many teachers who seek to register on higher degree programmes at universities are confronted with systems based on undergraduate registration processes. They have to fill in extensive registration forms and trek from table to table, queuing each time, in order to sort out finance, registrations, and so on when all they want to do is to provide a name and address and pay money. How often are processes considered from the consumers' point of view?

Other key concepts involve the radical redesign to achieve dramatic improvements. 'Radical' is defined as going to the 'root of things' and is a zero-based approach to find and treat causes of organisational ineffectiveness and not merely to treat the symptoms. 'Redesign' is where the old is thrown away and individuals start with the proverbial 'clean slate'. In education, where marginal increases in funding are not going to make significant differences to learning outputs, it is the fundamental redesign of learning that will make the difference. Finally reengineering involves making things dramatically better and not an incremental five per cent better.

For the purposes of this book, I should like to extend or interpret the definition of reengineering to focus on two major concepts. One is that we focus on reengineering processes in education and the second is that we give equal importance to reengineering 'mind-sets' so that the way in which individuals think about a situation and can achieve a significant paradigm shift in their thinking is seen as a prime achievement as well as the redesign of a core school process.

In this context it is clear that, instead of thinking about how we can get the most out of existing structures and resources, what is needed is *breakthrough* thinking. We have all been told many times: 'I should like to do that but we don't have the resources.' The speaker is either waiting for a fairy godmother (or should it be godperson?) to wave a magic wand, in order to get more resources, and will do nothing until that happens or s/he is incapable of rethinking how to tackle a particular challenge. One reality of public finance in the UK, the USA and Australia is that funds from public sources are not going to increase significantly; in fact they will become more constrained. If we are to lead and manage in this environment, a reengineering approach within existing resources would suggest that some basic questions are asked:

- Why do we do what we do?
- What do customers (pupils) really need?
- Does what we do contribute significant 'added value' to the education product?

We should be ignoring the *what is* and concentrating on the *what should be* framework for analysis. It could be considered as planning backwards; what are the outcomes which we want? We need to focus on what we must do as a school before we come to worry about how to do it. Then we have to think differently about how to do it. We cannot significantly improve the quality of our school by simply working harder. We have to work smarter not harder, and the smarter course involves not slicker ways of doing the same things but fundamentally different ways of

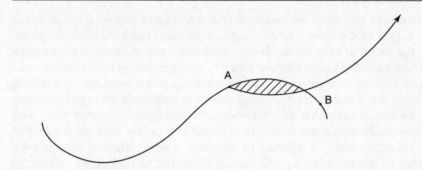

Figure 2.2 The Sigmoid curve

doing those things. A useful saying to remember is that 'sacred cows make the best burgers'. All organisations have things that they believe have to be done in certain ways or cannot be changed and it is by fundamentally rethinking those core factors that we are likely to achieve breakthrough thinking. It is clear why this should be necessary. There has been a vast improvement in the reliability and quality of consumer goods over the last twenty years, spearheaded by Japanese manufacturers. We now expect new cars to be perfect and not to have to return them for initial faults to be corrected. Yet in education, for a considerable period of time, reports from both Her Majesty's Inspectorate (HMI) and OFSTED have indicated a significant proportion of unsatisfactory lessons. We need a dramatic improvement in educational standards to achieve quality in present situations, let alone the standards which we will need to achieve in order to meet the educational demands of the next millennium. Thus, performance improvements to meet the challenge of the future will have to be dramatic.

The precise nature of such improvements in your school will depend in part on whether it is going through a period of success or not. Major improvement is critical in both cases but it is more difficult to demonstrate when the school is perceived to be successful. Charles Handy, in *The Empty Raincoat: Making Sense of the Future* (Handy 1994), employs an interesting conceptual tool called the Sigmoid curve (Figure 2.2).

Handy suggests that most organisations rise and fall or expand and contract in a way very similar to a sine wave. The challenge for leadership in successful schools is to spot when the organisation is at point A and to reengineer so that the school does not rest on its laurels when it is still improving. It must take the risk of moving on to a new Sigmoid curve and not wait to change until it is moving downwards at point B. Handy expresses this as follows:

> The right place to start that second curve is at point A, where there is time, as well as the resources and the energy, to get the curve

through its initial explorations and floundering before the first curve begins to dip downwards. That would seem obvious; were it not for the fact that at point A all the messages coming through to the individual or the institution are that everything is going fine, that it would be folly to change when the current recipes are working so well. All that we know of change, be it personal change or change in organisations, tells us that the real energy for change only comes when you are looking disaster in the face, at point B on the first curve. At this point, however, it is going to require a mighty effort to drag oneself up to where, by now, one should be on the second curve.

(Handy 1994: 51–2)

REENGINEERING: CROSS-NATIONAL EDUCATIONAL INSIGHTS

Considerable interest is being shown in the reengineering and reinventing of education by leading thinkers and authors in different countries. In England, David Hargreaves, in *The Mosaic of Learning* (D. Hargreaves 1994), challenges many conceptions about the nature of schooling in the next century. This finds strong parallels in North America with Louis Gerstner and colleagues in *Reinventing Education* (Gerstner *et al.* 1994) and Andy Hargreaves in *Changing Teachers, Changing Times* (A. Hargreaves 1994). This is also true in Australia with Brian Caldwell's well-known work on the future of self-managing schools (see, for example, Caldwell 1994). What fundamental trends can be seen as emerging across these countries? Here are some interpretations:

- The development of state and national curriculum and testing frameworks is providing measures of output and value-added, thus increasing information for parental choice.
- Relating value-added educational gains to resource levels allows schools to be compared in terms of 'value for money'. How can they achieve increased performance with the same resource level?
- Increased differentiation between schools encourages more specialised provision.
- Significantly enhanced levels of parental choice.
- Considerable changes in staffing patterns and arrangements, more para-professionals, core and periphery staff, fixed-term performance-led contracts, school-site pay bargaining.
- Radical changes in the nature of teaching and learning as the impact of the new teaching and learning technologies gathers pace.
- Greater varieties of finance with blurring between state-only and private-only funding of schools.
- Contracting out of educational as well as service elements of schooling.

- A re-examination of the boundaries between different stages of education and between education and the community.
- Redefinition of the leadership and management functions in schools.

These are all trends that are apparent now but what will be their impact in the future? How will we think of the nature of schools and schooling? What we need to do is to think differently about the nature of schools. While these macro trends are apparent, how do we get this sort of thinking down to the level of the day-to-day operation of the school? This is not very easy. A simple case study illustrates how the problem of incremental thinking predominates. A school in the UK, 'Moortown', is oversubscribed by sixty pupils each year. It is an 11–18 school with no other school nearby. The Local Education Authority refuses entry to these extra pupils each year, stating that the school is full to capacity. A closer examination of the case study school reveals some interesting factors. The school opens for pupils for 190 days a year (i.e. 52 per cent of the time), and during those days pupils operate an 8.30am to 2.30pm day (25 per cent of the time). As a result the building, as a fixed asset, is used for 13 per cent of the total possible time. This raises some interesting questions. Do children only learn in that 13 per cent or does learning also take place in the other 87 per cent of the time? The answer is obviously the latter. Once the perspective of schools being facilitators of learning and not the sole providers of education is accepted, then a little more creative thinking can be encouraged. Can Moortown School only be expanded by extra capital expenditure which produces buildings that are used only for 13 per cent of the time? Or can different patterns of attendance for different age groups be used? Can staff have different working hours and conditions? Can greater use be made of technology so that 'learning' takes place when teachers are not there? Can other adults be used as coaches as well as fully trained staff? The ideas that can be generated are many but our traditional way of thinking usually does not encompass them. We need far more radical interpretations of possible future scenarios. Will all the children be attending for five days in ten years' time? Will part of the lessons be conducted at home using the computer? Will traditional libraries become information centres bringing all pupils the best of the best all the time by using available technologies? Will the teachers work in support teams and facilitate the access to differing learning resources? What will the internal organisation in terms of buildings look like? Will they be the traditional classrooms of four hundred years ago or be radically different? Redesigning learning processes needs a radical shift in the 'mind-set' of our educational leaders.

What seems clear is that, even if marginal extra resources were available, a reduction in class size by one or two children is not going to improve the learning process radically. In fact, more of the same instead of radical rethinking is not going to engage those children who currently do not actively commit to education. Different patterns of education and resource use would seem to be the answer.

In order to break out of our current ways of thinking and to do things differently, two questions to ask are 'what leadership skills are needed to reconceptualise the learning process?' and 'what degree of organisational autonomy will be needed in order to do things differently?' The leadership skills and competencies form the basis of Chapters 4, 5 and 6 while Chapter 3 undertakes a radical reassessment of the organisational unit of the self-managing school by developing a taxonomy to assess possible future developments.

Chapter 3 asks how we can apply this sort of thinking to the self-managing schools operating as Locally Managed Schools (LMS), Grant-Maintained Schools (GMS) and City Technology Colleges (CTCs) in the UK and similar site-based reforms in Australia, New Zealand and the United States of America. It engages in a critical review of the nature of school autonomy in its present form and then poses questions about its potential over the next ten years.

REFERENCES

Beare, H. and Slaughter, R. (1993) *Education for the Twenty-First Century*, London: Routledge.

Caldwell, B. J. (1994) *Resourcing the Transformation of School Education*, Inaugural Professorial Lecture, University of Melbourne.

Davies, B. (1994) 'TQM: a theory whose time has come and gone', *Management in Education* 8 (1): 12–13.

Drucker, P. F. (1993) *Post-Capitalist Society*, New York: Harper Business.

Gerstner, L. V., Semerad, R. D., Doyle, D. P. and Johnson, W. B. (1994) *Reinventing Education: America's Public Schools*, New York: Dutton.

Hammer, M. and Champy, J. (1993) *Reengineering the Corporation: A Manifesto for Business Revolution*, New York: Harper Collins.

Hammer, M. and Stanton, S. A. (1995) *The Reengineering Revolution: A Handbook*, New York: Harper Business.

Handy, C. (1994) *The Empty Raincoat: Making Sense of the Future*, London: Hutchinson.

Hargreaves, A. (1994) *Changing Teachers, Changing Times*, London: Cassell.

Hargreaves, D. (1994) *The Mosaic of Learning: Schools and Teachers for the New Century*, London: Demos.

OFSTED (1996) *Annual Report of Her Majesty's Chief Inspector of Schools*, London: HMSO.

3 Reconceptualising the nature of self-managing schools

Gib Hentschke and Brent Davies

INTRODUCTION

The impact of the trends outlined in the previous chapter requires us to rethink the nature of education and, in particular, that of schools. Does their decentralised management and autonomy place them in a position to achieve radical redesign and rethinking? Autonomy for schools can be thought of in a paradigm of 'whales and minnows'. Previously, regionally organised 'whales' (the LEAs) were slow and laborious creatures to turn and change direction. Conversely 'the minnows', hundreds of schools linked by information (like a neural net), should be able instantaneously to react and change direction. But have we set up autonomy for schools (the minnows) to give them that freedom or are they still encompassed in the larger bureaucracy (the whales)? The possibility exists of course for all of the minnows to be swimming in different directions!

Developments in school autonomy have received enthusiastic promotion and support from politicians and the community. But has anything significantly changed in the internal organisation or in the performance of schools? Early research has focused on describing what has happened, identifying perceived initial managerial improvements and hoped for future benefits (see, for example, Bullock and Thomas 1994; Levačić 1995). Very little research has tried to identify the fundamental shifts in decision-making in schools that could lead to significant improvements in school performance. What is needed is a framework to examine whether any fundamental reengineering changes in school decision-making practice have taken place. However, a clearer understanding of the nature of managerial decisions in general, and decision-making in autonomous organisations in particular, is necessary before an analysis of decentralised schooling is undertaken. To engage in fundamental rethinking of the nature of self management, this chapter examines what is meant by organisational autonomy and then establishes a taxonomy of managerial decisions which is then used to consider the nature of autonomy in schools.

THE MOVE TO SCHOOL AUTONOMY

Throughout many parts of the world governments and educators are promoting the benefits of significantly increased autonomy for those who work in local schools. These arguments for increased autonomy in schools are similar arguments to those directed at organisations in the business sector: 'Get the decisions about how to run the firm down to the people who know best what needs to be done.' Current arguments about changes in school governance and management all aim in this one direction, although they travel under a variety of names – 'local management of schools', 'school-based management', 'shared decision-making', 'self-managing schools', 'self-governing schools', 'locally autonomous schools', 'devolution', and 'restructured schools'. Regardless of the specific label applied, the terms are meant to describe 'a school in a system of education where there has been significant and consistent decentralisation to the school level of authority to make decisions related to the allocation of resources' (Caldwell and Spinks 1992: 4).

The justifications for this move are several and persuasive in their logic, at least if the premises are accepted. The political justification for decentralisation – the argument that the closer government is to 'the people' the more likely it is to be responsive to their demands and interests – assumes the worthiness of people getting what they want for themselves from government. The economic arguments for decentralisation – that decentralised units foster necessary competition in sheltered monopolies and are more likely to produce offerings in line with the preferences ('needs' and 'desires') of local, more homogeneous, groups of consumers/citizens – add efficiency and effectiveness to the other worthy goal of public sector responsiveness. Thomas (1987) argues that decentralised unit managers are better able to make choices to maximise efficiency because:

> The unit managers are (i) closer to the clients; and (ii) better able than more remotely sited managers to identify the needs of the clients. In addition unit managers (iii) will give primacy to satisfying these needs; and (iv) will also know the best (i.e., most efficient) way of combining available resources to meet as many of these needs as possible. Finally, in making decisions on resource combinations the unit managers will vary the proportion of different resources as (v) production requirements and (vi) relative prices change.
>
> (Thomas 1987: 26)

These arguments about the improvements through increased school autonomy are part of similar arguments about the benefits of decentralisation in all organisations. These, again, include the benefits of increased flexibility in response to changing circumstances, enhanced effectiveness, greater rates of innovation, higher morale, greater worker commitment, and greater productivity.

Although the intensity and variety of arguments for decentralisation in general, as well as the scope of associated legislative activity over the last two decades, is impressive and compelling, it does not seem to follow automatically (to us at least) that these arguments point to an effective degree of decentralisation that provides sufficient autonomy in decision-making that could significantly enhance the teaching and learning process and in turn significantly enhance the input/output equation of educational productivity.

We have examined reform efforts in the United States of America and in England (in general terms, both are heading toward increased autonomy for schools but are doing so in ways which appear to be fundamentally different) in order to assess the degree of decentralisation and subsequent real autonomy in decision-making. In our attempt to understand the variety of changes within and between both countries we have sought first to gain some sense of the shift in management rights. What has really changed *managerially*?

UNDERSTANDING INCREASED SCHOOL AUTONOMY IN THE CONTEXT OF OTHER ORGANISATIONS

In order better to appreciate the relevance of those specific changes in schools, we have sought to place them in a broader context of management decisions and management rights in all organisations (see Davies and Hentschke 1994). This, for us, has meant asking two other questions. What might be the taxonomy of all major management decisions within which we might locate 'traditional' (non-decentralised) as well as 'restructured' (decentralised) schools? Then, in the context of that taxonomy, we seek to ascertain if 'restructured' schools are in some fundamental way different from 'traditional' schools, and if so, by how much.

We are using 'management decisions' as a variable for placing schools on a continuum of organisational autonomy. We felt that if we could identify the major categories of managerial decisions made in organisations and then ascertain whether managers inside or above the organisation had the right to make those decisions, we would have some sense of how realistic and useful are the current arguments for, and changes in, school autonomy. At one extreme of this continuum is an organisational unit such as a division of a larger company in which, in theory, all of the major management decisions reside with the 'parent organisation', that is, authorities above and/or beyond the organisational unit. At the other extreme is an organisational unit which is essentially an 'autonomous business', wherein those same major management decisions sit *within* that organisational unit. All organisational units, including US and English primary and secondary schools, would fall somewhere within the boundaries of totally autonomous organisations at one extreme and, at the other extreme, totally 'dependent' organisations.

The concept of using management decisions as a variable is a difficult one for several reasons. First, managerial decisions may be 'sector bound'. Some of the decision rights which describe the autonomy of an organisation are exclusively associated with one economic sector and not others. The following generalisations which characterise differences between public and private sector organisations are not uncommon:

> Government and business are fundamentally different institutions. Business leaders are driven by the profit motive; government leaders are driven by the desire to get re-elected. Businesses earn their income from their customers. Governments get most of their money from taxpayers. Businesses are usually driven by competition; governments usually use monopolies. Because politicians tend to be driven by interest groups, public managers – unlike their private counterparts – must factor interest groups into every equation. ... All of these factors combine to produce an environment in which public employees view risks and rewards very differently than do private employees.
>
> (Osborne and Gaebler 1992: 21–2)

If sectoral differences are so inherent and so fundamental, then it may necessarily follow that the actual form and theoretical benefits of organisational autonomy may vary dramatically depending on the economic sector in which the organisation is located. State-funded schools are basically public sector organisations, and managers in public sector organisations have a fundamentally different set of rights and responsibilities from their colleagues working in profit-orientated business firms.

Second, managerial decision rights have numerous interdependent dimensions. Regardless of the sectoral location of an organisation, the full impact of decision rights is often only understood when their interdependencies are considered. A given decision right will be 'different' when seen in the context of other decision rights. Consider the example of the decision right of determining changes in compensation of employees, for example, bonuses, pay increases, wage cuts. Changes in employee compensation are inherently linked (strongly or not) to evaluations of employee performance, changes in the content of employee work, and changes in the economic circumstances of the organisation. Although a given manager may have the technical right to determine changes in an employee's compensation, that decision right is severely limited if that manager does not also have the associated decision rights of evaluating that employee's performance and of determining (or approving) the content of work of that employee. Managerial decisions about the content of work, performance evaluation, and compensation are highly interdependent.

Third, managerial decision rights are inherently complex. Managerial decisions that can be easily identified as 'simple decisions' are, in fact, complex webs of many smaller decisions about rights and procedures, all of which make up the 'simple decision'. It is the composition of these many smaller decisions that, in the end, describes how the 'simple decision' is made and how 'real' it is. Indeed, the simple answer to the question 'Where does the decision sit?' is so coloured by a web of intimately related decisions that the answer may turn out, in practice, to be almost the opposite of the technically correct answer. For example, a school principal may have the 'right' (even the responsibility) of sacking an incompetent teacher, but the constraints and conditions imposed by trade unions, or LEA policies, may be such that the right exists in only the most extreme cases.

Fourthly, management decisions are owned and can be delegated via a wide variety of relationships. There is more to delegation than delegation! Stated another way, we tend to think of delegation as taking place when a manager 'above' an organisation says to a manager 'in' an organisation, 'You have the authority, subject to various constraints, to decide about (fill in the blank).' While this is perhaps the most commonly understood sense of the term delegation, there is a variety of alternative forms of this relationship between the manager 'above' and the manager 'in'. These alternative relationships may be formal, looking like, for example, a contract, or a franchise, or joint venture relationship. School caretaking services may be contracted to a private company instead of using school (or LEA) employees. These alternative relationships may be more informal and nebulous, involving relationships such as bartering, referral processes, and bonus or commission arrangements.

If managerial decision rights have numerous interdependencies, then it would be useful to understand, through a taxonomy, which types of management decisions are mutually dependent. If managerial decision rights are complex and made up of many small decisions, then 'the devil may be in the details', that is, the devil of successful school reform may be in the details of clusters of small decisions, not in the generalities and abstractions about school autonomy. Finally, if decisions can be delegated via a variety of mechanisms, then the form, as well as the content, of school-based decision rights may determine the impact of school autonomy.

So, even (or especially) in the face of these confounding circumstances, we think it helpful to attempt to identify the range of possible management decisions that can be decentralised, if only because so much has

Table 3.1 Taxonomy of managerial decisions

1 Decisions about the business to be in.
2 Decisions about how to organise and operate the production process or service delivery of the organisation.
3 Decisions about the kinds of labour to employ and how that labour is compensated.
4 Decisions about the customers or clients to be served.
5 Decisions about the categories of revenues to pursue in order to operate the business.

been claimed for the benefits of increased autonomy in general. What are the natural limits to that logic, and what special circumstances, if any, refine or actually refute that logic?

MANAGERIAL DECISIONS: A TAXONOMY

An appropriate taxonomy should allow an analysis to take place of key management decisions in autonomous and non-autonomous organisations. Items to be considered in the comparative analysis are those which vary in terms of whether they are made by the larger organisation for the unit or whether they are made within the organisational unit itself. Although there is a wide variety of such decisions, we think that they cluster around five broad issues (Table 3.1) which an autonomous organisation would have to confront.

These 'decisions' are really large bundles of many, more specific decisions, which themselves are complex and interdependent. It is difficult to separate, for example, people who make decisions about growing and shrinking a business from people who have the authority to raise revenues for the business. However, we believe that this five part taxonomy is a useful analytical approach and we now propose to examine each part in turn.

1 Decisions about the business to be in

Decisions about the business to be in start with determining the basic mission of the organisation. Who sets the overall mission of the organisation? Who can change it? Who can decide to go out of business? Who (if anyone) assumes the risk of the failure of the organisation and captures the benefits of success (if any)? Who has the right to redeploy financial assets as a consequence of changes in the mission of the organisation, including acquiring and disposing of assets?

Who creates the mission for an organisation? Who identifies, focuses, clarifies, and modifies the mission? Mission closely relates to market niche. Market niche is the 'client side' of mission in that market niche defines the mission in terms of the people served and often how they are to be served. All organisations can be described by what they choose to do (and for whom). Apple Inc. focuses on *personal* computing needs, Jet focuses on self-service, *low priced*, petrol, and Hyatt Hotels focus on the *business* traveller, because top management in those organisations have made decisions about missions and the connection to market niches.

Examples abound among schools as well. The Rossier School in Southern California focuses on high quality, full service, special education programming for children aged 5–18. Within this niche, the school takes in only students who are referred by local school districts: it does not take private students. Ombudsman Educational Services in Illinois and Arizona, on the other hand, focuses on no-frills, technology-rich general education programming for students aged 14–18 who are at risk of dropping out of school. Like the Rossier School, Ombudsman only takes referrals from school districts. Chetham's School of Music in Manchester takes only musically gifted students and is funded by the pupils' Local Education Authorities. In all of these examples, the focus or mission of the school is defined in terms of (1) the students and (2) the curriculum emphasis.

Closely associated with determining the focus of an organisation is being able to decide which lines of business to grow and which ones to shrink. Typically in an organisation, some of the discrete products/services it produces are more successful than others in the marketplace which leaves management with decisions about which products/services to develop in the future and which ones to allow to diminish or to be discontinued. By describing the areas in which the organisation seeks to be particularly proficient, it is also indirectly announcing to itself and to others those lines of business (and client interests) that it will be less concerned about. These rights, that is, rights to determine the direction of the organisation, are lodged *somewhere* in the organisation. Are they lodged largely within the organisational sub-unit or above the sub-unit?

2   Decisions about how to organise and operate the production process or service delivery of the organisation

Delivering educational services is the embodiment of the mission in real life. Who decides how the organisation will function, including who in the organisation will decide how each of the parts of the organisation will function both separately and in relation to other parts? Who determines whether these separate parts fit well or need to be refashioned? Who has the authority, for example, to intensify the labour or capital component of the production process? Who can determine the degree of 'self-service' in services, that is, how much to integrate the 'customer' or 'client' into service delivery processes? Who has the authority over where to locate the various parts of the operation of the organisation? How much leeway do individuals have in making these decisions? What are the natural boundaries? When does a change in production process become so major that the new process is really producing something different and who has the authority to decide? How much service will be provided?

In a school setting those general questions translate into specific questions of educational organisation. Does the school serve children during the traditional school hours only or does it provide extended hours of service as well? To what extent and in what ways are parents encouraged (or made) to be involved in the schooling processes of their children? Are children with special needs routinely pulled from mainstream classes to receive individualised tutoring or is that tutoring provided in their mainstream classrooms? Is homework regularly set across all subject areas or only in 'academic subjects'? For how many children will the service be provided? Who decides these and other production processes?

3   Decisions about the kinds of labour to employ and how that labour is compensated

Who determines the labour force which flows into the organisation; the qualifications of employees to be hired; and the actual employees to be hired? Who terminates employment and on what grounds? What are the specific decision rights associated with each of these questions and which managers have the authority to exercise those rights?

There is a wide range of decisions to be made around compensation, including not only benefits, salary, commissions, and bonuses but also broader compensation-related conditions of employment such as holidays, sick leave and retirement. Compensation-related conditions significantly shape the applicant pools of prospective employees in the short run and the composition and quality of the employees in the long run. Who determines the compensation levels of the unit's employees; the changes in merit pay; the benefits components of compensation; the impact on compensation of personnel in the organisation when the organisation succeeds beyond or falls below revenue expectations (bonuses/cuts in pay)?

4   Decisions about the customers or clients to be served

Decisions about clients include not only the categories of people that the organisation will serve, but also the proportion of people in those categories that the organisation will serve (the share of client markets). Who has the authority to determine which individual clients will be served and when services to specific clients will be provided, curtailed or discontinued? Who can determine when individual clients receiving one kind of service should, instead, receive a different kind of service?

Also there are a number of client-related decisions concerning whether to induce clients to take up goods and services voluntarily or to use legislative means to coerce this take-up. We legislate to require children to attend school but encourage them to pay for individual instrumental music lessons. Beyond the voluntary/compulsory dimension of client relations, someone decides the price/cost relationship between service providers and service consumers. Which services will be provided at what price, and what relationships do those prices have to the costs of production of those goods/services? To what extent is the price of a service to be subsidised by third parties? Indeed, are education service providers even to be allowed to set prices, and will clients be allowed to supplement tuition charges from their own pockets if they so choose?

5   Decisions about the categories of revenues to pursue in order to operate the business

In addition to money which comes to the school from the government by virtue of the student being enrolled in that school, there is, theoretically, a variety of revenue sources which could provide income streams for a school. Among the major additional sources are fees from parents for schooling (private financing of school); parental fund-raising through donations and covenants; and sales from auxiliary services, such as catering, pre-school education or care, or after-school programmes. Another would be the increasing use of industrial/commercial sponsorship and various private finance initiatives in the public sector.

Who has the authority to raise financial resources for the organisation and from whom? This can be considered in terms of initial capital or development capital. It can be considered in terms of guaranteed revenue based on pupil numbers or revenue linked to specific projects or learning schemes. This can be considered further by asking who can incur debt on behalf of the organisation? For example, can the senior management of a school (headteacher, board of governors) secure a loan to construct a new wing of the school? Who has the authority to sell assets in order to raise capital for the organisation? Can, for example, senior management of a school sell off parcels of land in order to raise money for improving the premises? Who (if anyone) has the authority to shift income from operating accounts into interest-yielding accounts or the authority to establish endowments or covenants? Can the school management take cash out of the operating budget and invest it for possible future use?

APPLYING THE TAXONOMY TO SCHOOLS

The proponents of the decentralisation of decision-making argue that, by giving schools real autonomy, decision-making at the school level will have a significant impact on the teaching and learning process, leading to measurable improvements in outcomes. The key hopes for this reform may depend on whether we are witnessing real autonomy in decision-making or merely a degree of managerialism that decentralises administration rather than decentralising autonomous decision-making. Have we been in the process of reengineering the governance and management of schools or have we been merely incrementally shifting the administrative and accountability burden?

To analyse the effects of decentralised or autonomous management, we believe it is first necessary to understand the complexity of managerial decisions. Second, it is necessary to formulate key elements in autonomous decision-making that allow an analysis of whether decisions in the management of autonomous organisations lie within the remit of school managers. Only if managers in schools have the control over those key decisions can we expect the benefits of decentralisation to accrue. To that end we believe that the taxonomy proposed in this chapter will establish criteria against which to set any significant assessment of fundamental change in the system. As we move through the early years of the twenty-first century leaders at the school site will need to assess their knowledge and competency to make decisions about the five categories in the taxonomy. A brief discussion here may provide the basis for a more substantive analysis by the reader.

The first category of managerial decision, that of 'the business to be in', seems initially to be an obvious one in that schools are in the business of educating children. While no school has shifted from the core business of educating children, schools have set up companies to hire out their internal grounds maintenance, property maintenance and catering operations (see, for example, Southlands School in Kent). While it is inappropriate to suggest that schools could stop functioning as educational organisations and employ their capital elsewhere, at the same time the precise scope of their activities is loosening up and changing. The question is how far will this develop? With the advent of advanced information technologies, traditional schooling patterns may become obsolete. The way that schools choose to reinvent themselves will test the limits of the traditional boundaries of the business they are in.

The second category of decisions, 'the organisation and operation of the production process or service delivery of the organisation', would seem to be one where there is considerable autonomy for school managers to make their own decisions. Here the limitations seem to be ones associated with 'traditional mind-sets'. As was illustrated in Chapter 2, can full flexibility in the use of buildings, organisational groupings and technology be deployed to redesign radically the learning process? Can teachers be persuaded to move away from traditional class sizes of thirty and teaching pupils in age groups and to think more in terms of differentiated learning patterns with the teacher acting as facilitator and co-ordinator as well as director of learning?

The third category of decisions, 'the kinds of labour to employ and how that labour is compensated', demonstrates a significant difference between the reforms in the UK and those in the USA and Australia. Only in England and Wales do the financial reforms include the funding of schools based on the average cost of a teacher yet charging them the actual cost. Nevertheless other systems, such as some in Australia and New Zealand, are now considering or planning full staffing flexibility. Thus, initial attempts to consider the advantages and disadvantages of younger as against older staff and the increase in the number of non-teaching assistants by savings in the teaching staff establishment, are now being evaluated by many schools. While Grant-Maintained Schools and City Technology Colleges can operate their own salary remuneration systems, few as of yet have broken away from centrally agreed salary structures. Fixed term as against tenured positions have been introduced to a minor degree as have limited attempts at performance related pay. This, however, remains a major area for the development of site-based autonomy.

The fourth category of decisions, 'the customers or clients to be served', presents an interesting framework for analysis. Schools in the state sector, unlike their private school counterparts, were in the business of educating all of the children allocated to them by the LEA. That position is changing; open enrolment and oversubscribed schools have opened a debate as to whether schools choose pupils or pupils choose schools. Grant-Maintained Schools have, in a few cases, been able to change their status to allow secondary schools to start junior departments or for primary schools to borrow money to start their own nursery schools. Others have taken even more radical steps by changing their status to become selective schools in terms of intellectual ability, thus excluding a large proportion of their potential clients. Schools are also specialising in different subject areas, such as technology or languages. Thus traditional perceptions of the school's flexibility to determine its client base are changing radically.

The final decision category, that of 'the categories of revenues to pursue in order to operate the business', is one which is set in the context of the changes that are affecting the public sector as a whole where mixed private/public funding is being encouraged. The higher education example of the replacement of student grants with loans and increased parental contributions or the introduction of vouchers in the post-16 sector are evidence of significant change in the patterns of finance. In the school sector, private sector finance of City Technology Colleges and further education colleges is an example of the mixed funding of mainstream education. The legislation to allow Grant-Maintained Schools to borrow capital is a radical shift in this category as is the introduction of vouchers for nursery aged children.

LEADERSHIP AND MANAGEMENT: APPROPRIATE KNOWLEDGE AND COMPETENCIES?

We believe that the changes in autonomy which we have witnessed to date have only been the first wave of reform. The second wave is the reengineering within the school and not just decentralisation to it. This second wave is about to impact on schools to empower them to enact significant decisions in the five areas outlined, so a reengineering of attitudes as well as process needs to take place. Fundamental to this is the development of the requisite leadership and management competencies to act in this new environment. If a school has a high degree of autonomy in managerial decisions, it becomes critically important that the school pursues an agenda of reengineering; success or failure of the school will depend on what leaders of that school decide to do. If, on the other hand, a school is largely a 'dependent' organisational sub-unit, school-based educators there will not have the responsibility for rethinking and reengineering. Responsibility for success (and failure) in these dependent schools lies with the 'higher ups'.

We are seeing greater devolution of control to schools. We believe that school-based reengineering will be necessary, and the reengineering of 'mind-sets' to develop new competencies may be a critical factor in the success of school leadership.

Each of the five areas outlined in the taxonomy above can be unpacked in terms of the content knowledge needed to understand it. However, the way in which that knowledge is to be applied depends on the successful application of several leadership and management competencies. This link between knowledge and competency is the underlying principle behind the chapters in the remainder of the book.

Apparently simple questions in the taxonomy, such as 'decisions about the business to be in', reveal a complex mix of content-based knowledge needs and management competencies. Content chapters in this book such as Chapter 7 on developing a strategic perspective, Chapter 14 on marketing and Chapters 16 and 17 on global trends would only be a start. The leadership necessary to create a vision about the future direction of the organisation, discussed in Chapter 10, together with an understanding of key future aspects of teaching and learning (in Chapter 12) would also provide the necessary knowledge base for the discussion.

These content building blocks would then be activated alongside a series of personal competencies such as 'understand and keep up to date with current educational and management issues and identify their relevance to the school' and 'give a clear sense of direction and purpose in order to achieve the school's mission and inspire staff and pupils alike' as promoted in the UK's Teacher Training Agency approach to competencies.

As outlined at the start of Chapter 1, leaders and managers in the twenty-first century need to understand clearly the nature and extent of their own management competencies and content knowledge. The individual needs a realistic assessment of their own current abilities so that the gap between those and the likely skills needed in the future can be filled. This involves setting out a personal development map and action plan. To start this process, the next three chapters explore the nature of leadership and management competencies, providing a framework for competency and personal self-development. These will then be followed by the exploration of a series of content chapters that will provide a framework within which to apply the competency analysis.

REFERENCES

Bullock, A. and Thomas, H. (1994) *The Impact of Local Management of Schools: Final Report*, Birmingham: University of Birmingham School of Education.
Caldwell, B. J. and Spinks, J. M. (1992) *Leading the Self-Managing School*, London: Falmer.
Davies, B. and Hentschke, G. (1994) 'Locating US and English schools in the context of organisational autonomy' (session 38.43), American Educational Research Association, Annual Conference, New Orleans, April.
Levačić, R. (1995) *Local Management of Schools: Analysis and Practice*, Buckingham: Open University Press.
Osborne, D. and Gaebler, T. (1992) *Reinventing Government: How the Entrepreneurial Spirit is Transforming the Public Sector*, Reading, MA: Addison-Wesley.
Thomas, H. (1987) 'Efficiency and opportunity in school finance autonomy', in H. Thomas and T. Simkins (eds) *Economics and the Management of Education: Emerging Themes*, London: Falmer.

4 Understanding competence and competency

Alan Trotter and Linda Ellison

If we are to understand the competencies needed for leadership in the schools of the twenty-first century and to develop those competencies in ourselves as well as to promote the development of others, we must first understand and then rethink our own competencies. The purpose of this chapter is to help you to establish an overview and understanding of the importance of leadership and management competence and competency development in schools. The following chapter then provides a framework for you to engage in a fundamental rethinking of your personal skills and competencies.

Competence and competency are about the skills and characteristics that people bring to tasks and situations and what they do that results in successful outcomes. As they involve the study of success, these concepts are very relevant to management development in schools. A simplified explanation of the difference between them is that competence is the ability to do a particular task while competency concerns the underlying characteristics which allow a person to perform well in a variety of situations. These definitions are examined more closely on p. 39.

Figure 4.1 provides a map of the chapter and of the sequence in which the topics, concepts and techniques are to be presented. An appropriate approach might be to scan Figure 4.1 first, then to skim the text, before reading the chapter in more detail. This will allow you to obtain an overview before plunging into the detail of the text. Having understood the concepts in this chapter, you can then move on to Chapters 5 and 6 which show how to determine and develop competencies and then, in conjunction with the rest of this book, how to use competency development for your personal and professional development.

THE IMPORTANCE OF COMPETENCE AND COMPETENCY APPROACHES

To get a perspective on the increasing use of competence and competency approaches, it is worth doing a broad brush survey of what has

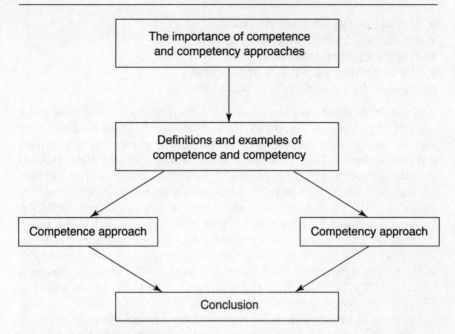

Figure 4.1 Structure of Chapter 4

happened in organisations since the end of the Second World War. From 1945 to the 1960s, the main priority of industry was to satisfy the steadily increasing demands for products and services. It was a period of stability and the emphasis was on increasing productivity. Organisations were structured hierarchically and work was divided into specialised tasks. Managers were the thinkers, planners, motivators and controllers. Hammer and Champy (1993) liken this fragmentation of tasks to a Humpty Dumpty model of management:

> Companies take a natural process, such as order fulfilment, and break it into lots of little pieces ... then the company has to hire all the king's horses and all the king's men to paste the fragmented work back together again.
>
> (Hammer and Champy 1993: 29)

In the 1970s and 1980s, the previous period of economic growth and stability gave way to new kinds of pressures on organisations. Uncertainty increased and change accelerated. Among the changes, some of which were discussed in Chapter 2, the following can be highlighted:

- Intensified and global competition.
- More power for customers.
- Structural changes through new technology.

- The availability of more information.
- Turbulence from financial deregulation.
- Turbulence from takeovers.
- The increasing influence of regulators.
- Pressure for profitabilty and short-termism.

To cope with these pressures, which at the present time appear to be intensifying, various responses have been tried. Organisations have carried out change programmes with the aim of promoting new organisational cultures. They have de-layered, downsized and decentralised in order to slim down, to give people more autonomy, and to increase profitability. Many jobs have been casualised (made part-time or short-term) in order to reduce costs and increase organisational flexibility. Fierce competition to attract and retain customers has led to the introduction of total quality management programmes and to a focus on 'closeness to the customer' (for example by emphasising the philosophy of the inverted pyramid where the organisation's structures are designed to support the interface with the customer). Currently, as discussed in Chapter 2, business process reengineering is being introduced, seeking even more radical solutions to restructuring organisations in order to meet the challenge of the rapidly changing economic situation.

As organisations responded to pressures in the environment, they increasingly saw the need to regard their people as assets who should be developed in order to become more flexible, resourceful and committed. This has been reflected in the nature of work in organisations which has also been changing as seen, for example, in the move from single to multiple tasks and skills, combining several jobs into one, and in horizontal and vertical compression with people being authorised to work across functions, deciding issues previously referred to line managers. Management work has also changed, with less emphasis on controlling and more on leading, coaching, and mediating interfaces, boundaries and resources (see Durcan and Oates 1994). So, work and management have become more fluid in scope and content: 'Defined jobs are gradually being replaced by those in which no one but the incumbent can tell the extent and the nature of the efforts needed to make things work' (Caretta 1992: 50). Organisations have realised that management training can no longer be a preparation for static jobs and roles:

> whereas in the past managerial competence went hand in hand with the possession of specific skills and abilities, it now seems to involve much more. Increasingly it rests on the development of attitudes, values, and 'mindsets' that allow managers to confront, understand and deal with a wide range of forces within and outside their organisations.
>
> (Morgan 1992: 11)

To develop people for modern jobs, organisations have seen the need to be clear about what kinds of work need doing, to analyse how effective performers do it and then to communicate this to a wider workforce and train them accordingly.

During the 1980s several national agencies in the UK focused on this kind of approach. The Manpower Services Commission (MSC) identified key skills and qualities for employability through the Youth Training Scheme (YTS). The Further Education Unit (FEU) promoted competence-based education and training in Further Education Colleges. These developments influenced the establishment of competence-based National Vocational Qualifications (NVQs). Concern about the quality of management education and development led to two reports (Constable and McCormick 1987; Handy 1987) which were influential in the formation of the Management Charter Initiative (MCI) and the development of the British version of management competences (MCI 1995).

Therefore, through the 1980s and especially during the 1990s, organisations in both the private and the public sectors have been turning to competence and competency in order to develop their people. Some firms such as ICI have been engaged in this for over twenty years while in others the focus has accelerated over the last few years. In the UK, government support has been provided for the competence approach through the Training and Enterprise Councils (TECs) and, more recently, competences and competencies have been identified by the Teacher Training Agency (TTA) for those entering teaching and for school leadership (TTA 1994a,b).

DEFINITIONS AND EXAMPLES OF COMPETENCE AND COMPETENCY

Competence is a concept which is used extensively in the UK; competency is a concept largely influenced by US thinking, particularly through the work of the psychologist David McClelland. Put simply, *competences* are about *outputs* to specified minimum standards while *competencies* are about *inputs* that a person brings to a job, resulting in superior performance. In everyday usage in the UK the word competence is used more than competency, although many people use the two concepts interchangeably.

The term *competence* has two common meanings. First, it can be the ability to do a task: we speak of the government's 'economic competence' or we might say of a person in a job or role, 'he's incompetent', meaning that he cannot get satisfactory results in tasks, or make adequate provision to deal with job challenges and contingencies. A second definition is that found in the Oxford English Dictionary, 'having the qualifications required by law to do some particular work'. The MCI defines competence as the ability to perform job requirements to a specified standard, and to be able to transfer the skills and knowledge to new situations. Similarly, for NVQ accreditation, 'Competence is the ability to perform activities to the level expected within employment' (Lloyd and Cook 1993: 14). So competence is about what you have to be able to do in a job to satisfy specified standards. In this sense a competence is like being a qualified driver – either you have passed the required standards of the driving test or you have not.

The concept of *competency* is different. As the Hay Group/McBer organisation state in their seminars,

> Competencies are the underlying characteristics which enable someone to perform a job better in more situations, more often, with better results. Competencies are those factors that distinguish the best from the rest in a given role. They are not the tasks of the job, they are what enable people to do the tasks.

ICI have their own version of the McBer definition: competency is the 'predisposition to behave in ways shown to be associated with the achievement of successful outcomes' (Esp 1993: 61).

The distinctions between competence and competency can be highlighted as shown in Table 4.1.

Table 4.1 Distinctions between competence and competency

Competence	Competency
1 Outputs for minimum standards	Inputs for superior performance
2 Concern for what the job requires	Concern for what people bring to the job
3 Sociological focus	Psychological focus
4 Reductionist	Holistic

Figure 4.2 (opposite) illustrates the stages in each process.

THE COMPETENCE APPROACH

A major example of competence in practice is provided by the United Kingdom's NVQ/MCI approach from which a variety of other frameworks have been derived. The aim is to set out standards of competence for occupations and, in the case of MCI, for the various levels of management. One of the National Education and Training Targets is to have 60 per cent of the workforce to be qualified to NVQ Level 3, Advanced GNVQ or two GCE A level standard by the year 2000. Competences for beginning teachers are set out in two DfE Circulars (DfE 1992, 1993) and are brought together by the Teacher Training Agency (TTA 1994b).

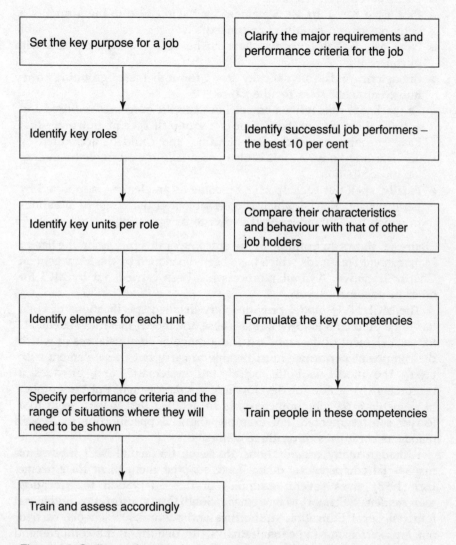

Figure 4.2 Outline and comparison of competence and competency processes

The NVQs and the MCI frameworks are developed using the same method. The steps to producing a competence specification through *top-down functional analysis* are logical and systematic:

- Work out a vision of where the organisation wants to be in five years.
- Produce a Key Purpose Statement showing the reason for the organisation's existence, in the format of a verb, object and condition or context.
- Specify key jobs in the organisation.
- Focus on one of these jobs.
- Produce a Key Purpose Statement for the job, also in the format of a verb, object and condition or context.
- Now ask, 'What outcomes have to be achieved to meet this key purpose?'
- Brainstorm and systematically trawl through these, grouping them into component roles for the job.
- For each job/role, refine and spell out specific outcomes required and arrange them into units. A unit is a group of specific outcomes that have 'meaning and independent value' and could be accredited by an awarding body. A unit is also potentially transferrable to another job or occupation.
- Finally, spell out each specific outcome as an element, supported by performance criteria, which is assessable and the range of situations in which the jobholder could expect to be operating.

Figure 4.3 shows an example of the outcome of this process in the Senior Management Standards which have been developed by the Management Charter Initiative. A similar process has been carried out by MCI for other management levels.

The MCI/NVQ model provides very detailed specifications of what has to be done in a job. As well as these, the model includes statements for each element of the standard and a range of circumstances in which the competent performer must be able to carry out these element sub-tasks. The model is both logical and systematic, and provides a comprehensive guide for development and assessment but the number of elements for a job competence is so detailed that it may seem to a learner too fragmented. For example, the MCI specification for senior managers comprises thirty-three elements.

Although many organisations are using the actual MCI models of managerial competences, others have adapted them to fit their needs. Esp (1993) gives several examples of this adaptation to education management. 'School Management South', a consortium involving fourteen Local Education Authorities and some 3,600 schools, carried out a project using Functional Analysis to determine the competences required for educational managers (Earley 1992). This resulted in the

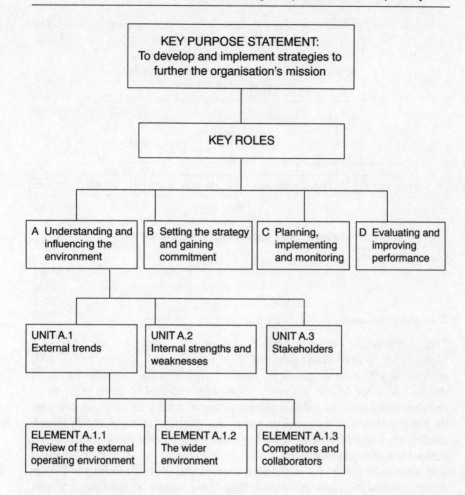

Figure 4.3 MCI Senior Management Standards
Source: MCI 1995

development of a series of key roles (Figure 4.4 overleaf) with associated units of competence and their elements.

Criticisms of the competence approach

Assumes static jobs and aims at minimum standards

The standards are pitched at threshold performance and are less appropriate for job situations where knowledge, attitudes, and autonomy to make discretionary decisions are part of the job (Tuxford 1989).

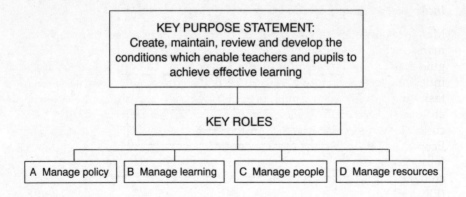

Figure 4.4 School Management South competence framework
Source: Earley 1992

Task/functional analysis too fragmenting

This analysis can be 'reductionist' and take the approach of 'analyse a competence to bits' (Tuxford 1989: 17). Spencer and Spencer (1993: 103) object that job analysis provides characteristics of the job rather than of the people who do the job well. Moreover, the lists of tasks tend to be too detailed (such as 3,000 motions to drive a car) to be practical, and do not separate out those tasks which are routine from the really significant ones. Pareto's rule of thumb would suggest that only about 20 per cent of the competences are critical to success. Against this, Mansfield and Mathews (1985) have devised a job competence model for NVQs which avoids fragmentation and uses the concept of contingency and discretionary features of a job. Those who are interested in designing a new MCI/NVQ type competence model for a particular job should consider their work.

It requires too much assessment

The MCI requires each of the elements of competence for managers to be assessed. For level M1 this involves 26 elements and for M2 it is 36 elements. Critics say that this can hardly be what Handy intended in his report (Handy 1987) which stimulated the formation of the MCI. Arguably, it is impossible to measure management competence objectively and reliably in a fragmented fashion. Some school managers have found the collection of evidence for the assessment to be onerous and not developmental.

Incomplete acceptance by employers

Many organisations have adopted a competence based approach to management development although only a few have adhered to MCI guidelines. This is because they believe that the MCI approach is inflexible and prescriptive, fails to recognise the diversity of managers' tasks and roles, and seems better suited to measuring competence at lower managerial levels. Some organisations feel that NVQs are costly to implement and that progress is slow. The Organization for Economic Co-operation and Development, in its country by country Jobs Study, said that NVQs have 'scant appeal because they lack credibility with employers and are even considered "a bit of a joke"' (Elliott 1995).

THE COMPETENCY APPROACH

The approach here is to take a particular job or role and to identify superior performers (taken to be the top 10 per cent) in that job or role. The researchers then observe highly successful individuals in the major responsibility and performance areas of the job or role, in order to look for the key characteristics and to formulate the major areas of concern and actions of these people. Others can then benefit from this information by using it to guide their own development.

Some of the competencies identified in this way are *threshold*, that is, they are the minimum needed to be able to do the job at all, while a few of the competencies are *distinguishing* and are the keys to outstanding performance. There may be a Pareto principle at work here: 20 per cent of the competencies determine 80 per cent of the success in a job. While it may be possible to differentiate between those competencies which are threshold and those which are distinguishing, it is probably sufficient to identify a complete list of competencies for a job and to give people the opportunity to develop all of them.

A competency is usually presented as: a title, a definition and statements of the kinds of behaviour used by successful performers. Table 4.2 (overleaf) provides a specimen.

The definition and behaviour examples of this competency illustrate *what* is involved. To practise and acquire a competency such as this one, it is worthwhile not just to copy these kinds of specific behaviours but also to consider the reasons *why* they contribute to effective results. Understanding the purposes and reasons underlying the specifics will enable you to use discretion in the distinct situations and tasks that you face, rather than to imitate the competency mechanistically.

Because competencies are not so much about the details of the job as about what outstanding performers bring to the job, the McBer

Table 4.2 The expression of a competency (information seeking)

Title	Information seeking
Definition	An active curiosity and a desire to know more about things, people or issues. Makes an effort to find out more, does not accept situations at face value, goes beyond routine questions, and scans for information that may be of future use.

Behavioural statements for this competency

Asks questions	Questions of people involved in a situation, even those not actually present. Even in a crisis takes time to gather any available information before taking action.
Personally investigates	Gets out and about and finds out from people closest to a problem.
Digs deeper	Probes below the surface to get at the root of problems.
Contacts others	Approaches people who are not personally involved to get their perspective.
Does research	Makes systematic effort over a limited time period to get data; uses media and other sources to gather information.
Establishes own systems	Employs means of gathering and using information, including walking the job and using meetings.

Source: Adapted from Spencer and Spencer 1993: 34–5

organisation has put a lot of effort into discovering the underlying characteristics of these performers which influence the orientation and ways in which they use their skills and knowledge. Spencer and Spencer (1993: 11) suggest an iceberg model (Figure 4.5) which shows the levels of characteristics determining a person's competencies and this highlights the fact that it is the hidden characteristics which are more difficult to develop. These are, however, very significant factors in effective school leadership.

Competencies are influenced by a person's 'natural tendencies' or motivations. The McBer model draws on the work of McClelland (1987) which claims that three motivations (achievement, affiliation and power) shape a person's concerns, her/his orientation and her/his disposition to act and use her/his skills and knowledge in certain focused ways. Although these concerns and actions may be affected by the person's values and her/his perception of the likelihood of success, the most enduring influence is one or more of the motivations which can be summarised in Table 4.3:

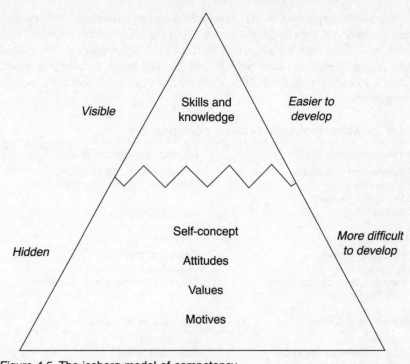

Figure 4.5 The iceberg model of competency

Source: Adapted from Spencer and Spencer 1993: 11

Table 4.3 Motivations influencing competency

Achievement	Affiliation	Power
Sets challenging targets	Likes to spend time with friends	Looks for chances to lead
Finds ways of improving things	Keeps in contact with people	Influences others to obtain leader roles
Values personal responsibility	Puts people before tasks and friends before experts	Willing to help others towards own or their goals
Seeks objective feedback in order to improve politics	Would rather work in a group than alone	Gets involved in organisational
Prefers working with experts to friends	Likes co-operating	Seeks and uses information to influence events.

Source: McClelland 1987

The McBer organisation has researched competencies for over twenty years across 200 jobs in 21 countries (Spencer and Spencer 1993). Their work produced 360 behaviour indicators which have been crystallised into 20 competencies and which can be clustered in various ways. Table 4.4 demonstrates how the McBer organisation clusters the twenty competencies.

Table 4.4 McBer organisation's Generic Competencies

Achievement and action	*Helping and human service*
Achievement orientation	Interpersonal understanding
Concern for order	Customer service orientation
Information seeking	
Initiative	
Managerial	*Cognitive*
Developing others	Analytical thinking
Directiveness	Conceptual thinking
Teamwork and co-operation	Technical/professional expertise
Team leadership	
Impact and influence	*Personal effectiveness*
Influence	Self-control
Organisational awareness	Self-confidence
Relationship building	Flexibility
	Organisational commitment

Source: Spencer and Spencer 1993

These competencies cover 80–95 per cent of the distinguishing characteristics of superior performance in the jobs studied. The remaining competencies differ for different jobs, such as a low fear of rejection (salespeople) or a sense of humour (nurses).

Specific sets of competencies have been generated relating to successful school leaders. The Gallup organisation has a strategy which profiles outstanding practitioners in any particular occupation (e.g. school leaders) and uses the profile of talents, predispositions and characteristics to furnish a template against which either development or selection profiling can take place. Whilst avoiding the language of competency, their approach does result in taxonomies of talents and themes for leadership. The North American Secondary School Principals (NASSP) model has been franchised in the UK to the National Educational Assessment Centre (NEAC). There is a set of competencies (Table 4.5) which can be assessed by a series of exercises designed either for heads and deputies or for middle managers.

Table 4.5 National Educational Assessment Centre competencies

Interpersonal competencies	Management competencies
Leadership	Problem analysis
Sensitivity	Judgement
Stress tolerance	Organisational ability
	Decisiveness
Communicative competencies	Personal breadth competencies
Oral communication	Range of interest
Written communication	Personal motivation

Competencies anticipating future needs

If the current focus on competencies is a response to changes in organisational, job and environmental conditions, then it is also logical to consider what competencies might be required in the future. The literature reports several examples of competency models for the future (Spencer and Spencer 1993; Quinn *et al.* 1990; Boam and Sparrow 1992). However, even if these have been formulated systematically by 'experts', they are still as much speculative as proven. Nevertheless, they are worth consideration.

One initiative (discussed by Boak 1991) does seem to be far ahead of any others: that led by Harry Schroder at the University of South Florida who has drawn on several areas of research to identify and test the validity of eleven High Performance Managerial Competencies (Table 4.6). These have also been tested out in the National Westminster Bank. Schroder's (1989) findings indicate that high levels of performance in changing circumstances are achieved when managers use these competencies.

Table 4.6 High performance managerial competencies

Information search	Concept formation
Conceptual flexibility	Interpersonal search
Managing interaction	Developmental orientation
Impact	Self-confidence
Presentation	Proactive orientation
Achievement orientation	

Source: Schroder 1989

When considering competencies for the twenty-first century, Spencer and Spencer (1993) conclude that a relatively few competencies should be concentrated on, for work and everyday life. They suggest that these should be included in Education and Parental Training as well as preparation for work roles. Not surprisingly, perhaps, the eight key competencies for the future (Table 4.7) turn out to be variants of McBer's Generic Competencies (see Table 4.4).

Table 4.7 Key competencies for the future

Achievement orientation	Initiative
Information seeking	Conceptual thinking
Interpersonal understanding	Self-confidence
Impact and influence	Collaborativeness

Source: Spencer and Spencer 1993

Criticisms of the competency approach

Competencies do not fully match management work

Burgoyne (1989) doubts the fit between competencies and management work, arguing that, unlike much other work, management creates and defines its own tasks and is subject to shifting boundaries. This is because much 'managerial work is characterised by pace, brevity, variety, and fragmentation'. Indeed as the reader will know, managerial work involves the ability to switch rapidly from one task to another within a complex range of personal relationships. The McBer organisation might respond by asking what a manager actually does who does these things well and what competencies s/he uses.

Competencies produce clone-like imitative behaviour

The criticism here is that individuals who try to emulate high performers, and do the things that they have done, may do so unthinkingly and inappropriately. If people learn only the behavioural examples of high performers, that is surely possible. However, if people learn the purpose and principles underlying a competency, they can choose appropriate rather than imitative actions.

Competencies for individuals undervalue collective competency

It is true that some organisations do have integrated competencies, over and above the separate competencies of their members. However, the two forms of competency are not incompatible, although recent emphasis has been on individual competencies.

CONCLUSION

Although this chapter has focused on approaches for individuals, it can be argued that the current emphasis on individual competences and competencies undervalues the collective effort of groups and whole organisations because much of our work nowadays takes place in teams, project groups and working parties. For this reason, leading thinkers (such as Hamel and Heene 1994; Hamel and Prahalad 1994) are working on the area of core competences, a term which they use in a general way to cover competence and competency. Hamel and Prahalad (1994) characterise core competences as the collective learning in the organisation, especially the co-ordination of diverse production skills and technologies. Core competences are about what an organisation can do particularly well that gives it competitive advantage and creates value for customers. A core competence 'represents the integration of a variety of individual skills and it is this integration that is the distinguishing hallmark' (Hamel and Heene 1994: 11). They cite Honda's knowhow in engines; the expertise of Federal Express in managing complicated logistics; Sony's competence in miniaturisation. It is evident that there is a valid domain of synergistic core competences in groups and organisations that is greater than the separate contributions of their individual members.

Another area loosely related to the competence/competency approach is the study of successful organisations. There are dozens, possibly hundreds, of books and prescriptions offering various kinds of panaceas so it is impossible to keep abreast of these, let alone evaluate them. These writers do not usually label their findings and prescriptions as competencies, even though they are often writing about the same ingredients. So far as studies of successful individuals are concerned, there seem to be two types: 'quick fixes'; and recommendations based on the deeper development of character and principles. Stephen Covey's (1989; 1994) work is a good example of the latter type. It is worth getting to grips with a number of writers who claim to have studied and codified what highly effective individuals do in various jobs and walks of life, and what successful organisations do. In addition to the work of Covey, the references at the end of this chapter give other writers worth dipping into, such as Garfield (1986) and Fletcher (1993). Writers claiming to have studied what successful organisations do include Peters and Waterman (1982) and, for the UK, Goldsmith and Clutterbuck (1984).

When looking for approaches, you may choose either a competence or a competency approach or you may decide to use both. Whatever your decision, there are many models and lists from which to choose. If you want to choose a model 'off the shelf' to suit your purposes, there are plenty available. Three questions will help you to decide between approaches or models:

- Are the competences or competencies sufficiently plausible keys to success to be applied to my school?
- Are the costs (especially the time costs) of implementing the model reflected in the benefits for the individual and for the school?
- Would such a model be seen and perhaps resisted in my school as a kind of transplant of abstractions from somewhere else which do not suit my school's culture?

The advantages of choosing a tried and tested model would be that you could be confident that the competencies are thoroughly researched and valid and that you would save a lot of time and money by not having to research to identify competencies specific to your organisation. However, the more generic and universal a competency is, the less it may fit a particular organisational culture so there is a case for taking the trouble to discover the competences or competencies that are crucial to success in your own organisation. This would involve members of staff in producing data, and this involvement would be more likely to gain their acceptance and willingness to learn and use the model once it has been formulated.

In this chapter we have discussed the reasons why we believe that competencies are important for school leadership and management. The processes by which readers can determine the competencies which are needed for their own roles and can establish a competency development framework are discussed in the next two chapters.

REFERENCES

Boak, G. (1991) *Developing Managerial Competences: The Management Learning Contract Approach*, London: Pitman.

Boam, R. and Sparrow, P. (eds) (1992) *Designing and Achieving Competency*, London: McGraw-Hill.

Burgoyne, J. (1989) 'Opinion', *Transition*, February.

Caretta, A. (1992) 'Career and succession planning', in A. Mitrani, M. Dalziel, and D. Fitt (eds) *Competency Based Human Resource Management*, London: Kogan Page.

Constable, J. and McCormick, R. (1987) *The Making of British Managers*, Corby: British Institute of Managers..

Covey, S. R. (1989) *The Seven Habits of Highly Successful People: Restoring the Character Ethic*, London: Simon and Schuster.

Covey, S. R. (1994) *First Things First*, London: Simon and Schuster.

Department for Education (1992) Circular 9/92, *Initial Teacher Training (Secondary Phase)*, London: HMSO.

Department for Education (1993) Circular 14/93, *The Initial Teacher Training of Primary School Teachers: New Criteria for Courses*, London: HMSO.

Durcan, J. and Oates, D. (1994) *The Manager as Coach*, London: Pitman.

Earley, P. (1992) *Final Report of the School Management Competences Project*, Crawley: School Management South.

Elliott, L. (1995) 'OECD damns British skills training', in *Guardian*, 24 May: 18.

Esp, D. (1993) *Competences for School Managers*, London: Kogan Page.

Fletcher, J. L. (1993) *Patterns of High Performance*, San Francisco: Berrett-Koehler.

Garfield, C. (1986) *Peak Performers*, Hutchinson Business.

Goldsmith, W. and Clutterbuck, D. (1984) *The Winning Streak*, London: Penguin.

Hamel, G. and Heene, A. (eds) (1994) *Competence Based Competition*, New York: Wiley.

Hamel, G. and Prahalad, C. K. (1994) *Competing for the Future*, Boston: Harvard Business School Press.

Hammer, M. and Champy, J. (1993) *Reengineering the Corporation*, New York: HarperCollins.

Handy, C. (1987) *The Making of Managers*, London: NEDC.

Lloyd, C. and Cook, A. (1993) *Implementing Standards of Competence*, London: Kogan Page.

Mansfield, R. and Mathews, D. (1985) *The Job Competence-Model*, Further Education Staff College.

McClelland, D. C. (1987) *Human Motivation*, Cambridge: Cambridge University Press.

Management Charter Initiative (1995) *Senior Management Standards*, Sheffield: MCI.

Morgan, G. (1989) *Riding the Waves of Change: Developing Managerial Competences for a Turbulent World*, Oxford: Jossey Bass.

Peters, T. J. and Waterman, R. H. (1982) *In Search of Excellence*, New York: HarperCollins.

Quinn, R., Faerman, S. R., Thompson, M. P. and McGrath, M. R. (1990) *Becoming a Master Manager: A Competency Framework*, New York: Wiley.

Schroder, H. M. (1989) *Managerial Competence: The Key to Excellence*, Iowa: Kendall Hunt.

Spencer, L. M. and Spencer, S. M. (1993) *Competence at Work: Models for Superior Performance*, New York: Wiley.

Teacher Training Agency (1994a) *Headteachers' Leadership and Management Programme – Consultation*. (4 November).

Teacher Training Agency (1994b) *Profiles of Teachers' Competence – Consultation on Draft* (4 November).

Tuxford, E. (1989) 'Competence-based education and training, background and origins', in W. J. Burke, (ed.) *Competency-based Education and Training*, Lewes: Falmer.

5 Determining and developing competencies in schools

Alan Trotter, Linda Ellison and Brent Davies

INTRODUCTION

This chapter provides a framework for the reader to engage in a fundamental rethinking of her/his personal skills and competencies. This is the
'reengineering mind-set' referred to earlier, in Chapter 1. It is important
to understand our own capabilities and how we develop them before we
engage in process and organisational redesign. Rethinking and redesigning our skills and capabilities is the first priority. In this chapter, we build
a framework based on the competency understandings established in
Chapter 4 which outlined the nature of job competences and of competencies associated with successful job performers. Personal competencies
seem to be more fitting than competences to the changing and fluid
nature of many modern jobs, especially school leadership and management, so this is the model used throughout the remainder of this book. If
you would like to follow up the competence models, useful references
would be Fletcher (1991), Lloyd and Cook (1993) and Management
Charter Initiative (1995).

We hope that you accept that to do your job effectively in these fast
changing times, it is important to develop your repertoire of competencies. We believe that the competencies identified by the National
Educational Assessment Centre and by McBer (see pp. 48 and 49)
provide a useful starting point for those in leadership and management
roles in schools. If readers wish to work with colleagues to determine
and validate a set of competencies from 'first principles', we would refer
them to the excellent detailed guidance provided by Spencer and Spencer
(1993) on the conduct of expert panels and Behavioural Event Interviews.

The four components in this chapter are:

- Competency assessment.
- Competency development.
- Coherence and progression in competencies.
- Tools for competency development.

COMPETENCY ASSESSMENT

The reasons why organisations or individuals may be concerned to assess individuals' competencies are, for example, in order to determine individuals' development needs, to match people to jobs or to look for candidates for promotion. You can utilise this book when considering your own competencies or when working with others on their profiles.

The approach or combination of approaches chosen for competency assessment will be influenced both by the purpose of the assessment and by a linked consideration relating to who should be responsible for assessing an employee's competencies. There are three possibilities:

- The organisation may take the responsibility, and set up a formal system to determine people's competencies and development needs.
- An employee and her/his boss or a mentor may jointly assess the employee's strengths and needs and agree a plan for development. This puts more 'ownership' and responsibility on the employee.
- Complete responsibility can be given to the individual employees by having them assess themselves and inviting them to decide what competencies they need to develop.

We would favour a shift towards more personal responsibility, with the individual making a 'learning contract' with her/his manager. This approach has the advantage of ownership: in our experience, staff are more likely to believe in a profile which they have been involved in developing, rather than one which has been handed to them by assessors. Indeed, the responsibility of individuals for assessing, developing and keeping records of their competencies is likely to increase, partly because the nature of work is changing and because of the trend towards more short-term and part-time contracts. Individuals will have to be prepared to switch from one job or contract to another more frequently in the future. People will find it useful to keep a record of the competencies that they have displayed in their work in order to show what they have achieved, and, equally important, to demonstrate their employability to future 'customers'.

Approaches to competency assessment

Although various approaches are available, we have found that any particular assessment approach used alone gives a one-dimensional snapshot. We are trying to build a multi-dimensional, complex perspective which is generated in such a way as to be accepted by the individual concerned and not seen as having been 'done to her/him' and thus to be unrepresentative. We believe that the following seven methods of assessing can be combined in a variety of ways in order to provide this multi-dimensional perspective.

360 degree method

This involves self-assessment plus assessment of the person concerned by peers and by those 'higher' and 'lower' in the organisation. This shows up any differences in perception by the different groups. For example, a leader may believe s/he is strong in 'sensitivity', but others may rate her/him low in this competency.

Assessment Centres

Here, exercises and simulations are designed to replicate situations calling for the use of key competencies. Individuals work through these, alone and in groups. Assessors observe and collect evidence, then make final judgements about each participant's profile of competencies. The profile and recommended development needs are then discussed with each individual. Assessors need careful training to be able to do this work. The National Educational Assessment Centre (NEAC) in the UK and the National Association of Secondary School Principals (NASSP) in the USA use this approach (see p. 49).

Behavioural Event Interviews

These (and similar forms of structured discussion) can provide a very rewarding way of exploring key activities with others and of identifying some of the key competencies which you bring to your work and which are associated with success or dealing with difficulties. We have found that the most effective approach is to work in threes, as follows.

A interviews B while C observes and takes notes and then the group rotates if required. An interview can last from twenty minutes to two hours. This is not an interrogation but is a process of drawing out and listening to a colleague in order to discover and pinpoint the things that s/he has done in specific incidents at work.

A asks B to recall about four to six critical incidents that s/he has handled and asks for the major responsibilities of the job (briefly, just enough to get the context for the critical incidents). The interviewee is asked to describe the first incident. To guide him/her through this, questions can be asked such as: 'What was the incident and what led up to it?'; 'How did you become involved?'; 'What were you trying to bring about, and what did you do about this?'; 'How did others see the situation and what did you feel about this?'; 'What was the outcome and how did you feel about this?' A question such as 'What characteristics does it take for someone to do your job?' may point up further incidents to probe.

Afterwards, the trio share their notes and observations and see if they can, together, crystallise the key competencies that were evident, looking for recurring concerns, thoughts, intentions and actions associated with success. Then, as well as reflecting on the incidents which have been described and the competencies which have been articulated, the interviewee can consider what has not been mentioned and can reflect on whether this is because the competencies did not feature during the events described or whether they are not a strength.

Assessment instruments

An example of such an instrument is the one developed by the Gallup organisation and used world-wide. This involves the nomination of outstanding practitioners by those in a particular occupational group. These 'experts' are then profiled in life themes and traits ranging from the general (such as ego drive) to the more particular (such as, for teachers, pride in learning). Assessment can be by taped face-to-face or telephone interview. An individual's responses are then analysed in relation to the research-based evidence to give a very thorough profile for developmental or selection purposes.

Psychometric tests

Tests such as the Myers–Briggs instrument, while not being designed to assess competency, can provide a picture of the whole personality as a basis for personal and professional development.

Appraisal or review systems

These systems can incorporate assessment – but there are risks of resistance by the people being appraised unless the system is integrated with the availability of development programmes.

Group exercises

When assessing competencies during our masters programmes, we would use a variety of well-known leadership and management exercises such as team role analysis (Belbin 1981; 1993), task and process dimensions of management (Blake and Mouton 1964) and learning styles analysis (Honey and Mumford 1986). The various exercises contribute to the building of a competency map and assist participants as they become more reflective and analytical about their competencies and styles of leadership.

We would suggest that you build up a map or portfolio of your competencies and then, having given some consideration to the pattern which appears, discuss these with a professional colleague, mentor or small group. The second person would, ideally, have been involved in some way in your competency assessment process. He or she would then be able to tease out from you some of the key features which you have demonstrated and to help to identify strengths and areas for development. This adds another dimension to the information presented.

COMPETENCY DEVELOPMENT

Once the competencies which seem to be appropriate for leadership and management roles in schools are understood and after a series of activities which point to individual strengths and areas for development is completed, a programme of competency development is needed. This will normally involve individual reflection and the guidance of peers and/or mentors.

Methods used for competency development

Group approaches

Here groups of individuals develop competencies together. This is likely to be the best method for getting people to become committed to competency development, with the added advantage that people can learn with and from each other and then maintain an ongoing mutual support network. One of the most highly regarded authors in this area is Revans (1980; 1983) who was the originator of Action Learning Sets, a method of putting together people from different organisations who actually have to face real management problems daily – as 'partners in adversity'. They meet regularly and help each other to tackle their respective challenges, with the group focusing in turn on the plight of each individual. These kinds of groups are sometimes used in schools (as discussed in Chapter 8), as part of Higher Education programmes and for MCI groups, with variations in the basic method.

Reflective logs/portfolios

When working on competency development with strategic leaders from schools, we encourage the use of a portfolio containing reflective analyses of critical incidents. We suggest that the following approach is used. First, give a description of your role and present management understanding. Secondly, describe a critical incident in which you were centrally involved and that had positive outcomes. Identify the management skills and competencies that were used that contributed to those positive outcomes. Thirdly, describe one management activity which had negative outcomes and try to isolate the management factors that were missing. This can be followed by entries which highlight other themes and critical incidents in your management practice. You can then draw out key factors relating to competencies demonstrated in practice and can identify further development needs. We have found that, in compiling the portfolio, individuals become more analytical about their own competencies. When their work is discussed with a tutor, mentor or senior colleague, another dimension is added as there can be further analysis and reflection and a wider perspective.

As well as acting as a device for personal development, the portfolio can be used to demonstrate progress and achievement to those inside the school or to potential employers. Esp (1993: 133–4) cites this type of approach. He recommends that managers could compile portfolios showing what they have achieved and explain these to another manager for competency appraisal or use them when seeking a job elsewhere. This reflects the use by pupils of personal Records of Achievement. New approaches to the continuing professional development of teachers are encouraging this approach, beginning with Initial Teacher Training and continuing throughout the career. This type of portfolio can demonstrate a person's experience and abilities through showing her/his track record of completed tasks, projects, initiatives, and the skills and knowledge involved.

Charles Handy puts a similar case for portfolios as proof of a person's employability:

> The intelligent society will inevitably be a credential society, one where certificates of competence become necessary passports in a more temporary and mobile workplace. We will move through life accumulating portfolios of competences and intelligences, portfolios which should start, but not finish, at school.
>
> (*Sunday Times* 27 February 1994)

Handy's view is that for the future we should look for customers requiring a specific piece of work to be done and show that we can do it, rather than relying on getting a lifelong job with the same employer. This view is echoed by Bridges (1995) who suggests that individuals will have to 'market' themselves as they move through a variety of types of employment.

Mentor/coach-learning partnerships

National schemes have been set up to establish pairings where an existing headteacher acts as coach or mentor to a newly appointed head-teacher to focus on competency development. Useful steps in this process are: (1) the pair identify what the learner is trying to achieve and the priorities; (2) they work out what has to be done to achieve these; and (3) they identify activities and behaviours required and relate these to the competencies that the learner already has and those that need to be developed (Esp 1993: 64). Boak's book (1991) is largely devoted to a similar approach using Learning Contracts.

Self-analysis and reflection

Learners identify parts of their job where the competency is important, and specific occasions where they have been successful in using the kinds of behaviour contained in the competency. Equally, learners pinpoint occasions when they could have been more successful by using the competency. This process leads to a self-assessment by learners of their development needs and what they want to practise and learn next.

COHERENCE AND PROGRESSION IN COMPETENCIES

One of the problems with the assessment and development of competencies is the fact that a competency is neither 'possessed' nor 'not possessed'. Those who are more 'expert' show this in one of two ways: through the degree to which they act intuitively or through the range of impact achieved when they demonstrate the competency.

Stages in competency development

Competency performance can be considered according to a person's progression towards proficiency. It is, of course, possible to get better and better at a competency just as one can get better and better at a skill. It is worth looking further at the nature of this progression because it is relevant to competency development (and also to assessment). The fact is that many jobs and associated competencies are characterised by gradations in performance. A person who has just passed a driving test is hardly likely to be as competent a driver as someone who has clocked up 100,000 miles' driving experience. Dreyfus' model (Eraut 1994: 118), which claims that there are five distinct stages of progression in a competency, was developed from studies of chess players and airline pilots. It encompasses skill and competency development including the role of routinisation and the place of strategy in performance. The five stages are as follows.

Novice

The person operates fairly rigidly, using facts and rules as they are learned. There is little situational perception or discretionary judgement.

Advanced beginner

The person's performance improves with experience as more situations are encountered. Understanding begins to go beyond facts and rules but situational perception is still limited – everything is treated as of equal importance.

Competency

The performer appreciates the scope and range of tasks, recognises more cues and can select and concentrate on the most important and can discern longer term goals. S/he acquires standardised and routine procedures.

Proficiency

The performer sees situations as wholes rather than aspects; sees what is most important in situations and can spot deviations from the norm. S/he can use rules of thumb and can call to mind things that have worked previously to deal with events.

Expert

The performer does not need to apply rules but has a deep, holistic recognition and intuitive understanding of situations. S/he has a repertoire of plans and stratagems to deal with changing situations, and often has a vision of how to rescue or make the most of situations.

The impact of the competency

One of the problems in the initial assessment of competencies or in the checking of progress is the extent of the impact that a person achieves by using a competency. Competency performance can range from a minimal level to a powerful, large scale effect. Spencer and Spencer (1993: 21–2) explain that the McBer organisation has identified five dimensions which indicate the strength of application of competencies. These are as follows.

Intensity or completeness of action

For example, the competency 'Achievement orientation' can range from 'wants to do a job well' to 'takes calculated entrepreneurial risks' with big pay-offs such as launching a new product.

Size of impact

The strength of the competency depends on the number and status of people or the size of project affected. For example a job performer might influence a peer or a boss, or the impact might be to influence the whole organisation. Superior performers are likely to take on challenges larger than their formal responsibilities require, whereas average performers take on tasks rather less than their job responsibilities.

Complexity

For example, the competencies relating to analytical and conceptual thinking may be applied to small scale issues, or, more ambitiously, may encompass more people, data, and systems.

Amount of effort

The time dedicated and the extra effort that a person applies to a given feature of a job can range from a little to a great deal.

Unique dimensions

The competency 'Self-confidence' includes not only positive strengths but also a dimension of 'dealing with failure', that is, how effectively a person gets over setbacks and avoids staying depressed. The competency 'Initiative' has a time dimension referring to how far into the future a person sees and acts. 'Superior performers see further ahead into the future and plan or act based on their vision' (Spencer and Spencer 1993: 22).

TOOLS FOR COMPETENCY DEVELOPMENT

It is difficult to know where to start when trying to work on competency development, particularly if you are working alone, for example when reading this book. We have outlined three tools from which to choose. You may find one or more of these to be useful in starting on the journey.

Tool 1

A process is set out below to analyse the demands of a school leadership role and to spell out the kinds of competencies which need to be developed.

Step 1: List personal tasks and challenges

In the light of your personal job purpose, make lists of your current and future tasks and challenges and select those that you will take personal responsibility for, and those that you will delegate to others. Use the matrix in Figure 5.1 and note on the top-horizontal axis the major tasks/challenges that you are or will be responsible for accomplishing.

Step 2: Spell out and cluster the competencies needed

Note down the competencies that you will need – what you will need to be good at and be able to do – in order to accomplish each of these tasks/challenges that you have earmarked as your personal responsibility. You will already have some of these competencies, but will want to develop others.

As you note them, try to assess whether a given competency is needed frequently – as in one or more routine, cyclical tasks – or exceptionally, for new or unexpected challenges such as dealing with a crisis or managing change. Cluster the competencies accordingly and note these on the vertical axis of your matrix. You may find that different tasks require the same competency.

Step 3: Identify the competencies which are strengths

Identify those competencies which are already your strengths. If you have not had recent assessment or discussion about this, you may wish to find a way of obtaining objective information (see p. 55–8).

Step 4: Set out priorities for personal development

Consider your matrix and set out priorities for personal competency development. As well as prioritising according to the criteria of frequently versus occasionally needed, you may also want to prioritise by the criteria of current versus future. At the end of this exercise you should have a list of competencies that you want to develop.

It will be useful to compare your results with the task and competency specifications for HEADLAMP in Figure 5.2 and, if you did not use them as a starting point, it is worth scanning the NEAC and McBer lists of competencies shown in the previous chapter, as well as the themes and topics in this book. This survey will help you to affirm or amend your own identified priorities.

COMPETENCIES (Inputs to the job)	TASKS (Outputs of the job)					
	CURRENT			FUTURE		
NEEDED FREQUENTLY						
NEEDED EXCEPTIONALLY						

Figure 5.1 Personal matrix of tasks and competencies

	Define aims	Develop and manage policies	Plan and manage resources	Ensure achieve-ment	Select and manage staff	Liaise with stake-holders
Give direction and motivate						
Anticipate problems, judge and decide						
Adapt to changes						
Solve problems						
Negotiate, delegate, consult and co-ordinate						
Follow through to implementation and review						
Keep updated on educational and management issues						
Communicate with all stakeholders						

HEADLAMP TASKS

Competencies and abilities

Other competencies discovered through personal analysis

Figure 5.2 HEADLAMP programme shown by matrix

Tool 2

The HEADLAMP Programme for newly appointed heads (TTA 1995) puts forward two sets of requirements for the role. These can be arranged as a matrix (Figure 5.2) with the tasks along the horizontal axis and the competencies and abilities along the vertical axis. You can use this matrix to reflect on the way in which the competencies are used to carry out the tasks. You can also use it to structure your self-analysis, to record examples of learning or to assess capability.

Tool 3

Kolb (1984) has shown that individuals, especially adults, learn best if they go through a cycle of four connected experiences (Figure 5.3).

Our interpretation of the process of adult learning involves proceeding round the four stages. Initially, there is the practical experience in school (concrete experience). The next stage, Reflective Observation, involves reflecting on the activity to work out what has happened. The process of Abstract Conceptualisation involves formulating a new concept, theory or method. This is followed by the Active Experimentation

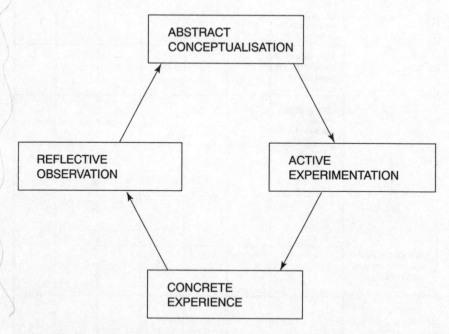

Figure 5.3 The learning cycle

Source: Spencer and Spencer 1993: 287

where the learner tries out the new material through exercises or simulations and then goes on to put them into practice in school.

Using this model, you can now think of a practical example from your school management role and apply the cycle to it. Can you identify all the above stages? In doing so, does it help you to rationalise the experience and to understand the processes involved? Now apply the framework to a future challenge that you face in your management role. In doing so, identify how you will encapsulate the four stages in your competency development process.

CONCLUSION

We believe that Kolb's model is reflected in the structure of this book in that the reader comes to it with practical experience. The focus on competency and knowledge throughout the book encourages reflection and conceptualisation. The reader can then develop her/his own practice. Kolb (1984) points out that although individuals may have a preference or inclination for one of these four types of experience, the most effective learning will result if all four stages are experienced in cyclical sequence.

REFERENCES

Belbin, M. (1981) *Management Teams: Why They Succeed or Fail*, London: Heinemann.

Belbin, M. (1993) *Team Roles at Work*, Oxford: Butterworth-Heinemann.

Blake, R. R. and Mouton, J. S. (1964) *The Managerial Grid*, Houston, Tex: Gulf.

Boak, G. (1991) *Developing Managerial Competences: the Management Learning Contract Approach*, London: Pitman.

Bridges, W. (1995) *Jobshift: How to Prosper in a Workplace Without Jobs*, London: Nicholas Brearley.

Eraut, M. (1994) *Developing Professional Knowledge*, London: Falmer.

Esp, D. (1993) *Competences for School Managers*, London: Kogan Page.

Fletcher, S. (1991) *Designing Competence-Based Training*, London: Kogan Page.

Handy, C. (27 February, 1994) 'To the head of the IQ', *Sunday Times*, pp. 8–19.

Honey, P. and Mumford, A. (1986) *The Manual of Learning Styles*, Maidenhead: Peter Honey.

Kolb, D. A. (1984) *Experiential Learning*, Englewood Cliffs, NJ: Prentice Hall.

Lloyd, C. and Cook, A. (1993) *Implementing Standards of Competence: Practical Strategies for Industry*, London: Kogan Page.

Management Charter Initiative (1995) *Senior Management Standards*, Sheffield: MCI.

Revans, R. W. (1980) *Action Learning: New Techniques for Management*, London: Blond and Briggs.

Revans, R. W. (1983) *ABC of Action Learning*, Bromley: Chartwell Bratt.

Spencer, L. M. and Spencer, S. M. (1993) *Competence at Work: Models for Superior Performance*, New York: Wiley.

Teacher Training Agency (1995) HEADLAMP, 19 May.

6 Establishing a development framework for this book

Brent Davies and Linda Ellison

The previous two chapters have given you an understanding of competence and competency. The chapters which follow this one will explore the concepts that need to be understood by strategic leaders in schools. This chapter acts as the link between the two parts of the book by providing a framework which you can use at the end of each chapter in Part II in order to focus on your own level of understanding of the concepts and perceptions of your own competency to be successful in the area. An individual undertaking a structured self-review after reading each of the chapters will find it helpful to use the following three-stage process: (1) identify the concepts in each chapter and the competencies which are significant; (2) evaluate both your personal knowledge and competencies in that area and that of your colleagues; and (3) devise an action plan to highlight development needs and identify suitable implementation strategies.

Stage 1: identify the concepts and competencies in each chapter

- What are the key concepts that are being explored in the chapter?
- What are the competencies that are needed to utilise the concepts?

Stage 2: evaluate your personal knowledge and competencies and that of your colleagues

- What is my level of understanding of the key concepts?
- What are my competencies in this particular area?
- What competencies reside in my senior management team in this area?

Stage 3: devise an action plan to facilitate appropriate development

- What knowledge of the key concepts do I need to develop?
- What competencies do I need to develop to support my existing competencies (and to complement those of the team)?

Stage 1: Identify the concepts and competencies in each chapter

	CONCEPT AREAS					
COMPETENCIES						

Stage 2: **Evaluate your personal knowledge and competencies and that of your colleagues**

1 What have I learned about my own skills, knowledge development and competencies in this area?

2 What have I learned about my colleagues' knowledge and competencies in this area?

Stage 3 : **Devise an action plan to facilitate appropriate development**

From the matrix in Stage 1, list the **concept areas** in which you feel you need to develop further/deeper understanding:

1...

2...

3...

4...

5...

From the matrix in Stage 1, list the **competencies** which you have identified as needing further development:

1...

2...

3...

Outline the strategies you will employ to implement a programme of development of the above concepts and competencies:

1...

2...

3...

4...

5...

As explained in Chapter 1, this book set out to help you to rethink, reconceptualise and reassess the educational context, the school and your personal leadership and management competencies. This should enable you to review key leadership and management areas and to envisage the future. Chapters 2 and 3 undertook a review of the educational context and the nature of the self-managing school. Chapters 4, 5 and 6 will have given you an understanding of competence and competency and the ability to work on your development in this area.

In Part II there will be the chance to work on some of the most significant areas of responsibility in school leadership. At the end of each chapter, there will be a link to Chapters 4, 5 and 6 by providing an opportunity for you to reflect on the competencies necessary to utilise the concepts outlined in each chapter. Putting together the competencies and the conceptual understanding should provide a firm basis for making the strategic leap into the future which is explored in Part III.

Part II

Developing a broad strategic perspective

Core leadership and management functions

Facilitating the leadership and management process

7 Developing a strategic perspective

Brent Davies and Linda Ellison

Earlier chapters have examined the changing educational context, emphasising the necessity to rethink fundamentally the nature of education in self-managing schools. Similar issues are also raised by Drucker (1993):

> What will be taught and learned; how it will be taught and learned; who will make use of schooling; and the position of the school in society – all of this will change greatly during the ensuing decades. Indeed, no other institution faces challenges as radical as those that will transform the school.
>
> (Drucker 1993: 209)

What sort of educational experience will learners have over the next ten years and beyond? Who will these learners be? How will schools plan to operate in this environment? The continued and increasingly rapid changes in both the educational and the global environment require that schools must think ahead about the types of organisations which they wish to be in ten years' time and that those who lead each school must be able to take it in the right direction.

Although there is now a wider range of decisions taken at the school level and a wider range of options available with regard to strategic direction and more operational matters, much of the planning emphasis to date has been on the creation of development plans, usually outlining the school's proposed activities over a one- to three-year period. Considerable expertise has developed at the school level with revisions to earlier approaches taking place regarding both the format of the plans and the planning process itself. However, the approach used (alongside financial constraints on schools) has encouraged incrementalism rather than a more strategic and creative approach, as reflected by the comment of Hamel and Prahalad (1989: 75) that 'creative strategies seldom emerge from the annual planning ritual'. The tendency to short-termism has been exacerbated by the speed of technological change and also by a sense of not being in control of the change process because of government legislation imposing on schools.

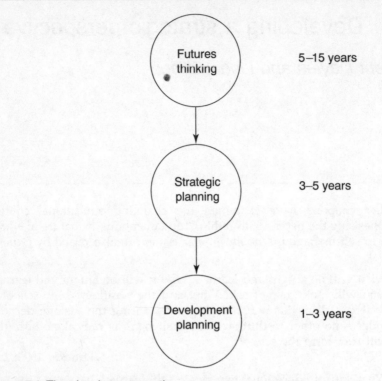

Figure 7.1 The planning perspective

Against this background, it is important to take a longer-term holistic perspective which considers what the nature of learning and the learning technology will be like in the twenty-first century and to avoid an incremental approach whereby a school would gradually alter its current provision. It is also wise to avoid some of the mistakes of industry and commerce where a rigid approach to strategic planning and an over-reliance on 'the planning department' (as pointed out by Mintzberg 1994) has produced inflexibility and an inability to grasp opportunities which would ensure the long-term effectiveness of the organisation. As Porter (1987: 22) detected, there is now 'a growing recognition that the processes for strategic planning were not promoting strategic thinking . . . meaningless long-term projections obscured strategic insight'.

A more appropriate model to incremental planning is to use 'futures' thinking in order to develop a vision about a desired future state and then to plan backwards from that desired state. Senior managers in schools must, therefore, develop knowledge and skills in the areas of futures thinking and strategic planning to complement and extend the existing development planning process. The link between these three activities can be seen in Figure 7.1.

The major sections of this chapter take each of the three processes and outline the key points to be considered by the leaders of self-managing schools. This will allow you to reflect on your knowledge and competency.

FUTURES THINKING

In order to develop visionary futures thinking in schools, we must move beyond simple incremental thinking and engage in radically different approaches to considering the school's future. Dent (1995: 12) uses the distinction between left and right brain thinking which he categorises as:

Left brain	*Right brain*
Repetitive	Creative
Systematic	Complex
Computational work	Intuitive powers and judgement

Do we, in terms of the administrative and managerial tasks undertaken by management in schools, develop more of the left brain as opposed to the right brain thinking? How do we develop more of the creative side of thinking? Dent (1995) goes on to build on this concept as a way of distinguishing between the incremental innovators and the radical innovators who can provide the breakthrough visioning that is necessary to operate in the twenty-first century (Table 7.1).

Table 7.1 Distinction between incremental and radical innovators

Tendencies of incremental innovators	*Tendencies of radical innovators*
To rely on the left brain	To rely on the right brain
To approach problems systematically	To approach problems from new angles
To be social and competitive	To be loners
To love results, progress and feedback	To love challenges and puzzles
To operate in neat, methodical environments	To operate in messy environments
To be stable and measured	To be eccentric and moody
To be more serious	To have a strong sense of humour

Source: Dent 1995: 269

It may be worthwhile considering how you fit into the left or right hand side of the table. It should not be considered as an either/or situation. Individuals exercise both sides of the brain: the point is that we should develop the characteristics of the radical innovators if we are successfully to envision the future.

When attempting to engage in futures thinking about the nature of schools and of the process of learning in the twenty-first century, it is necessary to consider some of the trends that will impact on schools over the next five to fifteen years. This should provide us with a useful starting point and help us to avoid falling into the trap of incrementalism. Some of the thinking that is available is provided in Chapter 2 and can be summarised as encompassing:

- Radical changes in the nature of learning and teaching – the core process of schools. This is particularly important with learning, as the new technologies will exert a powerful influence, giving students 24-hour access to high quality learning resources and thus altering the traditional role of schools and teachers.
- Increased differentiation between schools with wider parental choice.
- Considerable changes in the types of staff employed, in the nature of their contracts and in the way in which the leadership and management functions are distributed and carried out.
- An increasing emphasis on lifelong learning and the school as part of the community.
- Greater varieties of funding sources for education.
- Increased accountability at the school level, with an emphasis on value for money and value-added assessments.

How do leaders in schools assess the significance of these trends and consider how they will impact on their organisations? One useful approach is to utilise scenario building. Scenario building is a method of envisioning the future which involves assessing the trends and then building an outline or sketch of the major developments which might take place in the school. It is especially appropriate when the major trends affecting the provision will be the result of non-quantifiable factors. Many headteachers are sceptical of trying to look too far ahead. Scenario building recognises the unpredictability of the future and provides a means of preparing mentally for more than one future. The visions created are not to be seen as predictions but as possible scenarios. This should prove helpful to school leaders because it is important to recognise that decisions taken now will have long-term implications and that current decision-taking should allow for the uncertainties as exemplified in the scenarios.

At a practical level, two, three or four scenarios are built so that people can choose the one which seems most appropriate given current knowledge. When building the scenarios, it is important to involve people who have intuition, are creative and who have good judgement. This will help not only to ensure sufficient foresight but also to generate scenarios which are credible, useful and understandable. At this creative stage, the benefits can be seen of not having a senior management team whose members are all alike; a variety of views and some tensions and disagreements should result in better scenarios. A range of stakeholders, both internal and external, need to be involved at the scenario building and selecting stage, although much of the work will be carried out by the senior management team and the governors. Strategic leaders can consider what sort of schools would be best suited if a particular scenario were to become reality and what the challenges would be in the case of each scenario.

Having developed an understanding of the broader 'futures' trends and developed appropriate scenarios, the leaders of a self-managing school then need to move to developing a strategic plan for the school. This is the stage at which the understanding of the fundamental long-term shifts in society and in education begin to inform more concrete strategic plans.

STRATEGIC PLANNING

The problems of strategic planning

Once there is a clear 'futures' perspective of the world in which the school will be operating, there is a need for a more systematic means of ensuring that the school moves in a direction which will enable the vision to be realised. However, there is a major concern with simply applying the process of strategic planning because it is problematic in an era of rapid change. It assumes a rational and predictable process which in practical terms may not be possible in the current environment. In the most outstanding piece which we have read on the topic, Max Boisot (1995), in his chapter 'Preparing for turbulence: the changing relationship between strategy and management development in the learning organisation', provides two key areas of analysis. He suggests that control, which is inherent in the concepts of strategy, is rendered ineffective because of the turbulence caused by rapidly increasing rates of change. As a result he suggests, 'From the literature, we can identify four basic types of response: (1) strategic planning, (2) emergent strategy, (3) intrapreneurship, (4) strategic intent' (Boisot 1995: 32).

Strategic planning is based on there being a predictable environment which can be identified so that appropriate strategies can be implemented in a rational, steady way. The rate of change is assumed to be less than the organisation's ability to understand and adapt to those changes. In the educational context, rapid change over the last ten years and the future impact of technology on learning has cast doubt as to whether strategic planning over a three to five year period is possible.

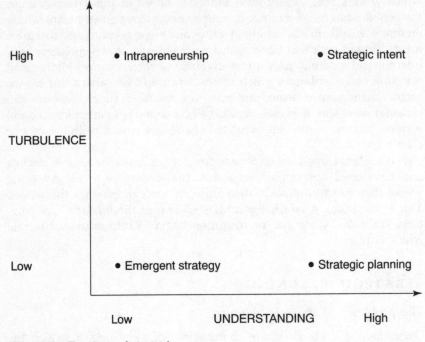

Figure 7.2 Typology of strategies
Source: Boisot 1995: 40

Boisot (1995: 33–5) suggests that alternative approaches should be considered.

Emergent strategy assumes incremental change with adjustment to the strategy as new information becomes available. Thus planners assume that a process of 'disjointed incrementalism' will change their plans as they go along. Another response is *intrapreneurship*, which assumes that the degree of turbulence in the system is so great that the centre cannot plan in an integrated way. As a result, decentralised units are encouraged to react to their specific circumstances and relate to the centre in a loosely coupled way. Thus localised success and failures build a direction for the organisation.

The final approach, and one which has a great deal of value for the educationalist, is that of *strategic intent*. Boisot (1995: 37) believes that an organisation 'operating in a regime of strategic intent can use a common vision to keep the behaviour of its employees aligned with a common purpose when it decentralises in response to turbulence'. This is a very powerful way of linking futures thinking and strategy as a means of providing direction and purpose for an organisation.

In an excellent typology of strategies Boisot links the four responses with conditions of turbulence and organisational understanding, as shown in Figure 7.2. We believe that schools operate partly in a highly turbulent environment and that, in such circumstances, the appropriate strategy is to use 'futures' perspectives to build a vision within the school in order to create a strategic intent for the school. Part of a school's environment is more predictable and less turbulent and, in those circumstances, techniques and approaches that are available from the traditional business school approach to strategic planning provide useful analytical tools. In this context, bearing in mind the limitations outlined above, we now propose to outline the strategic approaches that are available to the school manager, the outcome being a series of strategic objectives which will then be taken forward into the development planning process.

The strategic planning process

We would define strategic planning as 'the systematic analysis of the school and its environment and the formulation of a set of key strategic objectives to enable the school to realise its vision, within the context of its values and its resource potential'. Although, at this stage, there is a need to be fairly systematic in gathering information about the present and about future trends, creativity and intuition are still important (see Mintzberg 1994), particularly when generating options and deciding on the way forward. This stage, therefore, utilises both right and left brain thinking. Also, if the time spent on strategic planning is to result in a realistic and sustainable set of strategic objectives, the systems and processes used must encourage wide involvement and ownership of the decisions by all stakeholders.

The strategic planning process will, therefore, comprise: (1) *strategic analysis* to give a view of the current and medium-term environment; (2) *strategic choice*, that is, the generation of possible courses of action from which the school can choose in order to work towards the vision and then the evaluation of those options so that decisions can be taken about which ones to pursue; and (3) *strategic implementation* of a set of clear *strategic objectives*. Resulting from the first two stages these are to be taken forward for implementation through the *development planning* process.

Strategic analysis

The purpose of this analysis is to form a view of the strategic position of the school and of the key factors which will influence the school in both the short and medium term and which will, therefore, affect the

Table 7.2 Strategic analysis

Area for analysis	Need to know	Available tools or approaches

1 Environment:
   global
   national
   local
	Megatrends
	National trends
	Regional/local trends
		PEST (political, economic,
		   social and technological)
		   analysis

2 Approaches to
   teaching and
   learning
	Pedagogy, learning technology
	Effective schools characteristics
	School improvement data
		Research data and government
		   publications

3 School's product
   and service
	Areas of strength and weakness,
	   growth and contraction:
	   covering all aspects
		SWOT (strengths, weaknesses,
		   opportunities and threats)
		   analysis
		GRIDS (Guidelines for Review
		   and Internal Development in
		   Schools)
		Internal evaluation
		School inspection

4 School's
   customers/
   stakeholders:
   internal and
   external
	Existing and potential
	   customers/clients
	Perceptions of school
	Needs/objectives
	Values/expectations
		Market segments, demographic
		   and survey data
		Attitude surveys
		Preference surveys

5 Competitors	Strengths and weaknesses Perceptions of their provision Product/service offered	SWOT analysis Customer survey data Competitor analysis

6 The school and
   the market
	Product and service in relation
	   to the total market and other
	   providers
		Boston Consulting Group matrix
		Little's lifecycle analysis
		General Electric Screen

choice of strategy. These factors are drawn from a wide range of sources and the information will take some time to gather. A thorough approach is important as omissions or false assumptions at this stage could lead to the school making the wrong strategic decisions later on. Many classifications of areas for investigation are provided by the literature (for example Johnson and Scholes 1993; Luffman *et al.* 1991) and there are many detailed accounts of the tools which can be used. We have provided a checklist (Table 7.2) which shows the areas that a school would need to investigate and the tools and approaches which may be suitable. As we have indicated, many of the tools and approaches can be used to gather information for different areas. Sections (1) and (2) of Table 7.3 cover the broad environment in which the school exists while Sections (3) and (4) examine the school itself. These two can be brought together through the analysis in Sections (5) and (6) which examine how the school fits into the environment.

Although the information will usually be assembled by the senior management team, to appreciate fully the strategic position of the school it is necessary to understand how a wide range of stakeholders, such as pupils, staff, employers, governors and the community, view the situation which the school faces and its possible direction. Those responsible for aspects of the analysis need to look beyond their normal sources of information if the work is to have validity.

The section which follows takes the reader through Table 7.3, pointing out the key concepts and issues relating to each area under analysis. Further detail can be found in our other texts on this topic (Davies and Ellison 1992; 1994; in press).

1   The environment

One of the most significant strategic roles for school leadership is 'managing the boundaries', that is, seeing beyond the boundaries of the school and understanding the interface between the school and its environment. For the purposes of strategic analysis, the external environment can be sub-divided into global, national (or macro) and local/regional (or micro). This categorisation affects the degree of detail which is available and, sometimes, the degree of its impact over time. There are many acronyms, such as PEST, for the analytical frameworks which can be used. It is important to choose one which covers the relevant areas and which can be readily used by those in school without being too much of a drain on people's time. As broad a range of views as possible is needed because those in the school may not be aware of some of the information which is available to inform strategic planning.

2   Approaches to teaching and learning

Dimmock (1995) points to the importance of leadership which focuses on the curriculum and on pedagogy with the head and senior staff as instructional leaders. This reflects the earlier work of Caldwell and Spinks (1992) who prefer the term 'leader of learning and teaching' in its widest sense. As teaching and learning are the core business of the school, an understanding of current thinking and of future trends and possibilities is of considerable importance. This specific information will be essential to put alongside the more generic environmental data. In recent years there has been a tendency to neglect the area of teaching and learning while focusing on finance and structures. Approaches to teaching and learning should dictate structures and organisation, not vice versa, and the focus should be on ensuring teaching and learning for understanding. The well known strategic management maxim of 'structure follows strategy' is an important one to remember here. Spinks

(1991: 57) emphasises that successful schools will be those 'well able to predict future learning priorities for students and to shift resources and learning time to achieve those priorities'.

There have, over the last twenty years, been many research reports and inspection reports which offer evidence of effective teaching and learning strategies. An examination of these, in conjunction with environmental information and scenarios, can provide a reasonable basis for planning.

3   The school's product and service

There are various ways of categorising the school's product and service. In our experience, the headings which follow have proved useful in a great many schools. Further detail about the issues to consider under each heading are given in Davies and Ellison (1992; in press) The areas to be examined would be:

- Curriculum, learning and teaching.
- Human resources.
- Pupil/student welfare and pastoral care.
- Physical resources.
- Financial resources.
- Pupil/student roll and marketing.
- Management structures and approaches.
- Monitoring and evaluation mechanisms.
- Community.

Various tools and techniques are available to analyse the situation in each area. The suitability of each will depend on a range of factors such as the time available, the people to be involved and the culture of the organisation:

- SWOT analysis – an analysis of the strengths and weaknesses of the school, the opportunities which are available and the threats which it faces, as perceived by a range of stakeholders.
- GRIDS – Guidelines for Review and Internal Development in Schools provides a detailed and structured school-based review process (Abbott *et al* 1988).
- Internal monitoring and evaluation – part of the school's normal management cycle.
- School inspection – carried out either by OFSTED or by others brought in to give an external perspective, this provides a wealth of data which can be built into the planning process.

4   School's customers/stakeholders

Here the purpose is to identify three sets of strategic information using, for example, the following three approaches:

Information needed	Approaches
Who are the customers/clients and who might they be in the future?	Market segmentation
What are the perceptions of the clients/customers of the school?	Attitude surveys
What do the clients/customers want from the school?	Preference surveys

There are several caveats to offer to those who may consider these approaches. Vast amounts of data may be gathered with considerable time implications. It is better to think carefully about the type of information which the school requires before asking a lot of people a lot of questions. Also, the responses, particularly to attitude surveys, can be very disturbing. There needs to be careful preparation in relation to planning the dissemination of results. It is unwise to gather data and then to take no action on issues that arise, although the action may simply be to improve communication. Once the culture and processes have been established, these tools can be used to provide valuable information for strategic planning.

5   Competitors

The information gathered about competitors and potential competitors can be very significant in determining the appropriate strategic direction of the school. As was suggested in Chapter 2 there are considerable issues here because of parental choice, developments in the learning technology and changes in the funding of education and in the continuum of education itself.

The traditional product and service of the school can now, and increasingly will in the future, be offered by a range of other 'providers' such as satellite, the World Wide Web, private agencies, industry and commerce, parents and the community. The conclusion to be drawn here is that any analysis of competitors must go far beyond the usual brief consideration of what 'the school down the road' is doing.

6   The school and the market

In order to carry out an analysis of the way in which the school fits into the educational market, a variety of tools are available which were developed in industry and commerce for the analysis and positioning of business units or portfolios of activity in relation to the nature of the market. The examples which, in our experience, have proved useful to schools are the Boston Consulting Group (BCG) matrix, Little's lifecycle analysis and the General Electric (GE) Screen. These and other approaches are outlined in generic texts on strategic planning such as Johnson and Scholes (1993) and Greenley (1989) and in Davies and Ellison (1992; 1994; in press).

The strategic analysis will have provided a wealth of information on factors both inside and outside the school. The information then needs to be organised in order to form a clear view of those factors which are significant in influencing the school's future direction. At this point, it is appropriate to re-examine the school's vision to check that this is still a feasible reality. The mission statement may then be developed or re-examined in order to clarify the way in which the vision is translated into a set of guiding principles or goals.

The following checklist of questions may assist senior managers at this stage.

- Is there a shared and clear vision of what the school is trying to achieve and is this congruent with the context as revealed by the strategic analysis?
- Is there a mission statement which articulates the vision and does this statement have real meaning for the stakeholders?
- Does the school have a statement of broad aims/goals which reflect the vision and mission and which will guide strategic decisions?

Once the general direction of the school's development has been determined and there is a good understanding of the internal and external factors which are affecting it, choices need to be made about the strategies which might be followed in order to make a reality of the vision and the goals.

Strategic choice

The strategic processes described so far have resulted in the establishment of a clear understanding of the school's vision and values and of the situation in which it will be operating over the next ten years. The next stage is to identify a range of strategic options and then to choose those which are most likely to bring about the desired situation.

Option generation

When generating options, there is a need for creativity in exploring the possibilities. Again, a range of people should be involved so as to obtain a variety of options for consideration, especially by including those from outside the traditional school ways of thinking, for example from governors and the community. Something which seems to be an outrageous idea can lead, through creative discussion, to exciting opportunities. Unfortunately, many ideas are dismissed too quickly without considering whether, in the long term, they could be developed to increase school effectiveness. A good example is the way in which any attempt to alter the structure of the school day is vetoed because it sounds like 'extra work' whereas it could result in a more effective use of the premises, for example by running two tracks of pupils with two sets of staff. The scenarios created during the earlier stage of Futures Thinking should provide a stimulus.

Literature on strategic management (see, for example, Johnson and Scholes 1993; Bowman and Asch 1987) provides a range of possible options for future development which could be applied in any organisation. The framework which follows should be useful for schools.

- Withdraw from unsatisfactory or non-compatible areas of the school's portfolio of activities, e.g. the provision of hot meals or of minority post-16 courses.
- Consolidate (grow with the market, or defend the school's position in a stable market), e.g. maintain intake numbers, develop the marketing of the school in order to promote stability and a quality image.
- Gain market share by penetrating the market, e.g. raise intake numbers or take in more pupils at Year 12 or in a nursery unit.
- Develop new provision, either as products or services, e.g. start photography courses.
- Market development (entering new segments of the market or geographical areas): take post-16 students from mainland Europe, teach Information Technology skills to adults.
- Diversify into:
  (a) related activities, e.g. set up a music school or a Japanese school at the weekends or open up the reprographic facilities to commercial use;
  (b) activities with no clear relationship with the existing core business, e.g. set up a gardening or catering company for contracts in the community, workshops/business units in spare accommodation.
- Vertically integrate forwards or backwards, e.g. an infant school could develop a nursery, a secondary school could develop a primary department.

There is a further option, which is to do nothing by continuing to follow the current strategy that is proving to be successful. This 'if it ain't broke, don't fix it' strategy should be selected only after considerable thought and should not be seen as the normal option. In the rapidly changing environment in which education now exists, it is very likely that some strategic changes will be required if the school is to remain successful. The need to change, even when things seem to be going well, has been raised by Handy (1994) in his application of the Sigmoid curve and was covered in Chapter 2.

While generating options, it is worth considering how, broadly, the options could be made feasible. One strategy would be through internal development, for example by forming a grounds maintenance team within the school. An alternative approach would be through acquisition, such as when one organisation (say, a secondary school) decides to take over another (say, a primary school). Joint development, in which two organisations develop and manage a project such as a community arts facility, is an alternative which is increasingly considered as resources become more constrained. A final approach, which is well known in the world of corporate business but less so in education, is the demerger, in which part of the organisation breaks away to form a separate business, for example when a school loses its Years 12 and 13 to form a Sixth Form College.

Choice of options

Once the options have been generated and some attempt made at prioritising them, there remains the process of making the final decisions about which of them to pursue. This stage involves the evaluation of the various strategic options and the selection of appropriate ways forward. The strategies must be evaluated against criteria that take account of the information which is known to the school including: its vision and mission statement; the values of the school, its community and its leaders; the factors identified in the strategic analysis. At this stage, three groups of questions should be asked in order to evaluate the appropriateness of each option which has been generated in relation to its suitability, acceptability and feasibility. A matrix could be created in order to record results in a systematic and easy-to-read format.

Suitability   Is the proposed strategy congruent with global trends and does it:

(a) exploit the school's strengths and opportunities?
(b) integrate with the school's mission and goals?
(c) overcome difficulties identified in the strategic analysis?

Acceptability   This involves the school's value system and the effect which the proposed strategy would have on the school as it currently exists. It helps the decision-makers to consider the merits of the proposal:

- Does it accord with the values of the school and the community?
- Does it meet expectations?
- Does it have an effect on the functioning of the various parts of the school?
- Does it have an effect on capital structure?
- Does it involve risk?
- Does it incur costs/produce profit?

These last two are usually considered together in that a high risk strategy should have the potential to bring a high reward. It is recognised that the values and expectations of those in power will affect significantly the chosen strategy. Leaders need to consider whether power is currently in the right hands so that decisions are made in the best interests of the school and its community, rather than according to the influence of one or two individuals.

Feasibility   The prompt questions here relate to the competitive situation in which the school exists and to its strategic capabilities:

- Can the option be funded?
- Can the school perform at the required level?
- Can the necessary market position be achieved?
- Can the school cope with any competitive reaction?
- Can the school secure or develop the required skills?
- Is the technology available?

It is important to consider the gap between the present situation and the desired position in order to determine whether the school has the means to take the option or can develop the means, for example by acquiring the necessary funding or skills. There are recognised tools available such as resource deployment analysis (Johnson and Scholes 1993: 302–4). Although this practice is widespread in the planning of such things as staffing, timetables, and specific grants, it is not generally recognised by its official name. In many situations, the most significant determining factor relates to the competitive reaction of other providers of education. For example, there may be physical space in a secondary school whose mission is to promote continuity but the potential local outcry of a decision to recruit 5–11 year olds would probably be the most likely reason for rejecting the option.

The final decision on options for implementation would probably follow an extensive iterative process including negotiation and compromise and would normally be made by the governors, in consultation with the headteacher or with the whole senior management team.

Key strategic objectives

Once the choices have been made, the school can formulate a set of strategic objectives which can then be implemented through the school development planning process. These objectives should be:

- Realistic but challenging.
- Clear and concise.
- Communicated to all stakeholders.
- Used to create commitment in the various stakeholders, especially those working in the school.
- Used to inform decisions and activities during the school development planning process.

STRATEGIC IMPLEMENTATION: DEVELOPMENT PLANNING

Strategic implementation, we consider, is synonymous with development planning. This is the critical stage at which those within the school develop proposals and an action plan for achieving the strategic objectives and strategic options which have been chosen. As the focus of this book is on the strategic aspects of school leadership, we have given less emphasis to this significant but more operational part of the planning process. A much more detailed account of this stage of achieving the school's chosen direction can be found in Davies and Ellison (1992; in press).

In the early 1990s there was a lot of concern about those schools that did not have a formal, documented plan. Although there is no legal requirement to have a school development plan, the demands of OFSTED and of the various funding and auditing organisations then encouraged all schools to have one in some form. Despite this pressure, not all schools have a shared view of the purpose of the plan, the nature of the planning process or the format and subsequent use of the document itself. These are the areas to be outlined in this section.

The purpose of the plan

Caldwell and Spinks' definition of a development plan is clear and provides a useful model:

> a specification ... of priorities to be addressed, and of strategies to be employed in addressing those priorities, as the school seeks to achieve multiple objectives over a number of years.
>
> (Caldwell and Spinks 1992: 39)

It is important to realise that the objectives to be achieved include some relating to innovation and many which relate to the maintenance of existing activities. It is very discouraging for staff if they feel that their ongoing activities are undervalued and that all efforts are being put into new activities. Also, there needs to be realism about the balance between new developments and the maintenance of the existing activities, otherwise there will be work overload and a lack of resources.

The nature of the development planning process

The creation of the school development plan is a process, not an event. We would propose that this more operational part of the planning process comprises the following stages:

- Bringing together the strategic objectives and the activities to be maintained.
- Documenting and implementing the school development plan.
- Monitoring and evaluating.

The various steps take place over long periods of time throughout the year and each one is, in fact, iterative. For example, the evaluation has to be planned, resourced, implemented and evaluated. Schools need to decide whether to base the plan on academic or financial years. Many are moving to the latter so that planning drives the budget rather than vice versa. There need to be clear guidelines explaining when the planning activities take place and how the various participants in the process are to be involved.

Strategic objectives and maintenance activities

A list of strategic objectives will have been drawn up as a result of the strategic planning process and a wide range of maintenance activities will be continued from previous annual cycles. The senior managers will ensure that people are clear about the priorities.

Documenting and implementing the school development plan

In too many cases, the document becomes so detailed and unwieldy that it cannot be used as a working document. A useful phrase to remember is 'the thicker the plan the less it affects classroom practice'. It should, therefore, be set out in an easily read format and would cover the areas shown in Table 7.3 (overleaf).

We would see the development plan as a working document which would be set out in a list or matrix format. It can then be used to monitor progress and to provide a framework for modifications, should circumstances change. Suggestions for the layout of this document are provided elsewhere (Davies and Ellison 1992; in press).

Table 7.3 Areas covered by the school development plan

Core areas	Support areas
Curriculum and curriculum management	Management structures and approaches
Human resources	Financial resources
Pupil welfare and pastoral care	Pupil roll and marketing
	Physical resources
	Monitoring and evaluation
	Community

Teams/sub-units need to develop plans which will allow for the continuation of maintenance activities and which will ensure the introduction of new strategies as determined above. Some of these teams may have been created especially to plan a particular initiative such as the remodelling of the school grounds or the introduction of a new reporting system. Others will be part of the ongoing structure of the school, such as a Key Stage team or a faculty.

The plans should state detailed objectives over one year and indicative plans over a further two years leading towards the strategic objectives. Objectives should be costed. The costing should take account of staff development and time as well as materials. For each objective there should be performance indicators and success criteria, a named person who is responsible for the achievement of the objective and a date by which it should be achieved. It is important that these unit or project plans are created within the boundaries set by the whole school objectives and priorities. Draft proposals would be passed to a planning group for comment and discussion and then returned for refinement. When the whole school plan has been put together, it should be supported by data relating to expected pupil numbers, staffing and premises requirements.

The detailed activities will usually have financial implications for the school so it is important that the planning and budgeting cycles are linked. It is also important to review resource use and challenge existing patterns of spending. While planning over a three-year period is problematic, the financial implications of staffing structures and associated salary costs and incremental salary increases can be built into a spreadsheet to produce scenarios under different funding conditions. The same is also true for capital replacement and repairs to property and equipment. Further detail on this area can be found in Chapter 13.

The final plan will be approved by the governors while the responsibility for leading its implementation will lie with the school's senior management team. Considerable senior management time needs to be devoted to the successful implementation. For effective implementation, the way that the process is led can be as important as the content.

Monitoring and evaluating

The plan should be a working document which can guide those with responsibility for managing the activities and which can provide a framework for monitoring. This should involve those at all levels in the school in checking that they are working towards the targets set. At intervals, managers need to meet with those for whom they have responsibility in order to discuss progress. This will allow them to support those whose projects are showing some slippage in reaching the targets and will allow for revisions to the plan if appropriate. Members of the senior management team would monitor the major sections of the plan in the same way and need to consider the most appropriate way to keep governors informed of progress. Evaluation of the effectiveness of the chosen activities and strategies as well as of the process of creating and managing the plan will provide important data to inform the way forward.

CONCLUSION

The approach we have adapted in this chapter is one which incorporates three stages:

- Futures thinking
    Key trends and developments
    Vision, mission and aims/goals
    Building of strategic intent
- Strategic planning
    Interpretation of strategic intent
    Strategic objectives
    A central plan giving medium-term developments
- Development planning
    An action plan to include:
    (a) short-term objectives
    (b) targets, tasks, timing and indicators success
    (c) resource implications
    (d) person responsible.

Initial work on planning in schools has emphasised the management elements of operational planning in terms of one-year plans with two-year projections following. It is now important that the leadership dimension of strategic intent and futures thinking is given far greater prominence to enable schools to set their activity in a longer-term framework. We believe that this chapter provides the perspectives to enable this to happen.

It is important to reflect on the concepts that are central to this chapter and the competencies necessary to utilise them. To enable you to do this and to form an action plan, we suggest that it would be of assistance to make an enlarged photo-copy of the three pages in Appendix A.

REFERENCES

Abbott, R., Steadman, S. and Birchenhough, M. (1988) *GRIDS School Handbooks* (2nd edn, Primary and Secondary versions), York: Longman for the SCDC.

Boisot, M. (1985) 'Preparing for turbulence: the changing relationship between strategy and management development in the learning organisation', in B. Garratt (ed.) *Developing Strategic Thought*, London: McGraw-Hill.

Bowman, C. and Asch, D. (1987) *Strategic Management*, Basingstoke: Macmillan.

Caldwell, B. J. and Spinks J. M. (1992) *Leading the Self-Managing School*, London: Falmer.

Davies, B. and Ellison, L. (1992) *School Development Planning*, Harlow: Longman.

Davies, B. and Ellison, L. (1994) *Managing the Effective Primary School*, Harlow: Longman.

Davies, B. and Ellison, L. (in press) *Strategic and Development Planning*, London: Pitman.

Dent, H. S. (1995) *Jobshock*, New York: St Martin's Press.

Dimmock, C. (1995) 'Restructuring for school effectiveness: leading, organising and teaching for effective learning', *Educational Management and Administration* 23(1): 5-18.

Drucker, P. (1993) *Post-Capitalist Society*, New York: Harper Business.

Greenley, G. (1989) *Strategic Management*, Hemel Hempstead: Prentice-Hall.

Hamel, G. and Prahalad C. K. (1989) 'Strategic intent', *Harvard Business Review* 67 (3): 63–76.

Handy, C. (1994) *The Empty Raincoat: Making Sense of the Future*, London: Hutchinson.

Johnson, G. and Scholes, K. (1993) *Exploring Corporate Strategy* (3rd edn), Hemel Hempstead: Prentice-Hall.

Luffman, G., Sanderson, S., Lea, E. and Kenny, B. (1991) *Business Policy: An Analytical Introduction* (2nd edn), Oxford: Blackwell.

Mintzberg, H. (1994) *The Rise and Fall of Strategic Planning*, Hemel Hempstead: Prentice-Hall.

Porter, M. (1987) 'Corporate strategy: the state of strategic thinking', *Economist*, 23 May: 21–8.

Spinks, J. M. (1991) 'Difficult decisions', *Managing Schools Today* 1(1): 55–7.

8 Managing change

Viv Garrett

INTRODUCTION

The management of change is fraught with tensions: tensions between desired change and imposed, often unwanted, change; between planned and unplanned; between systematic planning and evolutionary change. It can always be guaranteed to cause a great deal of upset and disturbance in a school system. This is not always a bad thing if it is well managed, but what is the best way to manage change? Is there in fact one best way, or should it depend on our circumstances? Where do we begin? We need to start by attempting to understand as much as possible about the process of change in order to have a fair chance of managing it effectively.

The purpose of this chapter is to help to give you that fair chance. I will first discuss two key aspects of understanding change, then examine the dilemma of planning for change in a dynamic environment, and finally explore some important considerations for managing successful change. In order to do this, I will draw on my own experience and on recent interviews I have had with a range of headteachers. All agree that change is normal, is persistent, and is becoming ever more complex. When one considers the number of changes affecting schools over the last ten years, one can see that change is now so frequent as to be almost continuous. In addition, it is multi-dimensional in that it has an effect on several if not all parts of the school system. If one adds to that the normal unplanned disruptions to school life, such as the turnover of staff, illness, disagreements and the like, it becomes impossible to predict accurately the complexities of any particular change. That is not, however, an excuse for a *laissez-faire* attitude; it is a reason for *managing* the change instead of merely allowing it to happen. Fullan (1993: viii) acknowledges that those people with 'a knowledge of how to view, cope with and initiate change' will manage it better than others. He argues that change mirrors life in that one can never be perfectly happy or in harmony. The ability to manage change is an essential skill for all those in schools, whether they be managing at classroom level, middle management or senior management. This chapter, then, is for anyone involved in the management of change: to avoid any possible confusion, I will address all concerned as *change managers*.

KEY ASPECTS OF UNDERSTANDING CHANGE

Understanding the individual

One of the first considerations is to understand how change affects the individual. Let us look first at the tensions between planned and unplanned change, and whether changes are wanted or unwanted. All changes involve some form of transition from an old state to a new (Adams *et al.* 1976). These transitional events may be both *desired* and *expected*: examples of this could be starting at university, getting married, having children, or starting a new job. They may be *desired* yet *unexpected*, such as winning the lottery, or meeting up with old friends. These two kinds of change are generally pleasing to the individual. On the other hand are changes which are *not desired*, yet are *expected*. Examples of these are the death of parents, saying goodbye to close friends, or the end of a project. The most stressful of all are those changes which are *neither expected nor desired*, such as a sudden crisis resulting from unexpected illness or redundancy. All of these changes will cause a certain amount of stress to the individual but it will not necessarily always be negative stress. As change managers we need to be aware of these dimensions of desirability and predictability in individual approaches to the change process.

Change events happen to individuals whether they like it or not; whether they learn and grow from the experience is up to them. What does change mean to the individual? How does it make her/him feel? In order to answer these questions, it may be worthwhile reflecting on your own experience. What sort of feelings did you experience during a period of change? Did those feelings change during the process? Change can mean stepping out of a position where you feel confident, where you know the rules and the script, and where you are able to function comfortably, into an altogether more uncomfortable position where there is uncertainty about role, relationships and responsibilities, and where you have less confidence in having the skills and knowledge necessary to function effectively. Plant (1987) refers to these positions as *firm ground* and *swampy ground*. It is the area of swampy ground which offers the greatest opportunities and challenges; later on individuals will note that the greater choice is offered here too, although that might not be apparent at first. It is a big step for people to move into the unknown and can be likened to visiting a new part of the world. Will I like it?

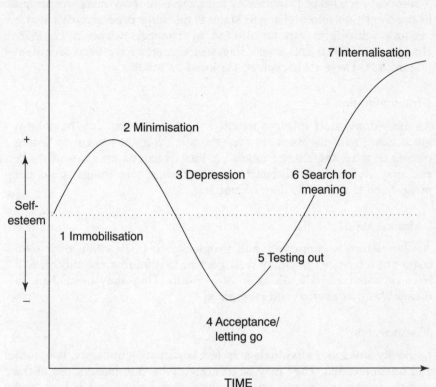

TIME
(usually longer than is thought)

Figure 8.1 Self-esteem changes during transition

Source: Adams *et al*. 1976

How will I cope? It is both risky and exciting. Different responses are normal and to be expected. They can range from the 'I'll try anything for a bit of excitement', through the more normal initial reticence until persuaded, to the 'I'm not going anywhere, and you're not making me'. These attitudes may well be affected by what else is going on in a person's life. Everyone has a need for a certain amount of stability, whether it be personal or professional. The stress factors of moving house, getting married (or divorced), or starting a new job are well documented. How reasonable is it to expect a teacher who is experiencing a combination of these stresses to view yet more change with enthusiasm? By recognising that need for some stability, change managers can show understanding and provide support.

Support can also be provided by taking note of individuals' responses to the transition into a changed state. It has long been accepted that a person's self-esteem can be affected by change (Adams *et al.* 1976; Hopson *et al.* 1992) and seven stages of changes have been identified (Figure 8.1). These stages can be explored as follows.

1 Immobilisation

As individuals start to piece together the information they have been given along with the rumours they are collecting, they begin to form a picture of what the change might be. First reactions are ones of shock and may well include disbelief and the feeling that things could not possibly be that bad, so they do nothing.

2 Minimisation

As the picture is confirmed, and people try to fit it within their own frames of reference, they may well attempt to minimise the effect it will have on them as individuals or as a group. They may even deny to themselves that change will take place.

3 Depression

As reality sinks in, individuals may feel particularly unhappy, confused and unappreciated. They may be trying very hard to make sense of the change, trying to reconcile it with their own values and beliefs, and trying to find where they actually fit into the new reality. They may feel powerless and not in control.

4 Acceptance/letting go

This happens at the lowest point when individuals do at last accept reality. While they do not know what the future holds, they accept that there will be a future and that they cannot go back.

5 Testing out

Individuals start to examine ways in which they can work with the change. This may involve discussions with peers or with senior managers, or trying out new materials or techniques. 'Where do I stand now?' is the prime question.

6 Search for meaning

This is the stage when self-esteem starts to rise again as individuals begin to understand the new ways and to see how they can use them and adapt them. They may continue to test out ways of working until they feel comfortable and ready to move to the next stage.

7 Internalisation

The change has now been understood and adopted. Individuals have the confidence to adapt and develop even more what is now an accepted way of working. They can now start to build on their newly developed strengths.

The crucial thing for the change manager to understand is that everyone will go through this process at her/his own pace, and that s/he should be allowed time for this process. Change managers have to allow others to make sense of the change in exactly the same way as they had to; it could take others longer if they are at different starting points. People come from different backgrounds with different experiences and this needs to be acknowledged. Change managers cannot force people to act and think differently but they can show understanding and support at the key points in transition. Fullan (1993) quotes Marris (1975) to demonstrate this:

> When those who have the power to manipulate changes act as if they have only to explain, and, when their explanations are not at once accepted, shrug off opposition as ignorance or prejudice, they express a profound contempt for the meaning of lives other than their own. For the reformers have already assimilated these changes to their purposes, and worked out a reformulation which makes sense to them, perhaps through months or years of analysis and debate. If they deny others the chance to do the same, they treat them as puppets dangling by the threads of their own conceptions.
>
> (Marris 1975: 166)

In providing support it should be noted that the stage from *depression* to *acceptance* is an important one and needs to be monitored. Patient reassurance and help should be given so that individuals do not feel that they are suffering alone. While some will come through this stage relatively unscathed, others will undoubtedly suffer. This is the stage of change when some staff development is usual; however this can cause even more anxiety in cases where the individual feels that s/he cannot cope. Once the individual indicates that s/he will let go of the past, then further development will be beneficial and will hasten the last stages.

This understanding of individuals' response to change is crucial and needs to be considered along with the second key aspect of managing change: that of understanding the organisation.

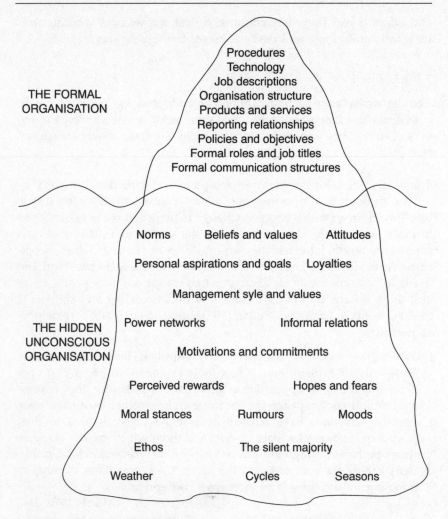

Figure 8:2 Organisation iceberg

Source: Adapted from Plant 1987

Understanding the organisation

An understanding of the organisation in which the change manager works, that is, of not only the pattern of formal meetings and lines of reporting and accountability but also the more informal ways of getting things done, is essential to the successful management of change. Schools may all have a similar purpose in that they provide an education for the students in their care, but the ways in which they go about this are very different. It may help to refer to the iceberg diagram adapted from Plant (1987) and shown in Figure 8.2.

The visible part of the iceberg indicates the formal organisation of the school: the ways in which the school is structured, its pattern of lessons and meetings, the explicit parts of its philosophy and purpose, i.e. *what is immediately apparent*. The underwater portion depicts the informal or hidden organisation: the ethos or culture, the ways things really happen, i.e. *what becomes apparent after a period in the school*.

The *formal organisation* is the normal vehicle for the working of the school. Schools have always been complex organisations, and they are even more so as they become more outward-looking and take into account the views of all their stakeholders. A deceptively simple way of describing a typical school is to think of it as made up of a number of transparent layers. The first layer is the physical nature of the buildings and grounds. The second is the arrangement of the students and the teaching: the students are divided into classes, the curriculum is divided into subjects, the timetable is divided into lessons, and the teachers are divided into subject or year groups. Students and teachers are surrounded by a framework of supporting personnel, including administrative and clerical/technical staff, welfare and classroom support staff and those taking care of the physical fabric and environment of the school. On top of this is a layer of responsibilities and reporting structures; a further layer of strategies contains communication procedures and meetings, and this is covered by a blanket of stated policies and procedures on the running of the school. This multi-layered kaleidoscope is then managed by the governors, headteacher and senior team, and influenced by parents, community, education officials and government, as well as staff and students.

The *informal organisation* is the cultural dimension of the school. This hidden part of the organisation includes the way in which individuals and groups relate to each other in an informal sense, and how they establish power groups which are apart from the formal structure of curricular areas and working parties. The most powerful staff members may not hold formal positions of responsibility in the school, but nevertheless teachers look to them for leadership in times of decision-making. They may be particularly charismatic individuals, they may be acknowledged experts who attract a certain level of respect, or they may hold influential positions outside the formal school structure. Examples of these might be a teacher union representative, a teacher with several years of experience who does not hold a post of responsibility, or a teacher serving as a local councillor. Interest groups may have developed within the staffroom: the ubiquitous bridge corner, the staff football team, a group with similar values or political beliefs; and outside the staffroom: those who prefer to take their breaks elsewhere in nooks and crannies around the school, and the outcast smokers. Each of these groups will have its own unstated, yet understood, code of practice which may well include how its members react to new initiatives. While change managers may be using the formal structure and procedures of their schools to introduce and implement a change, they need to be very aware of the informal rules and relationships current in the school and take account of this dimension both in their planning and in their day-to-day management.

Planning change is something that can be either almost totally over-looked, or else completed in such detail that there is no room for manoeuvre. The issues of *when* to plan and *in what detail* are addressed in the next section.

PLANNING FOR CHANGE

The process of the planning of change is currently undergoing much discussion and debate. Should the implementation of changes be incremental and controlled? Or should changes be allowed to evolve in an unplanned way? Where is the powerbase for change? Wilson (1992: 12) explores these issues in his discussion of approaches to organisational change, and comments that planned change relies upon a model of organisation in which there is uncritical acceptance of the managerial role, which is particularly true of North America and the UK. He compares this situation with other countries such as Sweden and Japan where ideas can emanate from all parts of the organisation and planned change requires careful consultation with the workforce. This is an interesting issue with regards to education in the UK. There is no doubt that government policies favour the acceptance of the hierarchical model of management with planned incremental change. However the majority of managers in schools would not accept that the onus of change lies solely with management; I know of several schools which have systems in place actively to encourage staff involvement in the initiation and implementation of change. I would argue that effective implementation of change relies on the active involvement of staff at each stage of the process, otherwise the change will never become fully operational and incorporated into everyday practice. Morgan (1993) addresses the empowerment of staff in his innovative book *Imaginization*:

> We are leaving the age of organised organisations and moving into an era where the ability to understand, facilitate, and encourage processes of self-organisation will become a key competence.
>
> (Morgan 1993: frontispiece)

Of course, school staff are not the only people to be involved in the change process. There may well be other individuals and groups outside the organisation who have an interest or stake in the changing situation. Fullan stresses the need to take into account the views of all participants and stakeholders as the change progresses. He warns us of the dangers of planning down to the last detail and reminds us that 'change is a journey not a blueprint' (1993: 24): one can never accurately predict what is going to happen. The active involvement of key stakeholders in the change process is crucial for effective implementation. The more say individuals have had at each stage of the process, the more likely they are to support developments. It is worthwhile referring to Berman's (1980) work at this point and noting his concept of *adaptive implementation* which is reliant on stakeholder input and participation. By allowing participants to adapt, form and reform their approaches to initiatives, internalisation of the change is more likely. This loosely-coupled attitude is in contrast to his alternative concept of *programmed implementation* which has, as its core, tightly controlled incremental steps towards agreed goals. These are but two ends of a continuum; actual practice takes place at various stages in between and is dependent on the internal situation and the external environment.

Fullan (1993) takes these perspectives into account and suggests that we do not spend too much time on strategic planning at the outset of complex change processes. He supports the *evolutionary perspective* as described by Louis and Miles:

> The evolutionary perspective rests on the assumption that the environment both inside and outside organisations is often chaotic. No specific plan can last for very long, because it will become outmoded either due to changing external pressures, or because disagreement over priorities arises within the organisation.
>
> (Louis and Miles 1990: 193)

As a result of the turbulent environment in which we now find ourselves, Fullan proposes a new order of events in preparing for educational change: *Ready! Fire! Aim!* (Fullan 1993: 31). He argues that the *Ready!* state encompasses the idea of direction, *Fire!* is the stage of enquiry and action where knowledge is formed, and *Aim!* is the stage when vision, mission and strategic planning are addressed. This is a direct challenge to the systematic approaches to change which first encourage us to shape the vision, then define the mission, then formulate the strategic plan, and only then follow it by action, that is, Ready, Aim, Fire.

Fullan maintains that the *Ready!* state embraces direction but that one should not become bogged down by vision, mission and strategic planning before learning about the dynamic reality (Fullan 1993: 31). An example which immediately comes to mind as an illustration of these three stages is an external inspection. Any school which is awaiting inspection is in a state of readiness; the staff have an idea of the direction in which they should be going. Once the school has been informed of a date for inspection, the long lead time enables the staff to complete informal audits of their information systems and their teaching and learning processes in preparation for the formal procedure. *Fire!* is the process of the inspection itself where all concerned share in a great deal of learning; and *Aim!* is the agenda discussed and formulated as a result.

I will use this framework of *Ready! Fire! Aim!* to examine how these states can be translated into concepts and strategies for the school workplace. I will then explore some key considerations for the successful management of change.

A state of readiness

We have seen above that Fullan (1993) believes that vision-driven change is the old paradigm, that vision should emerge from, rather than precede, action. He stresses the importance of the shared vision, and believes that the process of merging the personal and the shared visions takes time, and can only be achieved after much discussion and interaction. In my experience, schools are addressing this state of readiness and vision creation in different ways. All have become very conscious of the power of the marketplace and this becomes one of the key drivers of the ready state. What does a state of readiness actually mean for schools? I give three examples below of schools in various stages of creating readiness for change. The first school has raised awareness by initially focusing on classroom practice; the second by voluntary involvement of staff in regular think-tanks; the third by a new headteacher determined to turn a school around.

The first headteacher stressed that the intellectual stimulation of change is quite critical for the success of a school, but emphasised that the need for change has to be based on a knowledge of what is happening – that change *evolves* from a felt need. But where does this knowledge come from? He acknowledged that anticipation about particular situations comes from two sources in the school: from management and from the classroom. He has a very strong philosophy that the key function of a school is what happens in the classroom, and that the quality of interaction between the teacher and the pupil is one of his most important responsibilities. In order to learn about this, he and his assistant heads have targeted Faculties in the school, have observed lessons and held discussions with staff. In checking out the different subject areas, they have asked questions and posed challenges and made this part of accepted practice. In this way they have become sensitive to the need for change. As teaching has improved and examination pass rates have increased, the staff in turn have learned about their situations and have become far more sensitive and welcoming to the idea of change. The concept of staff development plays an important part in the life of this school.

Another headteacher stressed the importance of continuous thinking about the future and harnessing the best ideas from any member of the school, students included. She holds regular think-tank meetings with open agendas at which anyone can present a paper and share her/his ideas. The only proviso is that each area of the school must be represented at the meetings. These ideas are then discussed at various levels within the school. During this process, the ideas are shaped and reshaped before being given to a small working group to investigate. This headteacher felt that it is extremely important to indulge in the process of innovative lateral thinking: to focus on what is best for students and not to get demoralised by working to others' agendas all the time. An emphasis on the development of individuals through the appraisal process and training programmes, together with a climate of support, ensures that there is a buzz of involvement and achievement in the school.

Both of the above schools are led by experienced headteachers, are deemed to be very successful, and have recently gained Investors in People (IIP) awards. The third school is at a different stage of development with a relatively new headteacher. He has had a different starting point in attempting to achieve a ready state in his school. He inherited a school with low staff morale, poor results and no whole-school identity. Notice of an OFSTED inspection just one year after his appointment gave focus and impetus towards an agenda for improvement. The inspection findings coupled with his own ideas have set the subsequent agenda. He concedes that he has had to adopt a fairly autocratic style in order to introduce the necessary challenges for thinking about the future. The question of leadership style is an interesting issue in this context: this head differs very much from the above examples of experienced heads in established schools. In preparing this school for a state of readiness, this head has had to take into account various situational factors: those of *relationships* within the school (trust, respect and support for him and for one another), of the *nature of the tasks* to be undertaken, and of the *maturity* of the staff in terms of ability, experience and motivation. It is largely the factors of relationships and levels of maturity which may differ in the three schools described. Long established theories from researchers such as Fiedler (1967) and Hersey and Blanchard (1982) bear out these influences on leadership style. As this school works through its agenda and individuals develop in maturity, so the head should be able to soft-pedal on the 'telling' dimension and encourage a more participative climate. In practice the perceived and real culture change, as a result of the appointment of a new headteacher, often results in a turnover of staff which can contribute to the development of maturity in the organisation. In addition to this turnover, this school has now increased its student numbers and has been able to appoint other new members of staff. Staff development also plays a significant role in this school.

Each of these schools is working towards a culture of readiness for change, where individuals feel they have responsibility for their part in the overall agenda for school improvement.

Let us now consider the next part of the framework.

Prepared to fire! Investigating wicked problems

This is the stage of enquiry and learning; the action preceding the stage of strategic planning. Before making detailed plans for the future, we must ensure that we learn as much as possible about our particular problems. The term 'wicked problems' was coined by Rittel and Webber (1973) and could have been devised especially for the problem situations faced in schools. A wicked problem is one that does not have an easy solution; in fact it is probably not solvable. There is no right answer to the problem, and any possible action will be dependent on the nature of the problem, the situation and the individuals involved. The danger is that we get so close to our problem that we lose sight of the whole picture and make assumptions as to its real nature. When a problem occurs, we automatically search our frames of reference and slot in our previously tried solutions – we use our programmed knowledge. This ready application of programmed knowledge is not always appropriate in complex situations and denies learning taking place until after a solution has been tried out, sometimes unsuccessfully.

Fullan (1993) has a comment to make on this:

> we cannot develop effective responses to complex situations unless we actively seek and confront the real problems which are in fact difficult to solve. Problems are our friends because it is only through immersing ourselves in problems that we can come up with creative solutions.
>
> (Fullan 1993: 26)

We need to focus actively on the problem itself and try to build up the richest possible picture of the situation rather than begin by focusing on the possible solutions. In order to do this, we need to learn to ask questions of ourselves and others and to explore the situation afresh. As Pascale (1990: 14) states, 'Inquiry is the engine of vitality and self-renewal.'

This questioning is an integral part of Action Learning, an approach to management education developed by Revans (1983). Questioning and careful reflection should precede the use of programmed knowledge; learning is achieved when both are added together. This technique is used in Action Learning groups which bring together small groups of

committed people on a voluntary basis in order to help and support one
another through management problems. By the use of careful questioning, an individual is helped to explore the fullest possible picture of
a problem, then to focus in on possible ways forward. Strict rules
regarding technique and confidentiality apply. A commitment to action
completes the first stage of the process with follow-up meetings to check
progress and provide continuing support. Action Learning groups are
used in and across a wide range of organisations and are particularly
valuable in providing support to individual managers who would otherwise feel very isolated in their organisations.

Action Learning can be used in schools in a number of ways. A group
of classroom teachers or members of a department can explore ways to
improve teaching using examples of problem situations; a group of heads
of department can explore the problems besetting the introduction of
new assessment methods; a senior management team can actively
support one another in their responsibilities. In addition to extending
their knowledge about the particular situations being addressed, individuals will learn more about themselves and their styles of managing,
and will experience the challenges of commitment and accountability to
the group.

Other groups and working parties can be set up in schools in order
to investigate problem areas more deeply, to consider proposals and
suggestions, to consult, and to conduct feasibility studies. All of these
functions are examples of further enquiry and learning and fulfil the
necessary components of the *Fire!* stage.

Aim! Now can we plan?

The investigative processes outlined above begin the process of shaping
and reshaping ideas to form a vision of the future. By developing further
the circles of involvement and participation, knowledge and understanding is increased, not only about the vision but also about the
changes that may be necessary. Each stakeholder has had the opportunity to provide some input into the shared vision of the future. The
personal vision presented to the school think-tank, described earlier, has
now been investigated, and has been shaped and reshaped as it has been
discussed formally and informally in various corners and at various
levels in the organisation. Although this process can be lengthy and difficult, as individuals form and reform their positions, implementation now
has more chance of success because of the early involvement of those
affected. The planning in turn can be less affected by the negative actions
of individuals who feel that their opinions have been ignored or, worse,
were never sought. There is also more chance of the implementation
involving more creative changes and challenges to the normal accepted

pattern of the school. These more far-reaching changes have been described as *revolutionary transformation* (Wilson 1992) or *second-order* changes (Cuban 1988).

Wilson (1992: 20) has identified four levels of organisational change:

Level 1   Status quo – staying the same (or even running to stand still?).

Level 2   Expanded reproduction – doing more of the same.

Level 3   Evolutionary transition – making changes within the existing structures.

Level 4   Revolutionary transformation – making fundamental changes to the structures of the organisation.

Each level of achievement may be the result of a conscious decision. It may be that a school decides, after much consultation and reflection, to maintain the status quo for the time being (Level 1). Discussions of a successful pilot scheme may well result in replicating it elsewhere in the organisation: doing more of the same (Level 2). Similarly, fine tuning of extensive developments may be necessary, that is, making changes within the existing structures (Level 3). However, it is the level of making fundamental changes to the structures of an organisation which is the most difficult to achieve (Level 4). Cuban (1988) has a simpler model of *first-order* changes similar to Wilson's Levels 2 and 3, and *second-order*, similar to Level 4. He comments on the difficulties of second-order changes in relation to his analysis of school reform in North America:

> Most reforms foundered on the rocks of flawed implementation. Many were diverted by the quiet but persistent resistance of teachers and administrators who, unconvinced by the unvarnished cheer of reformers, saw minimal gain and much loss in embracing second-order changes boosted by those who were unfamiliar with the classroom as a workplace. Thus first-order changes succeeded while second-order changes were either adapted to fit what existed or sloughed off, allowing the system to remain essentially untouched. The ingredients change, the Chinese saying goes, but the soup remains the same.
>
> (Cuban 1988: 341)

We can learn from his experience and should never lose sight of the fact that educational change involves people. Systems seldom fight back, but human beings can and will!

MANAGING SUCCESSFUL CHANGE

It is tempting to say that once the three stages of *Ready! Aim! Fire!* have been addressed, there is every chance that the change will be

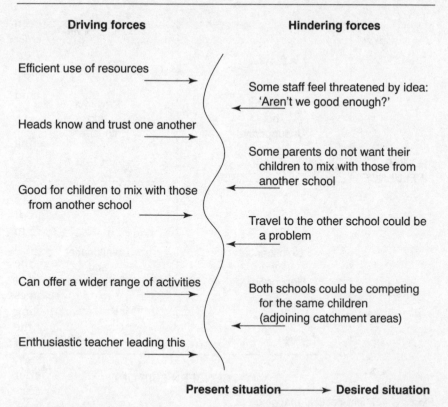

Driving forces   **Hindering forces**

Efficient use of resources

Some staff feel threatened by idea: 'Aren't we good enough?'

Heads know and trust one another

Some parents do not want their children to mix with those from another school

Good for children to mix with those from another school

Travel to the other school could be a problem

Can offer a wider range of activities

Both schools could be competing for the same children (adjoining catchment areas)

Enthusiastic teacher leading this

Present situation──────▶ Desired situation

Figure 8.3 Force field analysis: two schools wishing to combine their extra-curricular activities

successful. However, we need to recognise that resistance to change can be normal and natural. It is important for the manager to be sensitive to this and to be aware of the barriers which can exist (Dalin 1978; Pugh 1993). They may be *personal* barriers, built up as a defence where an individual feels that her/his values and beliefs are being threatened or undermined, or *psychological* barriers in response to an inherent unwillingness to change. There may also be *organisational* barriers, where the structure of the organisation is not flexible enough to permit particular changes, or *power* barriers, where individuals or interest groups are unhappy about possible redistribution of power.

There are two diagnostic tools which may be of use in raising the awareness of the change manager and others to the barriers which exist in a particular situation. These are: force field analysis, and micro-political mapping (for more details see Aspinwall *et al.* 1992). Force field analysis (see Figure 8.3) is commonly used to identify whether there is a critical mass of support for a proposed change, and to analyse the

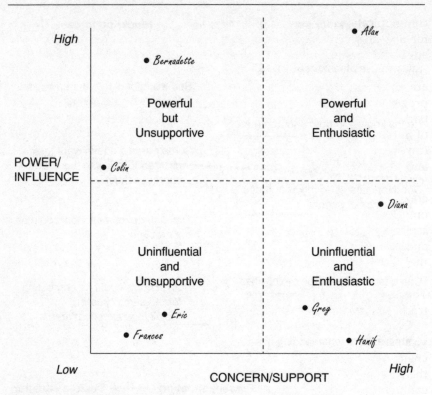

Figure 8.4 Micro-political mapping

reasons for any blockages later on. An open discussion of the driving forces and hindering forces of a change can be of considerable advantage and can aid identification of ways forward. By ensuring overt analysis, change managers open up the problem to encourage participation and ownership of possible solutions.

The second tool, micro-political mapping (see Figure 8.4), focuses more on people and their behaviour. This exercise aids the identification of individuals in terms of their power or influence, and their concern about or support for the change in question. For an individual change manager, or a small group managing a change, this mapping of the redistribution of power and the identification of winners and losers is a useful exercise to undertake. However, it should be noted that the analysis can be quite subjective, and any results should be sensitively handled.

Both of these exercises can help to identify areas, and agents, of resistance. The next stage for the change manager is to try to understand the reasons for resistance and to introduce strategies to remedy the situation. One particularly common reason is the *perceived* lack of communication: 'Nobody's told me what's happening' is a good excuse for non-involvement. Ensuring that everyone has the necessary knowledge and understanding of the proposed changes is the first step. Yet communication does not finish there. There are further questions which are often overlooked. What are the procedures for communicating progress and achievements to others? Are there mechanisms for feedback? A busy change manager can become so caught up in the intricacies of implementation that the business of reporting and receiving feedback can seem relatively unimportant. Yet it is the sharing of the successes and difficulties that ensures the continued involvement of people. 'Communicate like never before' (Plant 1987) and 'Communicate like crazy' (Clarke 1994) are the constant cries of advice. This applies not only to the supply of information *down* through the organisation and *across* it but also to the *upward* movement of information, comment and feedback. Only then can all feel properly informed. There is always the danger of not providing enough information: in those cases, the resultant vacuum provides opportunities for rumour and assumptions. Then additional work is required of the change manager to discover the truths and deal with the false situations which have arisen.

Even if communication is satisfactory, there will still be some individuals or groups who can be identified as resistors. This is when the change manager needs to consider specific strategies to overcome the negative attitudes displayed. A short-term strategy of immediately counteracting any negativity can prove its worth and nullify mischief making, but requires considerable vigilance by the change manager and can expend much time and energy. An understanding of 'what makes people tick' can help to identify additional strategies for providing support where needed, helping to build confidence, working together and sharing hopes and concerns, all are recognised remedies for the difficulties of the transition curve described earlier in this chapter.

Although the above may be effective strategies for managing resistance to change, they do not address the cultural issues of helping a school to achieve Fullan's (1993) *Ready!* state. It is in the quality of people and their interactions where ultimate success lies. We have agreed that change depends on people, on their feeling confident enough to take on change: confident both in the role they are playing and in their relationships with other people. We have discovered that we need to be sensitive to the need for support, particularly when individuals are afraid or depressed. We have established that we need to nurture the skills of individuals and help them to develop, in order to achieve their potential both as individuals and as members of the larger organisation. We need to empower them to do this.

Staff development plays an important part in any organisation, and managers have to try to achieve a balance between the needs of the individual and the needs of the organisation. It is becoming increasingly the case that the needs of the organisation come first; although any wise manager will take account of the individual's interests and needs in developing her/his role in the organisation. The appraisal system, although often maligned and under-rated, can provide a vehicle for the effective integration of personal and organisational needs. The resultant consolidation of personal and school development plans provides the basis for a programme of staff development. One school's example of six middle managers working with six middle managers from industry on a training programme demonstrates the learning that can be achieved by the sharing of experiences across two very different organisations. As well as gaining a qualification, they are providing a support group for each other where they can safely work through their ideas and frustrations. Middle managers are now being recognised as the target group for development. It is acknowledged that they can be a significant influence in schools: both on classroom practice and on whole school management. Professional development can play a large part in not only providing them with appropriate teaching and management skills, but also in helping them with the wider issues of developing confidence, clarifying their role, and being prepared to take on their responsibilities. As one head said to me, 'You can never have enough help for all the changes a school needs to take on board.'

It is now generally acknowledged that the quality of ideas and creative thinking is greater in a collaborative situation where individuals can bring and share their specific knowledge and expertise. 'People need one another to learn and to accomplish things' (Fullan 1993: 17), which is demonstrated by the forming of relationships, teams, partnerships and alliances. But these are not static: relationships by their very nature will change and develop. Collaboration is a dynamic process requiring awareness of the potential of forming and reforming relationships all the time. Collaboration means accepting that everyone's contribution will be encouraged and valued. It does not, and should not, mean that everyone will always agree, because the quality of interaction will depend on the contributions of the individual. These in turn depend on the individual's experience, their values and beliefs, their intuition, their capacity for independent thinking and their confidence in themselves and in the collaborative situation. Sometimes the contribution may be an initiating one, at other times it may move matters on by involving others inside and outside the group. It may also be a dissenting one, advising caution or proposing a different mode of action. This position of dissension is not a comfortable one, but the resulting conflict is essential for healthy group working and learning: 'You can't have organizational learning without individual learning, and you can't have learning in groups without processing conflict' (Fullan 1993: 36).

Tuckman's (1965) writings show agreement with the importance of conflict and he argues that the process of *storming* is an essential one for effective group performance. It is only after a group of people have been through the uncomfortable experiences of initiating and responding to personal challenge that they can call themselves a *team*.

Belbin (1981; 1993) takes this idea of teams further. His research is based on the belief that individuals fulfil a team role as well as a function within the organisation. There are nine such team roles: Plant; Resource-investigator; Co-ordinator; Shaper; Monitor–evaluator; Team-worker; Implementer; Completer–finisher, and Specialist. Some of these roles are inward-looking towards the maintenance and development of the team; others look outwards towards the organisation and the wider environment. It is not expected that any one person would be able to fulfil all of these roles; her/his team role will depend on her/his pattern of behaviour in the team situation. This behaviour pattern is established by a combination of the factors of personality, mental abilities, values and motivations, field constraints, experience and role learning (Belbin 1993: 30). There is an art to building a team, and, for a team to be effective, each of these team roles should be covered. That is not to say that each team should have a membership of nine people, but that each role should be represented within the membership. For example, one team member may fulfil a dual role of monitor–evaluator and completer–finisher, another of resource-investigator and plant, another may fulfil the specialist role alone.

It is recognised that one cannot always set up teams from scratch, and that it is often politically desirable to include certain members in a team, but it is worthwhile using Belbin's framework to analyse problems of non-performance and then taking remedial action. One headteacher who uses short-term working parties to initiate and implement change selects a small nucleus of workers: 'doers', 'facilitators' and 'thinkers'. The working party is then opened up for free membership to enable everyone to have the opportunity of serving. The importance of a clear brief is established with agreed dates for reporting back. In this respect, the role of the completer–finisher is important; different skills and roles are useful at different stages of a change process.

Provided that teamwork is not forced upon people or, worse, that lip service is paid to teamwork by merely appearing at meetings, there are very real benefits. Most individuals have an affiliation need – they like to feel part of something. Success or adversity can help the bonding of individuals into a team. One headteacher remarked to me that this was especially noticeable before, during and after an OFSTED inspection. The staff organised a celebration as soon as the last inspector's car disappeared down the school drive! These sort of informal social activities can encourage bonding and the breaking down of barriers. They can aid the development of an understanding that everyone in the organisation is a human being with different needs and different vulnerabilities even though s/he may be at a different level in the organisation. Improving relationships within the staff group as a whole can facilitate teamworking throughout the school. In turn, as individuals begin to realise both their potential and that of others in small working groups, so a better level of understanding and appreciation of others' strengths can influence relationships within the larger organisation.

But what happens when a short-term working party disbands? The members have succeeded in working well together to achieve their targets and have begun to realise their potential. They do not want to break up as a group; they are back on Plant's (1987) *firm ground*. However, there is a good opportunity here to use the expertise developed. Individuals can be encouraged to use their teamwork skills to develop other working groups. And the group as a whole can be used, in one headteacher's words, as a 'building block' for the future, for example a successful group working with other groups on relevant change issues.

However, it is not only inside the organisation that collaboration takes place. Working with the wider environment can provide new perspectives and the stimulus necessary to view the future creatively. Although this means moving into Plant's (1987) *swampy ground*, this can be particularly beneficial for the smaller school where the staff may feel under more pressure to be creative and might welcome an influx of new ideas. Fullan is continually advising teachers to 'connect with the wider environment':

> There is a ceiling effect to conceptualising inspiring visions, to investigating and solving problems, to achieving greater and greater competencies, and to engaging in productive relationships, if one does not connect to varied and large networks of others involved in similar and different pursuits.
>
> (Fullan 1993: 87)

Schools cannot develop in isolation from their environments. The best schools will always take account of the local and wider context in recognising opportunities for development, but without losing sight of their fundamental beliefs and values. This may range from school staff being active members of local community groups, through joint management of a sports centre, to an active Education–Business Partnership. The development of an interactive relationship with external bodies can be very challenging as well as potentially extremely rewarding. It is essential to respect each other's cultures and ways of working; it is by recognising and incorporating the strengths of each other's culture that learning and development occurs. But ease of working together does not happen overnight. It can take some time, and much hard work, to build up, particularly if the cultures are very different. However, once a working relationship is established, the results are worthwhile and can provide the impetus for further developments and future alliances. It is by learning to work with others that we start to learn more about ourselves. As schools work with new partners outside the education system, they can also begin to discover how others perceive them. Some perceptions and assumptions may be wrong and can then be challenged and corrected; others may well be uncomfortable but correct. The group of middle managers from school and industry working together provides one example. Not only are they learning from their tutor and facilitator, but there is also a great deal of cross-cultural learning taking place as they interact with one another. Some schools too have joined together for mutual support in all sorts of areas, for example, a more efficient means of offering training courses, or a sharing of specialist facilities.

A paradox here is the idea of collaborative working, and the establishment of alliances and networks, set against the reality of competition in the marketplace. This is another interesting tension leading to the careful choice of partners. But it is worthwhile seeking out more challenging partners and establishing an atmosphere of trust: the ultimate sharing may be beneficial to all. Some schools are taking advantage of the wider national and international context to enhance their development opportunities even further.

CONCLUSION

All of the above strategies refer to empowerment of the individual: ensuring that s/he has involvement in the processes of change, is able to work in collaboration with others, and has the necessary skills to implement any change. This form of power-sharing is crucial to successful implementation and eventual internalisation of the change, but it does require a manager or headteacher who is secure enough to continue to see the whole picture and to live with the feeling of possible loss of control. Headteachers can empower others by giving individuals the opportunity to share the power and control of a change. Individuals can empower themselves by learning about the change process and taking responsibility for their part in it. This acceptance of the potential of individuals is summed up in De Pree's (1994) description of *elegance*:

> Most of the time, when we consider ourselves and others, we are looking at only parts of people. The measure of individuals – and so of corporations – is the extent to which we struggle to complete ourselves, the energy we devote to living up to our potential. An elegant company frees its members to be their best. Elegant leaders free the people they lead to do the same.
>
> (De Pree 1994: 142)

Acknowledgements

I should like to acknowledge the help of the following people in the preparation of this chapter: Cheryle Berry, Ken Cook, Chris Pickering, Brian French, Tim Simkins and Kath Aspinwall.

> It is important to reflect on the concepts that are central to this chapter and the competencies necessary to utilise them. To enable you to do this and to form an action plan, we suggest that it would be of assistance to make an enlarged photocopy of the three pages in Appendix A.

REFERENCES

Adams, J., Hayes, J. and Hopson, B. (eds) (1976) *Transition: Understanding and Managing Personal Change*, London: Martin Robertson.

Aspinwall, K., Simkins, T., Wilkinson, J. and McAuley, M. J. (1992) *Managing Evaluation in Education*, London: Routledge.

Belbin, M. (1981) *Management Teams: Why They Succeed or Fail*, London: Heinemann.

Belbin, M. (1993) *Team Roles at Work*, Oxford: Butterworth-Heinemann.

Berman, P. (1980) 'Thinking about programmed and adaptive implementation: matching strategies to situations', in H. Ingram and D. Mann (eds) *Why Policies Succeed or Fail*, Beverley Hills, CA: Sage.

Clarke, L. (1994) *The Essence of Change*, Hemel Hempstead: Prentice-Hall International.

Cuban, L. (1988) 'A fundamental puzzle of school reform', *Phi Delta Kappan* 70 (5): 341–4.

Dalin, P. (1978) *Limits to Educational Change*, London: Macmillan.

De Pree, M. (1994) *Leadership is an Art*, London: Arrow.

Fiedler, F. (1967) *A Theory of Leadership Effectiveness*, New York: McGraw-Hill.

Fullan, M. (1993) *Change Forces: Probing the Depths of Educational Reform*, London: Falmer.

Hersey, P. and Blanchard, K. (1982) *Management of Organizational Behaviour: Utilizing Human Resources* (4th edn), Englewood Cliffs, NJ: Prentice-Hall.

Hopson, B., Scally, M. and Stafford, K. (1992) *Transitions: The Challenge of Change* (new edn), London: Mercury Books.

Louis, K. and Miles, M. (1990) *Improving the Urban High School: What Works and Why*, New York: Teachers College Press.

Marris, P. (1975) *Loss and Change*, New York: Anchor Press/Doubleday.

Morgan, G. (1993) *Imaginization: The Art of Creative Management*, London: Sage.

Pascale, R. (1990) *Managing on the Edge*, London: Penguin.

Plant, R. (1987) *Managing Change and Making it Stick*, London: Fontana.

Pugh, D. (1993) 'Understanding and managing organisational change', in C. Mabey and B. Mayon-White (eds) *Managing Change* (2nd edn), London: Paul Chapman/Open University.

Revans, R. W. (1983) *ABC of Action Learning*, Bromley: Chartwell-Bratt.

Rittel, H. and Webber, M. (1973) 'Dilemmas in a general theory of planning', *Policy Sciences* 4: 155–69.

Tuckman, B. (1965) 'Developmental sequence in small groups', *Psychological Bulletin* 63: 384–99.

Wilson, D. (1992) *A Strategy of Change: Concepts and Controversies in the Management of Change*, London: Routledge.

9 Leading and managing for quality

John West-Burnham

The purpose of this chapter is to evaluate the extent to which the total quality movement offers an appropriate response to the issues identified in Chapter 2. Total quality has existed in one form or another for fifty years; it is only since the mid-1980s that its application to the public sector in general and education in particular has been considered as a significant option. One of the myths surrounding the total quality movement is that it is a coherent package which is bought-in to an organisation. Nothing could be further from the truth. It is more appropriate to see it as a set of axioms which have to be understood, interpreted and applied. To claim, as Davies (1994) does, that 'TQM is a theory whose time has come and gone' is to sign a death warrant without the benefit of charge, trial, evidence and verdict! It is not the purpose of this chapter to defend total quality, rather to demonstrate that its full potential has yet to be understood and applied.

This chapter therefore focuses on five main issues:

- An analysis of the need for school management to change.
- A definition of total quality.
- An analysis of the components of total quality.
- A consideration of objections to total quality in education.
- A demonstration of total quality's consistency with other educational initiatives.

One semantic issue needs to be clarified at the outset. This chapter will refer to total quality rather than total quality management. This is consistent with practice in many organisations which have felt that the inclusion of 'management' inhibits and diminishes the proper emphasis on vision, values and leadership as well as strategic thinking. One of the crucial and distinctive features of total quality is its emphasis on the contextual as well as operational aspects of organisational development. A major problem for schools has been the lack of an integrated and legitimated approach to issues of leadership and management; indeed this has been an issue for organisations in most Anglo-Saxon cultures.

Legitimisation has been based on a historical and pragmatic basis that has justified practice on the premise of perceived success. As the next section demonstrates, survival is not an appropriate legitimisation for management systems.

THE NEED FOR SCHOOL MANAGEMENT TO CHANGE

Chapter 2 has already argued that the forces impinging on schools are individually and collectively so great that the management status quo is no longer an option. Indeed an attempt to sustain existing patterns of management may well be highly dysfunctional, not least in the pressures on individuals, manifested in stress and breakdown. In essence, most schools remain nineteenth century organisations in terms of structure, roles and technology. They are based on hierarchical and bureaucratic modes of operation and the deployment of resources – notably space and time – has its antecedents in the monitorial system. For most educational systems across the world the cumulative impact of policy changes over the past fifteen years challenges both existing practice and the presuppositions on which that practice is based. From a total quality perspective the imperatives to change can be identified as follows.

Polarisation   This phrase is used to describe the tendency for power to become increasingly centralised (i.e. with government) and for accountability to become increasingly institutionalised (i.e. located with the school). The traditional mediating vote of local government is being increasingly undermined and diminished. Schools are therefore far more exposed and have far fewer support agencies to draw on. At the same time they are far more visible as individual institutions in terms of their performance.

Accountability   This visibility is increasingly expressed in quantitative and data-based reporting which is public and which schools are unable to mediate, for example the publication of Standardised Attainment Test (SATs) scores and public examination results. The culture of inspection, notably in England and Wales, has created a model of accountability which uses generic criteria, tested by a limited and power-based process which takes little account of the situation of the individual school.

More for less   The demands on schools to meet externally determined outcomes has risen while the resources available have been static or actually reduced. This is partly a result of a world-wide movement to reduce spending by central governments and partly as a result of the use of formula funding which establishes a precise correlation between recruitment and income. These two pressures are mutually reinforcing in that if the unit of resource is being constantly diminished then schools that are successful in recruiting pupils are still faced with regular cuts in income.

Consumerism   Most developed countries are becoming what has been described as consumer democracies. These are characterised by an emphasis on choice, meeting customer requirements and penalties for failing to deliver a defined level of service. These trends have not yet been fully implemented in the school sector but are increasingly found in post-compulsory education. What is perhaps most significant is a change in culture, for example the loss of deference to professional knowledge, the articulation of expectations, the willingness to complain and the expectation of redress and compensation. Schools are increasingly having to function in an environment which is characterised by an increasingly sophisticated clientele.

Values   Somewhat perversely the emphasis on consumer satisfaction is being matched by an increasing emphasis on values. This is most clearly exhibited in environmental issues but is also manifest in the increasing emphasis on corporate ethics. In education this has found expression in the demands of religious and ethnic groups for educational provision that is consistent with their cultural and moral norms. There is an increasing expectation on public bodies to justify the ethical basis on which they function and to demonstrate consistency between professional values and actual behaviour.

Social change   The level of social change is increasing at an exponential rate. This is manifested in a number of significant ways:

- The number of children living in poverty continues to rise.
- Many parts of Britain are experiencing endemic unemployment.
- Traditional patterns of employment are changing with the loss of the concept of career, erosion of job security and movement of many low paid jobs to other parts of the world.
- Information technology is having a profound and systematic impact on every aspect of employment and learning.
- Patterns of family life are changing fundamentally.

The combination of these imperatives to change raises fundamental questions about the extent to which the way that schools are managed is valid, appropriate and effective. The issue concerns the criteria which are applied to demonstrate that schools are actually meeting the expectations on them. By historic criteria most schools are effectively managed; however the cumulative impact of the trends identified above and in

Chapter 2 is to question historic definitions of effectiveness. If education is not a self-legitimating process (and few would argue that it is), then it has to be viewed according to the extent that it contributes to society and, given the level of societal change, schools need to evaluate both what they do and how they do it. This raises the question of the extent to which traditional patterns of school management are congruent with their core purpose and serve as models for living and working in society as a whole. It must be difficult to legitimate a nineteenth century structure as the basis for educating young people who will be living and working in the twenty-first century!

There is an issue of the extent to which school management (roles, structures and processes) is 'fit for purpose'. This is emerging as a classic definition of quality, where purpose is defined by the customer. If purpose is the learning of individuals and fitness is the notion of congruence or focus with that purpose, then a number of concerns emerge:

- The congruity between the management and learning processes.
- The extent to which core purpose and values permeate every aspect of school life, e.g. development planning, appraisal, appointments procedures, budget allocations, etc.
- The way in which processes are implemented in a consistent manner, e.g. codes of conduct, assessment, learning and teaching strategies.
- The extent to which promises are kept, i.e. the translation of school aims into the school experience of each child, parent and teacher.

This chapter goes on to argue that total quality provides a means to realign school leadership and management.

DEFINING TOTAL QUALITY

One of the major problems with the total quality movement is that it has developed many of the characteristics of a religious movement. There are factions, schisms, apostles, disciples, creeds and heretics. This does little to recommend it to the cautious or wary. The purpose of this section is to provide an introduction to total quality, stressing that it is a broad framework to be applied, tested and improved rather than to be believed in. John Marsh (1992) offers the most useful definition:

> Total quality is a philosophy with tools and processes for practical implementation aimed at achieving a culture of continuous improvement driven by all the employees of an organisation in order to satisfy and delight customers.
>
> (Marsh 1992: 3)

A systematic inspection of this definition provides greater insight into the nature of total quality.

Philosophy   Total quality is a conceptual model which has to be applied in order to give it meaning. However, its distinctive nature is best expressed in the notion of total. Whatever an organisation does, its values and operating procedures should apply to everybody all of the time.

Tools and processes   Total quality does not operate by exhortation but, rather, offers specific techniques to help to translate principle into practice – the abstract into concrete experience. Thus the philosophy is underpinned by the means to implement it.

Continuous improvement   This is a core tenet of total quality, the principle that the purpose of leadership and management is to improve, enhance and develop products and services and not to perpetuate a perceived level of acceptability.

All the employees   Total quality argues for the significance and responsibility of every employee. This challenges notions of hierarchical control and an omnicompetent management.

Satisfy and delight customers   This is the distinctive characteristic of total quality; the organisation not only exists to satisfy its customers' needs but also accepts a responsibility to extend and enhance their expectations.

The focus on the customer is perhaps the most important characteristic of total quality and one which has caused most difficulties in the public sector in general and in education in particular. The problem has two closely related manifestations: first, the fact that total quality insists that quality is defined by the customer and, second, the problem of identifying the customer in education. These concerns are exacerbated by objections to the implications of using the notion of customer in schools, with its connotations of a cash relationship and (implicitly) a rather sordid type of transaction that education ought to be above. However these concerns are manifestations of models of thinking that are inappropriate given the analysis of change that started this chapter.

The major cause of the difficulties in education is that quality has been traditionally defined in a hierarchical sense and related to a platonic form, that is, it equates with truth, beauty or justice. This view pervades most educational systems and is expressed in a multitude of ways, significantly in the way in which knowledge is perceived and the implications this has for the perceived status (and related funding) for universities, sixth forms, secondary, special, primary and nursery education. To say that quality exists in a relationship and is defined by the needs of the customer rather than the status of the supplier is to challenge many cultural icons. A lesson may be claimed to be of high quality in terms of subject knowledge and modes of teaching but if it does not create understanding in pupils then it has limited claim to actual quality.

If the primary purpose of education is the learning of individual children (as many schools claim in their aims) then whatever labels are actually used there can be little doubt that the individual child is the primary customer. Parents, LEA, Department for Education and Employment (DfEE) and other groups in society all have claims to be customers in specific processes but the overriding definition of quality has to be in terms of the child. Thus quality is defined in terms not of proximity to a gold standard but rather of the extent to which actual needs are met. This does not imply a reductionist approach, as total quality includes in its definition the notion of 'delighting' the customer, that is, extending and enhancing possibilities and expectations.

Perhaps the most important feature of total quality, the one which distinguishes and differentiates it most significantly, is the emphasis placed on *total*. One of the abiding problems for any organisation, commercial or public sector, is the extent to which it satisfies all of its customers all of the time in every respect of its products or services. In manufacturing industry total quality has led to dramatic reductions in waste and scrap. An improvement from 25 per cent waste to 8 per cent is not unusual and many businesses aspire to 'zero-defects'. It is difficult to conceptualise what this might mean for schools; it is certainly a challenging if not actually intimidating objective. However it may be more appropriate to think in terms of processes which increase the possibility of zero-defects and to define zero-defects in terms of individual outcomes rather than generic and arbitrary standards. Thus the criterion is not the number of GCSE grades at A–C but, rather, demonstrating that every pupil has achieved the optimum possible level of performance, that is, the demonstration of value-added. Total quality in education offers the possibility of focusing the definition of quality on the attainment of every individual rather than on arbitrary standards in which the individual is lost. If the attainment of 100 per cent customer satisfaction is a problematic or overwhelming challenge, not to accept it is to institutionalise failure. Of course there are variables outside a school's control – total quality emphasises the importance of ensuring optimum performance in those areas which can be managed and of seeking to influence those that cannot be directly controlled.

THE COMPONENTS OF TOTAL QUALITY

Much of the early literature on total quality in education was dominated by the competing claims of the disciples of the various gurus. The cynicism generated about the movement was in response to the apparent lack

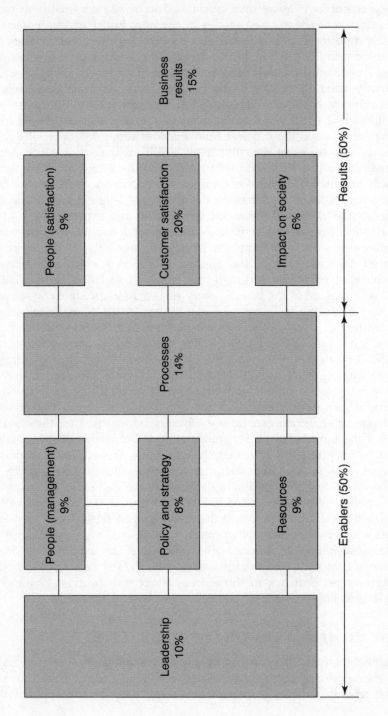

Figure 9.1 The components of the European Quality Award (EQA): criteria and assessment values

of agreement as to what total quality actually was. Experience over a number of years has allowed the evolution of a model which appears to be gaining increasing acceptance as a valid and appropriate typology of the components of total quality, their relative significance and interrelationships. The European Foundation for Quality Management's (EFQM) self-review model has been widely accepted by commercial organisations in Europe and is the basis of significant development work in schools.

The EFQM model is based on an analysis of the components of management in successful organisations. The key components are classified as *enablers*, including processes, which produce *results*. Processes are the mediating force between enablers and results. The European Quality Award (EQA) allocates a general weighting to each component to indicate its relative significance but stresses that these could be changed to reflect the different criteria of different types of organisations. The European Quality Award is shown in Figure 9.1 with the relative weighting of the importance of each of the components.

A number of significant factors can be implied from this simple structure:

- The interdependence of all the factors.
- Recognition of the weighted contribution of each.
- The centrality of processes.
- The emphasis on outcomes or results.
- The significance of leadership and people management.
- The emphasis on customer satisfaction.

A great deal of work has been done under the auspices of the Royal Mail and Sheffield LEA to apply this model to education (see Sisum 1996). A summary of the components of the model as applied to schools produces the following key characteristics.

Leadership

- Visible improvement in leading total quality.
- A consistent total quality culture.
- Recognition and appreciation of the efforts of others.
- Support through the provision of resources.
- Involvement with customers and suppliers.
- Active promotion of total quality outside the organisation.

People management

- How people resources are planned and improved.
- Development through recruitment, training and career progression.
- Individuals and teams agree targets and review performance.

- Involvement in continuous improvement and empowerment.
- Effective communication.

Policy and strategy

- Policy and strategy formulated on the concept of total quality.
- Based on relevant and comprehensive information.
- The basis for business planning.
- Clearly communicated.
- Updated and improved.

Resources

- Financial strategies support policy and strategy.
- Data systems are managed for improvement.
- Suppliers, materials, buildings and equipment support policy and strategy.
- Technology is applied to ensure maximum efficiency and effectiveness.

Processes

- Processes critical to success are identified.
- Systematic and consistent management of processes.
- Measurement and feedback are used to review and improve processes.
- Stimulation of innovation and creativity in process improvement.
- Implementation and evaluation of process changes.

People satisfaction

- Measurement of and response to employee perceptions.
- Identification and measurement of factors relating to employee satisfaction.

Customer satisfaction

- Measurement of and response to customer perceptions of products, services and relationships.
- Identification and measurement of factors relating to customer satisfaction.

Impact on society

- Analysis of the community's perception of the extent to which needs and expectations are met.
- Use of other indicators to demonstrate impact on society.

Business results

- Demonstration of financial indicators of the organisation's success.
- Demonstration of non-financial indicators of the organisation's success.

What the EFQM model offers to education is an integrated and holistic approach to (a) identifying the components of quality management and (b) indicating their interrelationship and relative significance. However, the model is only an indicative framework; it achieves meaning and significance in the context of a core purpose – the reason why the organisation exists. In this sense there is a problem in applying the principles of total quality to schools as, for the education system as a whole and also with individual schools, there are a number of claims as to the nature of the core purpose. The tension might be characterised as that between vocationalism and socialisation on the one hand and a liberal, humanistic approach on the other. Within the principles of total quality it is not appropriate for an external definition to be imposed on the school – it is for the school to respond to its environment as it sees fit. Thus a total quality school might see its primary function as GCSE pass rates or as social amelioration. What is important is that a core purpose is agreed and then applied consistently through the model, or an appropriate variant of it. It is clear from the components of the EFQM approach that organisations have to be responsive to customers on the basis of their needs and satisfactions and not those of the organisation.

If a school claims to be a 'caring and secure environment' then that has to be defined in terms of the perceptions of pupils, not those of teachers. Equally a school that presents itself as being focused on the 'learning of the individual pupil' has to ensure that every aspect of its structures and processes can demonstrably add value to the individual's learning. This could raise issues about the design of the school day, the compartmentalism of subject knowledge, the use of IT, the role of the teacher, and so on. The issue is one of demonstrated consistency between purpose or aspiration and the practical functioning of the organisation. In many organisations, including schools, there is a mismatch between intention and experience; total quality approaches can help to close the gap.

There are two approaches to quality management which are supportive of attempts to ensure consistency: Investors in People and BS EN ISO 9000 (previously known as BS 5750). Investors in People (IIP) works in the same way as the EQA; it distils best practice into a series of principles to which organisations can demonstrate their adherence and so receive external accreditation. IIP relates to the management of people, notably their involvement in organisational planning and the training and development necessary in order to allow them to contribute effectively to organisational objectives.

BS EN ISO 9000 is another form of external accreditation which is based on the comprehensiveness, specificity and rigour of work systems and practices in order to ensure consistent performance. In essence it works on the principle of definition in order to secure prevention of errors and thus enhance the possibility of removing variation.

Both approaches have been applied to schools, often with considerable success. IIP has probably achieved wider acceptance because it is demonstrably consistent with well established educational procedures such as development planning, appraisal and the provision and evaluation of INSET. However, the accreditation process has raised questions for school managers about the integration of management processes in a consistent manner. The 9000 series has been more problematic. Schools have found it to be valuable in designing, managing and improving many processes and systems. However there does appear to be some concern with the extent to which it actually impinges on the learning process. There is no reason why it should not but the emphasis in schools appears to be on the peripheral and supportive activities rather than on the core process itself. Both Investors in People and BS EN ISO 9000 can contribute to the implementation of a total quality strategy; of themselves they are only constituent parts and are not synonymous with total quality.

Implicit to the EFQM and other models are six key concepts that help to make total quality distinctive.

Fitness for purpose   This is the distinctive definition of quality, where the purpose is that defined by the customer and fitness is the extent to which a product or service meets the purpose.

Continuous improvement This means the institutionalisation of permanent commitment to find ways of enhancing every product or service, often through reference to customer feedback but also by 'delighting the customer'; in other words, finding new and better ways of presenting a product or service.

Eliminate variation This entails managing processes to ensure that outcomes conform to the agreed specification or exceed it; in other words, the guarantee that a customer can have confidence in the consistency of what is offered.

Measurement This is the basis for managing and monitoring processes so as to establish consistency and eliminate variation through the use of statistical methodology, as well as measuring customer satisfaction and outcomes.

Quality assurance   This means the prevention of waste and variation through definition and training and the provision of appropriate resources.

Closeness to the customer   This is the notion of integrating the customer into key processes so as to create an interdependent relationship (sometimes called the customer chain) which improves communication and so increases responsiveness and minimises the possibility of error.

Many of these characteristics are achieved in total quality organisations through an emphasis on teamwork. Teams serve both as the means by which processes are managed and as the basic unit of organisational structure. Teams are both more efficient and more effective when it comes to task completion and are a more appropriate vehicle for ensuring valid social relationships, one of the most important elements in employee satisfaction. Most total quality organisations have restructured themselves into a team-based culture not only for these reasons but also to help to ensure closeness to the customer. If customers are perceived as being internal and external, that is, all part of the same chain, then teams are much more appropriate vehicles for sophisticated levels of communication and thus for responsiveness.

The implications of total quality for school management can be exemplified in ten questions:

- How much profound learning is taking place in school and how do you know?
- To what extent are the values of the school (aims or mission) exemplified in the daily experience of every pupil?
- Does the school keep its promises to pupils, parents and staff all of the time?
- Is leadership, as opposed to management and administration, manifested throughout the school?
- Is there an emphasis on learning and development for all members of the school community?
- Is the organisational structure of the school appropriate for a learning community?
- Do the school's learning, pastoral and management processes work on a philosophy of prevention?
- Is data used as the basis of improvement?
- Does every aspect of the school's resources focus on the needs of customers?
- Is the school focused on meeting the needs of individual pupils?

The central theme of these questions is the notion of linkage between intention and experience. The quality organisation works to minimise the gap between its vision and values and what its customers actually derive from encounters with the services offered. This is a practical as well as a moral imperative. The closer the linkage the more likely is quality, the greater the gap the more the organisation is existing for itself.

OBJECTIONS TO TOTAL QUALITY IN EDUCATION

Objections to the implementation of total quality in education can be placed into categories: its commercial origins; innovation overload; and an inappropriate culture.

Commercial origins

The genealogy of total quality is not one to endear it to education professionals. It can be traced back to statistical process control techniques used in the American munitions industry in the Second World War. It was then developed in Japan and was largely taken up by multi-national manufacturing businesses. This would appear, superficially, to offer a somewhat inauspicious pedigree for its introduction into a small primary school. The concerns are largely focused on the perceived lack of relevance of a management theory which has at its centre the notion of profitability. There are also issues to do with professional autonomy in what appears to be a conformist and compliant approach to management. Most significant is the perceived problem of transfer from manufacturing industry to the education of children.

Four responses can be made to these concerns. First, no organisation has ever taken on total quality in its 'pure' theoretical form. It has to be modified, adapted and made to fit the culture and purpose of a specific organisation. Second, the management structures of many schools (hierarchical and bureaucratic) are a lot less concerned with individual integrity than are the structures of some other organisations. The secondary school, with its hierarchical structure, compartmentalised use of time and resources and assumptions of homogeneity, is much closer to the archetypal factory than are many businesses. Third, a business that focuses primarily on profit is unlikely to survive. The most successful businesses give priority to meeting customer needs and in doing so ensure their profitability. This is not a semantic distinction but a very real control shift manifested in many ways, most notably in retailing. The concern may be an expression of the British reluctance to provide a service. Fourth, as is demonstrated in the final section of this chapter, there is a very high degree of congruence between total quality and existing educational movements, notably school effectiveness and school improvement. The issue may be purely linguistic, that is, the introduction of an *alternative* jargon (never let it be said that schools do not employ a significant jargon of their own).

If we talk of management in education then it is inevitable that there will be a significant amount of cross-fertilisation of language, concepts and principles. All schools manage in some way and they all use concepts and principles that are found in other contexts. The problem is that 'management' and 'industry' are seen as homogeneous entities with education equally distinctive; this is patently not the case. There is as much diversity of practice in industry as there is in education and the issues that concern educationalists also concern industrialists.

Total quality will not transfer directly from a commercial organisation to a school, no more than it will transfer from one commercial enterprise to another. An essential component of the total quality process is the identification and agreement of core purpose, vision and values and the means of achieving them.

Innovation overload

If the introduction of total quality is seen as yet another innovation then teachers will be quite properly suspicious, if not actually hostile. However it is essential to see total quality as a means rather than an end. Schools have to be managed, therefore it seems reasonable to develop a model of management which is totally consistent with the purpose of the school and which facilitates the maximum amount of time on task. In the terms of one of the great clichés of the quality movement, it is all about 'working smarter – not harder'.

It is a fair guess that most of the schools that have needed to manage the fundamental, profound and demanding changes of the past ten years have not changed the way they lead and manage in an equally fundamental and profound way. Structures, roles, systems and processes are much the same as they were in the 1970s. It is no wonder that schools are often dysfunctional places, putting enormous demands on teachers and managers who are frequently working harder to diminishing effect.

Total quality offers a coherent and integrated range of tools and techniques which can actually help schools in coming to terms with the demand of 'more for less'. A further important point is that no organisation, and this is especially true of schools, will come to total quality as a *tabula rasa*. Many of the features of total quality will already be in place.

Inappropriate culture

Quite apart from the problems with its industrial origins, many educationalists object to total quality because of the implications which they perceive that it has for the nature of schools as organisations. Capper and Jamison (1993) have identified a number of concerns about total quality in education:

> Some aspects of TQM are laudable: viewing the interactions of an entire system, encouraging employee participation in decision making, fostering participant feedback, utilising data collection and analysis and viewing system improvement as a processual rather than terminal exercise. These few basic principles, however, can be used as tools of domination, control and coercion, or as vehicles for social change, descending on goals and how to reach them. It is only through the explicit, stated goal of providing an equitable education leading to full participation in society that TQM can hold hope of transforming education.
>
> (Capper and Jamison 1993: 30)

In response to this critique it could be argued that such concern could be expressed about any systematic approach to management. Total quality is not hostile to democracy and is not founded on a reliance on pseudo-objective statistical methods – it is the people who define the system that determine its nature. Total quality is not ideologically neutral: it has fundamental underpinning values about the nature of leadership, the importance of values, participation and a responsiveness-based model of accountability. These premises serve as a significant rejoinder to much of what passes for management in many educational organisations. Total quality does compromise the concept of personal autonomy but balances it with a respect for the integrity of all individuals within a school. Total quality does make use of a scientific/rationalist approach in its use of statistical data, but balances this through the development of an interpretative community which places the definition of quality in an individual and subjective frame.

Total quality as a concept is rather like democracy – many claim it but few actually practise it; and those that are furthest from its principles are likely to be the most fervent claimants, exploiting the label to mask the reality of how they manage.

The vast majority of the literature advocating total quality has conspicuously failed to come to terms with the essential nature of the educational process. If that is perceived to be learning then total quality offers a means of managing which is morally, intellectually and logically consistent. In essence the problem is not about the validity of total quality in an educational context but rather about educationalists agreeing what the purpose and nature of schooling should be.

Table 9.1 Key characteristics of effective schools related to components of total quality

School effectiveness	Total quality
1 Professional leadership creating consensus and unity of purpose	Emphasis on leadership, teams and open communication
2 Shared vision, high aspirations, consistent practice	Mission, continuous improvement, process management
3 Attractive, orderly learning environment	Fitness for purpose
4 High expectations	Vision, values, continuous improvement
5 Purposeful teaching	Fitness for purpose, delighting the customer
6 Positive reinforcement, clear feedback	Fitness for purpose, process management
7 Concentration on teaching and learning	Focus on core purpose, customer care, fitness for purpose
8 Progress monitoring	Process management, measurement, emphasis on results
9 Pupil rights and responsibilities	Individual development, prevention
10 Home–school partnerships	Integrating customers, prevention
11 Learning organisations	Investing in people

TOTAL QUALITY, SCHOOL EFFECTIVENESS AND SCHOOL IMPROVEMENT

By most criteria total quality is an alien concept to many schools, largely because the way in which they are managed is often not the result of an explicit and deliberate choice. It is, rather, a coalition of a range of factors in which the history of the school and the personalities of the principal protagonists are key variables. This is true of most organisations. There does appear to be an emerging consensus that it is possible to extrapolate a number of significant factors found in successful organisations and schools and make them universal in application. This is not to seek to create a management hegemony but rather to isolate and manage the variables. There remains the issue as to what constitutes success and this may well have to be expressed in terms which are contextually determined, that is, the result of political, social and economic criteria contingent to a particular time and place.

Such a process has resulted in the school effectiveness movement which has generated a range of indicators, derived from observed practice, which appear to be transferable. Sammons *et al.* (1995) have identified eleven key characteristics of effective schools. It is possible to relate these to the components of total quality identified earlier in this chapter to demonstrate congruity between the perceived components of successful schools and a compatible, integrated approach to management (Table 9.1). Most schools will demonstrate some or all of these characteristics to a greater or lesser extent. Total quality offers a means of working towards a situation where all of the components are displayed in every aspect of the school.

In this respect total quality has much in common with the principles of school improvement. The issue is one of translating the rhetoric of effectiveness into practical, specific and relevant processes. Again there is probably a high synergy between total quality and school improvement with the emphasis on shared leadership, vision, planning and the use of techniques to translate aspiration into practice. It is perfectly conceivable that a school could use effectiveness and improvement approaches, never having heard of total quality, and qualify for the European Quality Award, BS EN ISO 9000 and Investors in People. What total quality offers is a means of reconceptualising schools that is consistent with best educational practice. It does so by proposing a conceptual model that forces a focus on key processes and provides the specific techniques to ensure consistency with the core purpose. Schools achieve astonishing results but often at enormous cost in human terms. Total quality is as concerned with the suppliers as with the customers and measures success in terms relevant to all of those involved in the organisation. In other words it can help to redress the balance, reconciling the needs of adults, children and their parents and seeing them as part of a wider community with equal rights, obligations and expectations.

Total quality is not a panacea; more organisations have failed than have succeeded to implement it. What it offers is a means of conceptualising leadership and management with the same confidence that learning and teaching are understood in the effective classroom.

> It is important to reflect on the concepts that are central to this chapter and the competencies necessary to utilise them. To enable you to do this and to form an action plan, we suggest that it would be of assistance to make an enlarged photocopy of the three pages in Appendix A.

REFERENCES

Capper, C. A. and Jamison, M. T. (1993) 'Let the buyer beware', *Educational Researcher*, November.

Davies, B. (1994) 'TQM: a theory whose time has come and gone', *Management in Education* 8 (1):12–13.

Marsh, J. (1992) *The Quality Toolkit*, Reading: IFS International.

Sammons, P., Hillman, J. and Mortimore, P. (1995) *Key Characteristics of Effective Schools*, London: Office for Standards in Education.

Sisum, C. (1996) 'Introduction to the Scarman Papers', *Quality and Learning* 2 (1):4.

10 Reflections on leadership in self-managing schools

John West-Burnham

This chapter is a reflection on our understanding of leadership in education institutions. If the 1970s and 1980s were the decades of management in schools, then the 1990s have emerged as being much more concerned with leadership. The reasons are complex and various but are probably attributable to the increasing realisation that efficient management in itself will not create effective, successful or improving schools.

However, this increased emphasis on leadership as a distinctive phenomenon, as opposed to a subset of management, has led to a range of semantic confusions. Most of those are cultural in origin, such as the obsession with hierarchy so that the leader has to be 'top' and the emphasis on the masculine manifestations of the leader as a hero, as courageous and as a role model. Leaders in schools have to exist in a somewhat bizarre continuum between, at one extreme, a focus on learning as the core purpose and, at the other extreme, the formal models of accountability and historical perceptions of the 'headmaster'.

This chapter examines the manifestations of the current imperative for leadership, then explores some of the issues and problems in talking about leadership in the context of schools. It concludes with a review of some of the thinking that has taken place in evolving a new paradigm of what leadership might mean.

All of the discussions about leadership suffer from what Gronn (1995), when talking about transformational leadership, describes as 'a strong air of human perfectibility' and he goes on:

> the terminology about elevating people to previously unheard of levels of potential, altered levels of awareness, autonomy, mission and vision, and even the very idea of transformed individuals and organisations carries with it all the hallmarks of a religious crusade.
>
> (Gronn 1995: 25).

There is a clear tension between the ideal and aspirational as opposed to the proven techniques and strategies. This chapter seeks to help to clarify the vocabulary that is used in talking about leadership and management and so help to create a mental map to inform conceptualisation and, thus, to predicate action.

THE IMPERATIVE FOR LEADERSHIP

Irrespective of any problems of definitions, identification, development and sustainability, there does appear to be an overwhelming consensus about the relationship between leadership and effective, successful or improving schools (another interesting example of problems of terminology). Beare *et al.* (1989) are quite explicit:

> Outstanding leadership has invariably emerged as a key characteristic of outstanding schools. There can no longer be doubt that those seeking quality in education must ensure its presence and that the development of potential leaders must be given high priority.
>
> (Beare *et al.* 1989: 99)

This exhortation is given significant practical endorsement by the findings of a survey of successful schools carried out by the National Commission on Education:

> The right sort of leadership is at the heart of effective schooling, and no evidence of effectiveness in a school with weak leadership has emerged from any of the reviews of research.
>
> (NCE 1995: 335)

Confidence about the strength of the correlation between leadership and a successful school has now reached such a level that it has been formalised in the school inspection process in England and Wales:

> Evaluation of the role of the headteacher needs to focus on the extent to which his or her professional leadership and management are effective in those aspects of the school's work which bear most directly on the improvement of the quality of provision and the educational standards achieved.
>
> (OFSTED 1995a: 108)

This criterion reinforces the view of Her Majesty's Chief Inspector of Schools in his first Annual Report (OFSTED 1995b) where he argued for the proposition that the quality of teaching determines the levels of pupil achievement and that the quality of headship determines the quality of teaching. The strength of this correlation has been generally perceived as being so logically necessary and universal that it has led to such conceptual formulations as educative and instructional leadership.

Leadership thus becomes the panacea for all educational (not to mention social and economic) ills – put leaders in place and all will be well, problems will be solved and a new golden age will emerge shortly.

We search, so often in vain, to find leaders we have faith in. Our doubts are not about our leaders' talents, but about their trust-worthiness.

(Block 1993: 260)

The current emphasis on competencies might be seen as creating a technology of leadership with the balance of opinion moving towards specific components of the role which can be defined, assessed or measured. If we return to the swamp then technical competency may help us to stay afloat but it will not necessarily give us the will to struggle through. There is no doubt that leaders need knowledge (or access to knowledge) and a range of skills in order to be effective. However, these have to be contextualised in terms of personal values, self-awareness, emotional and moral capability. This is not to produce another set of formulations but rather to argue for leaders who have self-knowledge and are able to learn and so grow personally.

Duignan and Bhindi (1995) argue for the development of an inte-grated and holistic model of leadership based on the notion of authenticity:

In our recent experiences in research and consultancies, the authors are hearing managers of a variety of types of organisations using the concept of 'spirituality', not in any narrow religious sense but more in a sense of questioning as to the deeper purpose or meaning of their actions in the light of such values as trust, honesty in relationships, social conscience and justice in their dealings.

(Duignan and Bhindi 1995: 6)

This coincides with Greenfield's view that:

the ultimate training of a teacher would be a kind of philosophical withdrawal to look at the larger issues in a fresh perspective ... A deeply clinical approach ... is needed.

(Greenfield and Ribbins 1993: 262)

The a priori of leadership would therefore appear to be the capacity to understand and then to translate that understanding into action, and this is the essence of learning. This introduces the concept of the reflec-tive practitioner (Schön 1983) and systems thinking:

Leader as teacher does not mean leader as authoritarian expert whose job it is to teach people the correct view of reality. Rather it is about helping everyone in the organisation, oneself included, to gain more insightful views of current reality.

(Senge 1990: 10)

Insight can be seen as the outcome of reflection, the ability to see inter-relationships, to analyse complexity and to generate options and then have the capacity to choose. For Greenfield, Schön and Senge, these processes have to be set in the context of vision, values and moral confidence. There is nothing in this catalogue that is exclusive to any one individual. It could be argued that the person with designated formal authority should possess these qualities as a pre-ordinate but s/he is unlikely to achieve her/his full potential to influence organisational development and effectiveness unless her/his behaviour is replicated throughout the organisation.

There are a number of direct and practical implications of these insights for leadership and management in schools:

- Introducing the key terms – learning, reflection and review – into the terminology of the school, e.g. in its aims and mission statement, in job descriptions, in policy statements and all documentation.
- Generating a common language to help to create shared understanding about the vision and values of the school, especially in the key areas of learning and relationships.
- Creating interdependence through the introduction of teams as advocated in Chapter 11.
- Making review and reflection implicit to a range of processes, e.g. meetings, lessons, INSET sessions.
- Developing the capacity in individuals to become more reflective by example, training and the creation of space and time, e.g. time at the end of every lesson and meeting to ask the questions 'what did I learn?' and 'how did I learn it?'

However, none of this will work if it is in the context of a control culture based on hierarchy. The first, and perhaps most fundamental, realignment of thinking is to move into a notion of what Greenleaf (1977) describes as servant leadership:

It begins with the natural feeling that one wants to serve, to serve first. Then conscious choice brings one to aspire to lead. The difference manifests itself in the care taken by the servant – first to make sure that other people's highest priority needs are being served. The best test is: Do those served grow as persons; do they, while being served become healthier, wiser, freer, more autonomous, more likely themselves to become servants?

(Greenleaf 1977: 44)

It is important to reflect on the concepts that are central to this chapter and the competencies necessary to utilise them. To enable you to do this and to form an action plan, we suggest that it would be of assistance to make an enlarged photocopy of the three pages in Appendix A.

REFERENCES

Beare, H., Caldwell, B. J. and Millikan R. H. (1989) *Creating an Excellent School*, London: Routledge.

Block, P. (1993) *Stewardship: Choosing Service Over Self-Interest*, San Francisco: Berret-Koehler.

Duignan, P. A. and Bhindi, N. (1995) 'A quest for authentic leadership', paper presented at the British Educational Management and Administration Society (BEMAS) Annual Conference.

Gardner, H. (1995) *Leading Minds: An Anatomy of Leadership*, New York: Basic Books.

Greenfield, T. and Ribbins, P. (1993) *Greenfield on Educational Administration*, London: Routledge.

Greenleaf, R. K. (1977) *Servant Leadership*, New York: Paulist Press.

Gronn, P. (1995) 'Greatness revisited: the current obsession with transformational leadership', *Leading and Managing* 24(1): 7–30.

Hall, V., Mackay, H. and Morgan, C. (1986) *Headteachers at Work*, Milton Keynes: Open University Press.

Holmes, G. (1993) *Essential School Leadership*, London: Kogan Page.

National Commission on Education (1995) *Success Against the Odds*, London: Routledge.

OFSTED (1995a) *Guidance on the Inspection of Secondary Schools*, London: HMSO.

OFSTED (1995b) *Annual Report of Her Majesty's Chief Inspector of Schools*, London: HMSO.

Ribbins, P. (1995) 'Understanding contemporary leaders and leadership in education', in J. Bell and B.T. Harrison (eds) *Vision and Values in Managing Education*, London: David Fulton.

Schön, D. A. (1983) *The Reflective Practitioner*, New York: Basic Books.

Senge, P. M. (1990) *The Fifth Discipline*, New York: Doubleday.

Torrington, D. and Weightman, J. (1989) *The Reality of School Management*, Oxford: Blackwell.

11 Leading and managing staff for high performance

Max Sawatzki

As has been noted earlier, and in keeping with predictions by futurists such as Alvin Toffler (1971), John Naisbitt (1982), Charles Handy (1994), Peter Drucker (1993) and many others, a new era is with us – an era in which the global marketplace and the global economy have become the reality which they have been predicting for years.

Along with this new world order, a number of key themes and issues emerge as critically important. These include a far greater emphasis on national and international competition, or *hypercompetitiveness*; a major shift from a product-based economy to one in which greatest value is attached to information and services; a generally heightened demand for increasing levels of performance, in an era dubbed by Moses (1990) as the High Performance Era; and a preoccupation with restructuring, downsizing, reinvention and reengineering, as organisations grapple with the demands of this emerging era.

And whilst reengineering is the subject of a different chapter of this book, it is worth considering the impact of this phenomenon as it relates to this most critical task – the leadership and management of staff within high performing schools.

Following the lead of Hammer and Champy (1993) reflected in Chapter 2, I agree that

> Reengineering . . . isn't another quick fix . . . a new trick. What matters in reengineering is how we want to organise work today, given the demands of today's markets and the power of today's technologies.
>
> (Hammer and Champy 1993: 2)

But while emerging technologies have great implications for reengineering teaching and learning, within this chapter I would like to concentrate on the organisation of work as it relates to the leadership and management of staff.

THE NEED FOR BOTH LEADERSHIP AND MANAGEMENT

In keeping with Kotter's (1990) view of the world, it needs to be acknowledged from the outset that, in this era which is high on complexity and rate of change, there is a need for significant levels of both leadership and management in striving to develop and maintain world class

Table 11.1 Distinguishing leadership and management

	Management	Leadership
Creating an agenda	Planning and budgeting: establishing detailed steps and timetables for achieving needed results, and then allocating the resources necessary to make that happen	Establishing direction: developing a vision of the future, often the distant future, and strategies for producing the changes needed to achieve that vision
Developing a human network for achieving the agenda	Organising and staffing: establishing some structure for accomplishing plan requirements, staffing that structure with individuals, delegating responsibility and authority for carrying out the plan, providing policies and procedures to help to guide people, and creating methods or systems to monitor implementation	Aligning people: communicating the direction by words and deeds to all those whose co-operation may be needed so as to influence the creation of teams and coalitions that understand the vision and strategies, and accept their validity
Execution	Controlling and problem solving: monitoring results vs. plan in some detail, identifying deviations, and then planning and organising to solve these problems	Motivating and inspiring: energising people to overcome major political, bureaucratic, and resource barriers, to change by satisfying very basic, but often unfulfilled, human needs
Outcomes	Produces a degree of predictability and order, and has the potential of consistently producing key results expected by various stakeholders (e.g. for customers, always being on time; for stockholders, being on budget)	Produces change, often to a dramatic degree, and has the potential of producing extremely useful change (e.g. new products that customers want, new approaches to labour relations that help to make a firm more competitive)

Source: Kotter 1990: 6

organisations. Hence, there is little point in debating the virtue of one versus the other, or even bothering to dwell greatly on defining the difference between them, even though Kotter does this very neatly through the analysis illustrated in Table 11.1. Suffice it to say that in this high performance era it is pointless talking about managing staff, without at the same time talking of leading staff.

EMERGING TRENDS IN LEADERSHIP

Whilst it is not possible to examine fully here the nature of effective leadership, it is worth reflecting briefly on the changes to the concept of leadership that have occurred over a number of years. The American Telephone and Telegraph definition, for example, as presented by Moses (1990), has changed significantly in this time, as illustrated below:

1956   A man can lead a group to accomplish a task without arousing hostility.

1970–80 An individual can lead a group to accomplish a task.

1990   An individual elicits high performance outcomes from others.

Apart from the significance of the changed wording to include female leaders, which in itself is a major leap forward, the trend in this development is clearly towards the leader as facilitator of team performance, rather than as knight on white charger, or director and supervisor; and towards a situation wherein leadership is about the creation and maintenance of a climate and conditions for the achievement of goals and the attainment of high performance – a situation in which leadership involves working with and through others.

This does not suggest for a minute that the leader is simply a co-ordinator, because this is certainly not the case. Leadership is a far more active and deliberate process than this. Indeed, leadership will always be about helping the group to move forward by utilising the efforts of individuals who complement and enhance each other's skills, 'linking the group to the strengthening unit of a common purpose ... making the parts whole' (Adair 1986: 116).

Looking at these changes in another way, it is worthwhile reflecting, as Sharpe (1995: 17) does, that 'education for the twenty-first century is coinciding with a renewed interest in the concept of leadership. ' Tracing the emergence of the concept through two-dimensional leadership (1960s), situational leadership (1970s) and transformational leadership (late 1970s), Sharpe concludes that in the late 1990s leadership is regaining its rightful place in the scheme of things, having been relegated to second place by the 'more mundane and at times sterile diet of management efficiency' in the 1980s.

This analysis supports a currently dominant view of the need for what De Pree (1990: 1) describes as Strategic Leadership. In his terms, 'the first requirement of a leader is to define reality. The last is to say "Thank you". In between the leader must become a servant and a debtor.'

Within the schooling context, Caldwell and Spinks (1992: 92) define strategic leadership as:

- Keeping abreast of trends and issues, threats and opportunities in the school environment and in society at large, nationally and internationally; discerning the 'megatrends' and anticipating their impact on education generally and on the school in particular.
- Sharing knowledge with others in the school's community and encouraging other school leaders to do the same in their areas of interest.
- Establishing structures and processes which enable the school to set priorities and formulate strategies which take account of likely and/or preferred futures; being a key source of expertise as these occur.
- Ensuring that the attention of the school community is focused on matters of strategic importance.
- Monitoring the implementation of strategies as well as emerging strategic issues in the wider environment; facilitating an ongoing process of review.

Consistent with, but somewhat of an extension of these views, is the conception of leadership provided by Manz and Sims (1994). In their publication, *Superleadership*, they conclude that the leadership which is required today is best described as 'leading others to lead themselves' through, among other things, modelling effective leadership behaviours, and establishing self-leadership systems – culture, socio-technical designs, and teams. In their terms, 'superleaders have super followers'; a view which is endorsed by Chaleff (1995: 46), who argues that 'We need a dynamic model of followership that balances and supports dynamic leadership ... a proactive view of the follower's role, which brings it into parity with the [formal] leader's role.' In essence, we are therefore drawn to a model which suggests that leadership lies in all of us, and the high performing organisation will be one in which each member of the team is a self-led, growing and dynamic individual, prepared to contribute to the greater good of the team and the organisation.

But what of the *formal* or designated leader's position within this scheme of things? The final piece in the mosaic is provided by Wilson *et al.* (1994) who show visually the changes that have occurred over the years, arriving at the *highly empowering* leader who acts as mentor to a number of self-managing work teams. This formulation is shown in Figure 11. 1. The transition in conceptions of leadership commenced with

Autocratic leadership

Level 1
Autocratic

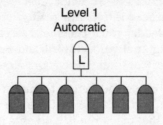

Participative leadership

Level 2
Central

Level 3
Transitional

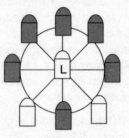

High involvement leadership

Level 4
Partnering

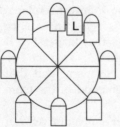

Level 5
Highly empowering

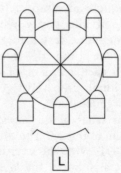

Figure 11.1 Five levels of leadership

Source: Wilson *et al.* 1994

earlier bureaucratic and often autocratic forms; moved through more participative leadership forms in which the designated leader allowed others to exercise a leadership responsibility; and into more recent high involvement models under which the leader is either a partner in leadership, or in its most highly developed form, a mentor to the self-led team.

Again, I emphasise that under these arrangements the role of the formal leader is no less important. Indeed, the opposite is true, as s/he must carry out her/his role by establishing and communicating the vision, by modelling, and by mentoring and coaching. This approach is consistent with the view of Bennis and Nanus (1985: 46) that 'Leaders acquire and wear their visions like clothes. Accordingly, they seem to enrol themselves (and then others) in the belief of their ideals as attainable, and *their behaviour exemplifies the ideals in action*' [my italics].

Such views of leadership also rely heavily on the concept of *empowerment* whereby the designated leader 'empowers others to translate intention into reality and sustain it' (Bennis and Nanus 1985: 80). Such empowerment, urges Bennis and Nanus (1985: 82–3), involves four major elements:

- Significance – a feeling of those involved that they are doing something important and significant, a feeling 'of being at the active centre of the social order'.
- Competence – development and learning on the job.
- A sense of community – a sense of 'family', of being 'joined in some common purpose'.
- Fun and enjoyment – derived from the work and interactions with others involved in it.

In summary, therefore, reengineering leadership in high performing schools of the future involves developing a form of leadership which is highly involving and highly empowering, which relies on leading others to lead themselves and which consequently has significant implications for the second major part of our picture, namely management.

EMERGING TRENDS IN THE MANAGEMENT OF STAFF

Of the many issues that could be addressed under this heading, I propose to concentrate here on three, viz. creating and developing high performance teams; utilising on-the-job development systems including mentoring and coaching; and developing performance feedback mechanisms.

Creating and developing high performance teams

As we saw earlier, new conceptions of leadership involve the formal leader acting as a mentor to largely self-led, self-managed work teams.

The outstanding emphasis being placed on these increasingly popular organisational forms mirrors Moses' (1990) view that, in the high performance era, the team, and not the individual becomes the major unit of analysis.

It should come as little surprise that such an arrangement is currently enjoying increasingly high levels of support from organisations of all kinds. This is because it is a manifestation of the belief that in high performing, responsive, customer-focused organisations which are striving for success in this era, power, information and resources need to be allocated as close as possible to the point of delivery of services; and the team represents a strong organisational form which can provide the basis for such an arrangement.

The emerging model suggests that, for high performance teamwork to occur, this alignment of power, information, resources and indeed rewards within the team structure is a fundamental prerequisite. This is in contrast with earlier approaches in which teams were sometimes used to deal with specific issues and/or solve particular problems without, necessarily, having large amounts of power and resources at their disposal. Under the new scenario, effective teamwork becomes far more than a nicety aimed at improving working conditions of staff, or even achieving improved outcomes, and moves to the central position of major driver in pursuit of high performance.

Putting it another way, we can talk all we like about teams and teamwork (when we may well often mean groups and group work), but unless we are prepared to put our money where our mouth is, we are not likely to achieve high performance teamwork, that is, teamwork that produces, in the main, consistently high levels of performance, or higher levels of performance than would normally be expected given all the circumstances.

If this is true of organisations generally, it is even more pertinent for schools and school systems within which the dominant paradigm is rapidly becoming one in which the school itself is the major self-managing team. Under this arrangement it is important that the paradigm shift, which has seen the transformation of large, bureaucratic education systems into new arrangements involving a strategic core steering a system of self-managing schools, is in fact institutionalised at the school level, so that the school itself consists of a strategic core steering a system of self-managing teams.

Carmichael (1993) portrays the change at institutional level as shown in Figure 11.2. Under the arrangement outlined, the hitherto bureaucratic scientific management model applying world-wide in years gone by is rapidly being replaced by a new arrangement featuring a very lean strategic core 'steering' a system of self-managing work units, with responsibilities as shown.

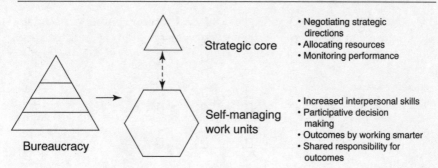

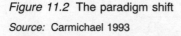

Figure 11.2 The paradigm shift

Source: Carmichael 1993

This is where the real challenge lies for schools because many school heads or principals, while endorsing the move from the centralised organisational arrangements which were typical at the system level in a previous era, have not, as yet, come to terms with the new paradigm as it applies at the school level. What to do? In implementing this central idea there are four key steps which need to be taken:

● Reorganising the school.
● Forming the teams.
● Building high performance teamwork.
● Aligning rewards and incentives with team performance.

Reorganising the school

The first of these steps, as suggested above, is to organise the school so that teams become an integral part of it. In other words, the school, as a self-managing work unit, needs to comprise a strategic core which

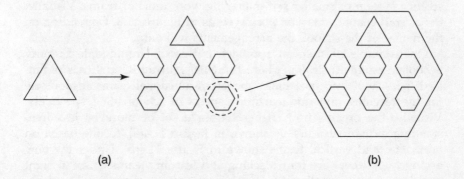

Figure 11.3 Restructuring (a) the system and (b) the school

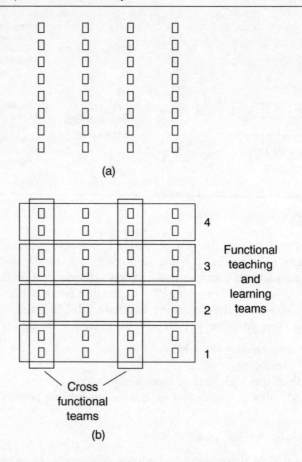

Figure 11.4 School reorganisation: (a) the previous arrangement and (b) the new arrangement at Huntingdale Primary School, Western Australia

steers a system of smaller self-managing work units or teams. Visually, the overall changes may be portrayed as in Figure 11.3. Depending on the nature of the school, the arrangements will vary.

One example of such an approach is that of Huntingdale Primary School, Western Australia, where principal Murray Randall has organised the school into functional and cross-functional teams responsible for the teaching and non-teaching aspects of school life respectively. Visually, the organisation changed from a set of more or less free-standing individual units, as shown in Figure 11.4(a), to one based on horizontal and vertical teams shown in Figure 11.4(b). Under the new arrangement, there are four teaching and learning teams of six to eight people, and cross-functional teams to cover areas such as school management, curriculum, and so on.

In explaining the very thorough culture building process the school went through, principal Murray Randall says they began by talking and moving towards a shared understanding and a common language. They then held a strategic planning workshop for the three members of the School Administration (Senior Management) Team, including sorting out their roles. Next they raised the level of debate through presentations at staff meetings, through holding targeted workshops, and by providing release time, for staff to plan and think. They gradually moved to implementation of Total Quality Management principles, and made a number of important modifications to teaching and learning.

Peer coaching is a significant feature of the new arrangements, and new leaders have emerged very clearly. What began as a good idea has become a vibrant new organisational structure which has overcome initial barriers and, as Murray tells it, the 'fierce individualism' that existed previously. The next move is to provide each team with its own budget which will operate within the framework of the overall school budget. This will provide the cement that binds the mosaic together.

Forming the teams

The second step that needs to be taken is to form the teams that will provide the basis for the organisation. Like the definition of team and leader, there are many theories on forming teams based on complementary roles, behaviour styles, personality styles and the like. Analytical instruments and psychometric tests range in sophistication and technicality from the more extreme, such as the Myers–Briggs Type Indicator and the Margerison–McCann Team Index, to far simpler versions, such the Briggs–Stratton behaviour styles inventory, the Belbin self-perception inventory, and the Gregorc style delineator. Each of the last three has a different role to play in helping with teamwork. The first deals with dominant behavioural styles, the second preferred team roles, and the third dominant thinking styles.

Of course care needs to be exercised in the use of such instruments as they are merely *indicators* of dominant styles at a particular time. These can change over time, and any one individual can display the characteristics of more than one style at any specific point. Hence caution must be exercised in granting to the instruments a level of accuracy and immutability that cannot be justified. Similarly, in arranging the mix of styles it is important to recognise the limitations of the instruments and our own ability to combine complementary styles in order to make the 'perfect' team. In short, this is not an exact science, and it should not be treated like one.

Having said all this, the fact is that instruments such as those mentioned above can play an important role in team building, and, whether we use the simple versions or the complex ones, whether we read widely and deeply to increase our own knowledge and understanding, or indeed use other methods, the major messages remain the same, namely that, in building effective teams, we must:

- Be aware of our own dominant behaviour styles, thinking styles, and preferred team roles.
- Be aware of the range of styles and roles that exist in others.
- Appreciate and respect other styles and roles as valid, indeed important to the success of the team.
- Compose teams using complementary behaviour styles, thinking styles, and preferred team roles.
- Assign individuals to appropriate roles, based on their individual styles, characteristics, and preferences.
- Vary team composition according to the nature of the task.
- Share functional team leadership according to the nature of the task.

And if high performance teams need very good leadership, leaders of high performing schools need to be thoroughly sensitised to this issue of diversity and complementarity, in order to ensure that the teams which are formed, the people who are recruited, and the systems which are developed, take account of these significant issues. This may require some form of technical analysis from the many that are available, but the least it will require will be conscious observation of the behaviour of team members or potential team members, and heightened sensitivity to their particular styles, characteristics, and individual needs.

Building high performance teamwork

Having formed the teams, the third step is to create the conditions for the achievement of high performance. What are some of the issues that need to be considered here?

First, one major discriminating characteristic of teams that ultimately reach high levels of performance is their preoccupation with outcomes, as well as their focus on measurements of performance. In essence, for such teams feedback is the fuel that powers performance and they are very active in gathering and analysing data in order to take their performance to even higher levels. Hence, whether it is data relating to the extent of achievement of goals, whether it is data relating to the performance of individuals within the team, or whether it is data relating to performance of the team as perceived by the individuals within it, one critical element of high performance is that of data gathering, analysis and feedback.

A second major element relates to the unification of the team around a common cause or, more often, a difficult or highly challenging task.

Those of us who have experienced teamwork in a personally challenging outdoor or wilderness environment appreciate fully the team cohesiveness and synergy that results from an extremely difficult and/or dangerous situation, whether it be in white water or on a sheer rockface. There are few other experiences which reduce individuals to a sense of common cause and genuine feeling and concern for other members of the team than this one. And of course there are many parallels in organisational life, with particularly challenging missions and their associated levels of risk having similar effects upon team members.

The point is, however, that without this single unifying challenge or threat teams can rarely rise to levels which might genuinely be called 'high performance'. Hence, it is in my view unrealistic to expect all teams within an organisation to be *high performing*. And yet, if there are insufficient such teams, the overall organisation is likely to lack the get-up-and-go to reach the very high standards necessary for the high performance era.

Critical questions that must be addressed, therefore, are what are the *real* challenges in this organisation? What are the issues which desperately need to be addressed? Who are the best people to address them? And how should we configure them as a team in order to achieve the outcomes required in as effective and efficient a manner as possible? Having said this, there is no good reason why all teams should not aspire to the features of high performing teams and it is therefore important to emphasise that, whilst not all will be high performing, there is no reason why they cannot still be highly effective 'real teams'.

Thus, in building high performance, as well as forming teams effectively, it is also critical to do the following:

- Identify clearly the specific challenge that needs to be addressed.
- Develop a clear focus on outcomes and performance.
- Collect and use high quality data to underpin judgement and action.
- Foster a culture of continuous improvement.
- Create a climate of development and learning on the job.
- Adopt common and agreed processes of decision-making, problem-solving, and innovative thinking.
- Develop a sense of caring for the team and individuals within it, that transcends personal success or well being.
- Create a working climate which offers fun and enjoyment.
- Celebrate success.

Aligning rewards and incentives with team performance

The fourth and final step relates to *alignment*, namely alignment of resources to programme outcomes and alignment of incentives and/or rewards to team outcomes. This is indeed a real challenge, which is occupying a lot of thought in organisations that have, since time immemorial, remunerated individual performance. Even now, with an increasingly high degree of emphasis on teamwork and team performance, the dominant reward paradigm continues to be based on the individual.

So how might it be done differently? In short, only with difficulty unless the school allocates a certain amount of its salary and/or other budget to a reward pool that may then be applied on the basis of performance. Like most things, the best approach would be one founded on common sense – one that has as its basis individual salaries and perhaps even an element of individual performance reward, whilst at the same time building in a capacity for incentives and/or rewards for teams, not necessarily in cold hard cash but in whatever form is negotiated between the team and the principal or the strategic core team. This could include, for example, professional development opportunities, fact-finding or benchmarking investigations, special technology for use by the team, or even celebratory events to mark the accomplishment of noteworthy high levels of performance.

From manager to mentor; from commander to coach

Under the arrangements outlined above, it becomes clear that approaches to leadership and management will be quite different, with a major emphasis being placed on mentoring and coaching both of teams and of individuals within teams. Consistent with Figure 11.1, it seems reasonable that the principal and her/his strategic team might be responsible for mentoring and coaching one or more teams within the school and might, in addition, be responsible for setting up a school-wide mentoring and coaching system which involves everyone in the school.

Within the overall context of performance development, the concept of mentoring and coaching has always offered great promise for supporting individual growth and development but, in the high performance era, the concept which might hitherto have been seen as an organisational frill becomes integral to performance. Little wonder that. in *The Return of the Mentor*, Caldwell and Carter (1993) note that mentoring as an issue has recently taken on far greater prominence as workplaces seek to respond to the needs of the emerging era, and the demands for service-driven, highly efficient organisations. They also note that this prominence spans a wide range of both private and public sector organisations, including many in Health and Education that seek to create what Senge (1990) refers to as *the learning organisation*.

Some commentators are inclined to use the terms 'mentor' and 'coach' interchangeably, but I prefer to differentiate between the two. In a sense, mentoring is a more inclusive, more embracing term which often includes the activity of coaching, but can be much more than that. Hence for me a mentor is a trusted, experienced professional, who is willing to assist a less experienced person by listening, sharing experiences, advising, guiding, and coaching; a coach is more of a trusted colleague who is willing to assist by observing performance, gathering and analysing data, and providing meaningful positive feedback. As suggested above, coaching may be thought of as a subset of mentoring, and a mentor, whilst s/he may well coach from time to time, will do far more than this. Other activities may include helping the person to identify and refine developmental needs, assisting with the creation of a personalised individual development plan, reflecting with the person on her/his handling of specific activities or initiatives which the mentor may not have seen personally, but which can provide the opportunity for what Hersey (1990) calls *reflective review and coaching*.

Whatever the tasks agreed upon, it is critical that the protégé takes responsibility for managing an individual developmental plan, whilst the mentor acts as supporter, helper and encourager. Consequently the role involves far more listening than it does talking, and is much more subtle than giving lots of good advice and suggestions based on experience. Indeed, the skilled mentor is able to assist the individual to draw her/his own conclusions about performance by having her/him articulate the issues, incidents, solutions and so on, and by working in a way that allows distillation of appropriate action plans.

It is important to note here that this concept of 'mentor' is a far cry from the earlier colloquial versions of the term which implied opening doors for fortunate individuals or giving them a leg up the organisational ladder, often at the expense of others who were not lucky enough to have key decision-makers as their 'mentors'. On the contrary, the model envisaged here is a very professional one, aimed totally at assisting the individual to grow and develop.

Developing performance feedback mechanisms

As has already been established, the quest for high performance needs to be built upon a platform of goals, outcomes, and feedback about performance, both at the organisational level and at the level of individuals within the organisation. Since this chapter deals predominantly with leading and managing staff, it is to this latter point that we now turn.

It has long been recognised that feedback about performance is essential to organisational improvement, and organisations all over the world are increasingly seeking such feedback from their clients/customers and from other key stakeholders. This is in fact one major characteristic that distinguishes high performance organisations and/or teams from others

– the extent to which they gather effective data, feed it back, and use it to drive the organisation to increasingly higher levels of performance.

Such approaches involve collection of performance data about a whole range of variables in the course of normal operations. Most also involve gathering customer response data through survey questionnaires and, increasingly, through face-to-face focus group meetings. Many organisations have found this approach to be highly effective, not the least of which is Qantas Airways, Australia's largest airline, and its sister British Airways. Both represent excellent examples of organisations that use feedback to drive their performance.

It is not just external customers that can provide this crucial feedback. Many high-powered organisations are seeking feedback from employees, some using very informal and/or unstructured approaches whilst others are using more structured approaches based around specially developed questionnaires such as the Service Organisation Profile (Georgiades 1990). The basis of such feedback models is the belief that employee satisfaction provides the basis for customer satisfaction. Hence, when an organisation obtains a clear view of its performance in terms of key variables such as Leadership, Service Mission, Management Practices, Group Climate, Job Satisfaction, Role Overload, Career Development and the like, and when this is shown relative to a world-wide database, the feedback can be extremely powerful in stimulating change and, ultimately, heightened performance.

Within education, increasing emphasis is being placed on annual survey data, with many school systems and individual schools gathering important data which they can use to improve their performance. As in other organisations, the trend is towards gathering this data from a wide range of stakeholders about a broad set of variables relating to school performance.

Feedback: an essential ingredient for the people of the organisation

If feedback is essential for driving organisational performance, it is just as critical for the individuals within the organisation. Outside education, increasing importance is being placed upon what is now being termed '360 degree feedback'. Under this approach, each individual systematically gathers data about her/his performance from a range of people, either once or twice a year, using specially prepared and agreed instruments. The range of people from whom comments are sought typically includes the person's manager, her/his 'peers', and her/his 'subordinates', whom we now prefer to refer to as 'team members', a term better suited to the flatter, team-based structures of today. By gathering data from these various sectors, the individual gets a multifaceted, rounded, or '360 degree' view of performance, as seen from a range of perspectives.

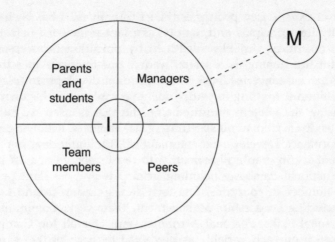

Figure 11.5 The 360 degree feedback model

Surprisingly, analysis of a range of models and instruments reveals that many omit reference to the client or customer served by the individual, either internal to the organisation or external. No doubt this is somewhat related to the difficulty of gathering meaningful data from the client sector, but for organisations that champion service excellence this appears to be a serious omission, and one which schools can hardly afford.

Hence within schools it is suggested that data should be sought from the person's manager, and an appropriate sample of peers, team members, parents and, where appropriate, students. The person also needs to analyse her/his own performance in order to compare perceptions with the feedback received from others. Thus, the 360 degree feedback model might be pictured as in Figure 11.5, with the individual at the centre of the process, and the person's mentor on the side, with the task of helping the person to make sense of the feedback and to determine appropriate growth plans.

It is important that the process be kept simple, through the use of an instrument which asks simple questions, and which is easy to complete and return. It is also important that respondents be free to rate the person according to the way they really think in answer to the questions asked, by providing the feedback anonymously.

Thoughtful construction of the data gathering instrument and accompanying analytical approaches can result in the individual receiving very specific feedback which can be presented in a simple and easily understood graphical format. One example of such an approach is provided by the Principal Development Inventory (PDI), developed by Performance Development International with input and assistance from a large number of experienced principals (PDI 1995). The PDI has been created especially for principals and deputy/assistant principals. It focuses on a range of critical variables identified by practitioners as essential to successful functioning as a school leader, and thus provides the basis for high performance feedback and individual development planning.

In addition to inviting the individual to complete her/his own assessment using the 40-item questionnaire, the PDI is used to gather 360 degree feedback from a full spectrum of stakeholders. Following analysis by Performance Development International, the individual is provided with feedback in graphical format, with results shown against those of an international database including principals and assistant principals from a number of countries. The forty items cluster around key variables including Leadership, Management, Teamwork, Communication/ Interpersonal Skills, Personal Attributes, and Overall Job Competence. Performance on each variable as perceived by each of the respondent groupings (parents, teachers, manager, and so on), is shown, relative to the perception of the individual, giving a solid basis for analysis and for development planning.

Of course, the place to start with all of this is with the designated formal leader and her/his leadership team. Apart from the fact that the performance of school leaders is such an important variable in school performance, there is another major reason for doing so. In Australia we call it *leadership by example*. As noted earlier, others such as Manz and Sims (1994) call it *superleadership*, or 'leading others to lead themselves, by modelling effective leadership behaviours' whilst Bennis and Nanus (1985) simply call it *exemplifying ideals through behaviour*.

Whatever we call it, it means being prepared to put ourselves on the line by demonstrating our own personal commitment to high performance and growth and then, having done this, by holding the quite reasonable expectation that all other staff will follow the lead. The overall outcome of this will, we hope, be a learning, growing, dynamic, high performing school of the twenty-first century, a school which is nourished by feedback, the fuel that powers performance.

DRAWING THE THREADS TOGETHER

This chapter has presented a range of issues relating to leading and managing staff in high performing schools. It began by emphasising the importance of both leadership and management, and the leadership theme has permeated the whole chapter.

It has also acknowledged that the changes required are more than fiddling at the edges or simply tweaking the systems. For many schools the changes envisaged represent a bold, adventurous step, and one that can only be met by comprehensive overhaul or reengineering.

Hence, major emphasis has been placed on creating and building high performance teams, on aligning rewards and incentives with team performance and on adopting approaches to leadership and management which place responsibility for performance with the team and the individual; which encourage performance feedback and developmental planning; and which begin with the leadership team leading by example in search of a new, great tomorrow in the truly high performing school of the twenty-first century.

> **It is important to reflect on the concepts that are central to this chapter and the competencies necessary to utilise them. To enable you to do this and to form an action plan, we suggest that it would be of assistance to make an enlarged photocopy of the three pages in Appendix A.**

REFERENCES AND FURTHER READING

Adair, J. (1986) *Effective Teambuilding*, London: Pan.

Albrecht, K. A. and S. A. (1987) *The Creative Corporation*, Illinois: Dow Jones.

Belbin, R. M. (1985) *Management Teams: Why They Succeed or Fail*, London: Heinemann.

Bennis, W. and Nanus, W. (1985) *Leaders*, New York: Harper and Row.

Bridges, W. (1995) *Jobshift: How to Prosper in a Workplace Without Jobs*, London: Nicholas Brearley.

Caldwell, B. J. and Carter, E. M. (1993) *The Return of the Mentor*, London: Falmer.

Caldwell, B. J. and Sawatzki, M. (1993) 'The school charter – linking strategic management with highly effective schools of the future', paper presented to Schools of the Future Charter Development Workshops, Victoria: Directorate of School Education.

Caldwell, B. J. and Spinks, J. M. (1992) *Leading the Self-Managing School*, London: Falmer.

Carmichael, L. (1993) 'The management paradigm shift', unpublished presentation to the National Project on the Quality of Teaching and Learning, Adelaide, 1992.

Chaleff, I. (1995) 'All hail the brave follower', *The QANTAS Club*, November.

Covey, S. (1990) *The 7 Habits of Highly Effective People*, New York: Simon & Schuster.

Covey, S. (1992) *Principle-Centred Leadership*, London: Simon and Schuster.

De Pree, M. (1990) *Leadership is an Art*, New York: Currency Doubleday.

Drucker, P. F. (1993) *Post-Capitalist Society*, New York: Harper Business.

Georgiades, N. (1990) *The Service Organisation Profile*, Chorleywood, Hertford-shire: NGA Organisation Consultants.

Hammer, M. and Champy, J. (1993) *Reengineering the Corporation*, Sydney: Allen and Unwin.

Handy, C. (1994) *The Empty Raincoat: Making Sense of the Future*, London: Random House.

Hanuschek, E. A. *et al.* (1994) *Making Schools Work: Improving Performance and Controlling Costs*, Washington, DC: Brookings Institution.

Hersey, P. (1990) *Mentoring and Coaching: A Development Program for Educational Leaders*, Reston, VA: NASSP.

Kaplan, R. S. and Norton, D. P. (1992) 'The balanced scorecard: measures that drive performance', *Harvard Business Review*, Jan/Feb 1992.

Kaplan, R. S. and Norton, D. P. (1993) 'Putting the balanced scorecard to work', *Harvard Business Review*, Sept/Oct 1993.

Katzenbach, J. R. and Smith, D. K. (1993) *The Wisdom of Teams: Creating the High Performance Organisation*, Boston: Harvard Business School.

Kotter, J. P. (1990) *A Force for Change: How Leadership Differs From Management*, New York: Free Press.

Manz, C. and Sims, H. (1994) *Superleadership*, New York: Berkley.

Mink, G., Mink, B. P. and Owen, K. Q. (1987) *Groups at Work*, Englewood Cliffs, NJ: Educational Technology Publications.

Moses, J. (1990) 'High Performance Leadership', unpublished paper presented to the Twenty-first International Congress on the Use of the Assessment Centre Method, Anaheim, California.

Naisbitt, J. (1982) *Megatrends*, London: Futura.

National Centre for Effective Schools Research and Development (1992) *School Based Instructional Leadership*, Trainers' Notebook, Wisconsin: University of Wisconsin.

Odden, A. (1995) *Educational Leadership for America's Schools*, New York: McGraw Hill.

Odden, A. and Odden, E. (1994) 'Applying the high involvement framework to local management of schools in Victoria, Australia', paper presented in a symposium on 'Improving School Performance Through School Based Management: A Systemic Approach' at the Annual Meeting of the American Education Research Association, New Orleans, 4 April.

Officer, G. (1995) 'Global trends shaping workplaces of the future', *Benchmark* 13.

Performance Development International (1995) *The Principal Development Inventory*, Fadden, Australian Capital Territory: Sawatzki Consulting Group International.

Riley, P. (1993) *The Winner Within*, New York: Berkley.

Semler, R. (1993) *Maverick*, Sydney: Random House.

Senge, P. M. (1990) *The Fifth Discipline: The Art and Practice of the Learning Organisation*, New York: Doubleday.

Sharpe, F. G. (1995) 'Educational leadership for the twenty-first century', *The Practising Administrator* 2.

Toffler, A. (1971) *Future Shock*, London: Pan.

Waterman, R. H. (1994) *Frontiers of Excellence*, New York: Norton.

Wilson, J. M., George, J., Wellins, R. S. and Byham, W. C. (1994) *Leadership Trapeze: Strategies for Leadership in Team-Based Organizations*, San Francisco: Jossey-Bass.

12 Managing learning and teaching

Tony Tuckwell and Michael Billingham

This chapter focuses on the core purpose of the school, an area which many believe has been somewhat neglected during the years of rapid administrative and managerial restructuring and imposed curriculum change. It sets the context of learning and teaching by initially examining the growth and restructuring of the education system. It then moves on to examine the nature of learning and teaching in the twenty-first century and the characteristics of a learning school in the next century.

GROWTH AND RESTRUCTURING

The expansion of state education in the first half of the twentieth century and the various administrative and institutional restructurings of the second half have, in the end, only tinkered with the core issue of improved teaching and learning. It is by default, rather than by design, that the very processes of teaching and learning have now been thrust into the spotlight.

It is argued that education has been too monolithically slow in its development compared with the speed of technological advance in the global economy. Marshall and Tucker (1992) describe the problem in the United States. Their analysis has echoes in the UK:

> The key to both productivity and competitiveness is the skills of the people and our capacity to use highly educated and trained people to maximum advantage in the workplace. In fact, however, the guiding principle on which our educational and industrial systems have been built is profoundly different ... the principle of mass-producing low-quality education to create a low-skilled work force for mass-production industry.
>
> (Marshall and Tucker 1992: xvi)

The need for a wider publicly financed education system emerged a century ago because the cruel social effects of the industrial revolution, the extension of the franchise and the challenge of German industrial militarism, made it a social and economic imperative. But the aim was greater accessibility and a reduction in inequality, rather than a search for quality. The founding legislation of Forster (1870) and Balfour (1902), completed by Butler (1944), created a state education system which was firmly embedded in Local Authority control and which ended with basic secondary education for the majority and a high quality academic challenge for the chosen few.

As far as the curriculum was concerned, Morant, President of the Board of Education in 1904, provided a stable subject framework whose labels, give or take technology, still ring true today (see Moon 1991). However, the detailed content and objectives of the curriculum were not questioned, let alone regulated, except where the descending requirements of the universities shaped the public examination system for the most able. The rest could be left deferentially to a school's professional judgement. In a relatively homogeneous society, with a factory industrial economy manned by semi-skilled and unskilled labour, mere exposure to education would, it was felt, be adequate.

Most of the legislated restructuring of education in the twentieth century has focused on the secondary sector, while changes in the primary sector have been precipitated by a range of reports beginning with Plowden (1967). If the Butler Act provided the first major restructuring of secondary education, then the mid-1960s marked the beginning of the second. The Newsom Report of 1963 focused attention on the educational and resource deprivation of the 80 per cent in secondary modern schools. The dismantling of the selective system was the first qualitative inference that universal secondary education was not delivering the goods: 'The trouble with the tri-partite system was not that grammar schools were bad but that . . . secondary modern schools never achieved the "parity of esteem" intended for them' (Hargreaves 1994: 18).

In a thrust of determinist optimism it was believed that the all-ability school would level up standards to provide grammar school education for all and end the class divisions which, it was said, the selective system perpetuated. Cross-party consensus on education saw fifteen years of secondary reorganisation, from 1964 to 1979, across nearly all education authorities and facilitated by governments of both persuasions. Areas of voluntary curriculum reform blossomed, most especially through the Schools Council, but there was no national strategy for the curriculum. Headteachers were still omnipotent. Governing bodies lacked teeth. In fact, in many primary schools, the balance of subjects to be taught was largely within the control of the classroom teacher. Whole school inspections by Her Majesty's Inspectors (HMI) were rare and confidential. Parents by and large accepted the professional expertise of the teacher and the Local Education Authority's decisions on school placement.

But the relative slowness of Britain's economic growth cast graver doubts on educational expansion as a simple panacea. Quality and value for money entered the educational vocabulary. Prime Minister Callaghan's 1976 Ruskin College speech opened the Great Debate. Among his areas of concern were the methods and aims of formal instruction, the case for a core curriculum of basic knowledge, monitoring the use of resources in order to maintain a proper national performance, and the role of the Inspectorate in relation to national standards.

Thatcher's electoral victory in 1979 intensified the debate although it took her two more General Election victories to reach the conviction that a centrally determined curriculum and restructuring of the management of schools were necessary. It was significant that her first election victory coincided with the findings of Rutter *et al.* (1979) that schools *do* make a difference. While not rejecting the notion that socio-economic background affects a child's educational performance, this first major longitudinal study showed that schools with similar cohorts of children achieved markedly different outcomes. The ensuing School Effectiveness movement (see Reid *et al.* 1987; Dimmock 1993) clarified the characteristics that typify an effective school: shared vision, strong leadership, high and consistent expectations, a clear and continuing focus on teaching and learning, well-developed assessment procedures, responsibility for learning shared by the pupils, participation by pupils in the life of the school, rewards and incentives to succeed, parental involvement, and extra-curricular activities to enhance learning and relationships. The value-added movement of the 1990s, which seeks to establish reliable base-line measurements against which later educational outcomes can be compared, was also the natural offspring of Rutter's research.

The 1988 Education Reform Act (ERA), however, challenged every curriculum assumption on which education had hitherto been based. The 'secret garden of the curriculum', over whose wall James Callaghan peeped, was now publicly opened by Margaret Thatcher with the introduction of the National Curriculum and its accompanying assessment procedures at ages 7, 11 and 14. The continued relative underperformance internationally of British children in mathematics and science necessitated clear structures and accurate measurements of attainment earlier than 16+. In short the structure of education, which may have served the production-line factory economy of post-war Britain, was, in common with education systems throughout the developed world, irrelevant to the globalised post-industrial information economy of the twenty-first century based on highly skilled electronics and technology and the need for a flexible workforce (see Chapman 1990; Dimmock 1993).

ERA also saw a major management and financial restructuring. Only market competition, it was felt, backed by accurate public information on schools, would drive up standards. The controlling role of Local

Education Authorities (LEAs) was swept away by the delegation of finances to schools through Local Management of Schools (LMS), the facility for schools to leave their LEAs for Grant Maintained Status (GMS), the institution of private sponsorship through City Technology Colleges (CTC), and open enrolment based on parental preference. Test results, examination grades and attendance figures were published annually by the Department for Education and Employment and have been turned into league tables of schools and LEAs by the national press. Catchment areas have become much more fluid, at least for those parents with the knowledge and determination to exploit their preferences. With state school finances driven by pupil numbers and parental preference, a free recruitment market, sometimes cut-throat, has emerged in all but the most isolated rural areas. Quite intentionally the market implication of funding through Age-Weighted Pupil Units has had much more effect on schools' responses to parents than the relatively damp squibs of increasing the number of parent governors and the Governors' Annual Report and Annual General Meeting. Media awareness and the internal marketing of the school to existing parents and pupils have become paramount activities so that the local grapevine at the school gate, still the most potent form of advertisement, may stay favourable. The 1993 Education Act supplemented these changes with four-yearly public inspections of all schools by the Office for Standards in Education (OFSTED), involving parents' meetings with the inspection team, publicised reports (although the less frequent HMI inspection reports had been public since 1982) and public post-inspection action plans.

Thus in half a century education has already experienced three major restructurings – 1944, 1964–79 and 1988–93. But it is only as we approach the millennium that the processes of teaching and learning have reached centre stage. Uniform restructuring of school systems has been tried but has not produced a truly comprehensive system (see Walford 1993). The delegation of finances and the demise of the controlling LEA has still not produced sufficient measurable improvements in educational outcome although it may yet be too early to assess the longer-term effects of the curriculum creativity which self-managed finances can release in schools.

Hargreaves (1994) sums up the opportunities and threats of the present position:

Virtually everybody – with the exception of the unreconstructed Left which believes our schools were doing a perfectly grand job until the dark ages of the Thatcher years – knows that our educational system, and especially our schools, ought to be better and have the potential to be better. Outside central government, most also accept that it is as unsuccessful as it is unwise to achieve this mainly through legislation and detailed regulation from the centre. We have had over ten years of this and the degree of success in improving schools has been limited, falling short of original aspirations.

(Hargreaves 1994: 1)

The National Commission on Education (1993) is equally direct:

A minority of academically able young people receive a good, if narrow, education and, for them, provision is well-suited and efficiently run. For a majority of young people, education is of more variable benefit ... The gulf in outcomes between our best schools and our worst is big, much bigger than in most countries.

(NCE 1993: 1)

The curriculum of the twenty-first century

Whatever its shortcomings, the concept of a National Curriculum is here to stay. What such a curriculum will contain at any point in the future is uncertain, though the National Commission on Education (1993) is clear about the fundamental values needed to underpin it.

A framework of real values ... makes sense only when the full reality of learning and teaching is taken into account. Thus an excellent framework:

● will motivate pupils towards learning and promote enjoyment in learning. It will do this by such means as challenging pupils and arousing their curiosity, by helping them both to acquire and to use the basic tools of communication, by opening out aesthetic and other experiences to which they can respond, by providing learning which individuals perceive as relevant to their own present or future needs and by helping them to mature as confident and self-reliant members of society;
● will challenge the acceptance of low expectations and low aspirations too often found in our system. Thus it will offer schools and teachers support and encouragement, and will in particular give them scope for creativity and innovation. It is the task of teachers to provide schemes of work best suited to the range of abilities and needs represented in any group of pupils;
● will aim to be appealing to all pupils, and will therefore be varied enough to enable each to develop her or his own range of 'intelligences' or abilities;
● will provide for progression, and will therefore follow naturally on from nursery education and will lead naturally on to further or higher education or employment and training;
● will provide a basis for measuring the attainment of young people.

   An excellent framework, above all, will offer to all pupils a means of succeeding and having that success recognised.

The shelf-life of gobbets of knowledge is limited outside those aspects of the curriculum that may be part of cultural transmission and, even here, recent attempts to secure agreement on those works of literature which constitute a basic canon have foundered. For the foreseeable future international benchmarking in at least the basic skills of literacy in native and foreign languages, numeracy, science and technology, will require a form of centralisation based on whatever criteria are current at the time. Globalisation of educational attainment criteria goes hand-in-hand with the global economy.

For the immediate future there is much to be said for providing a more satisfactory shape to the existing National Curriculum to take account, at the one end, of the importance of pre-school education, and, at the other, of the *de facto* extension of compulsory education and training for the majority of young people to age 18 or 19. The National Commission has tried to give a blueprint.

At the pre-school end the National Commission says: 'There is a case for regarding 0–5 as the first stage in our education system' (1993: 131). The needs of children under 3 years must be addressed. Then, the priority must be access to high quality publicly-funded education for all 3–4 year olds, the curriculum to be geared to young children's needs, with an emphasis on first-hand experience and the central role of learning through play and talk. For ages 5–7 the National Commission's recommended Key Stage 1 curriculum envisages a mandatory core of English (and Welsh in Wales), mathematics, and the rudiments of science and technology in 50 per cent of curriculum time, with early experience of humanities and expressive arts in the other half. At Key Stages 2, 3 and 4 the balance stays the same except for some broadening of the core to incorporate citizenship and a modern foreign language. Citizenship, related directly by Key Stage 4 to employment skills, is construed as including working in teams; effective communication in word and number to achieve practical ends; problem-solving; personal effectiveness; self-discipline in thinking and acting. The National Commission also argues for the retention of much of the current Key Stage 4 core elements. But it would confine the statutory core (English or Welsh, mathematics, science, technology, a modern foreign language, citizenship) to 50 per cent of curriculum time with the other half left to the discretion of the school, subject to the required inclusion of one subject from each of the humanities and the expressive arts. This, in effect, raises the core to 70 per cent and is not far removed from the 1995 Dearing compromise.

The National Commission sees national tests in Key Stages 1–3 as essential building blocks for other learning. Inspired by Scotland's example, the Commission would prefer the tests to be selected by teachers from banks of tests nationally devised to be used at the appropriate moment in relation to a pupil's progress. There is an emphasis on child-centred testing, which is primarily designed to aid diagnosis and differentiation, rather than on testing which is centralised in content and timing and is primarily designed to serve the needs of the market and public account-ability. The National Commission also argues for the replacement of current attainment levels 1–10 by a scale A–G, although this would exac-erbate the width of the current attainment levels, with their in-built appearance of prolonged academic immobility.

For post-16 the National Commission accepts that 'a national curriculum which assumes that formal education comes to an end at 16 is already inadequate by international standards' (1993: 53). It advocates a Key Stage 5 for 16–18 year olds which should, none the less, with Key Stage 4, provide a single entity for 14–18 year olds. The content of the curriculum at Key Stage 5 would be much more fluid leading to a General Education Diploma (GED) awarded at Ordinary Level (age 16) and Advanced Level (age 18). The GED would replace all existing acad-emic and vocational qualifications. All courses at Key Stages 4 and 5 would be modular with moderated teacher assessment playing the major role. The GED would be a 'grouped award' based on a minimum total number of credit points and, within that total, a minimum number of points from core subjects (Key Stage 4) and at least three core subject areas (Key Stage 5). The modular approach would permit the most able students to pursue Advanced Level modules before the age of 16 and even, in some cases, omit the GED Ordinary Level. It would also permit pick-and-mix combinations of courses which would blur the distinction between the academic and vocational for those students whose educa-tional development post-16 has been inhibited by the lack of esteem for the vocational and the academic exclusivity of A Levels.

It is eminently sensible that the first step for the next century must be to tie up the loose ends of the close of this century. But a good curriculum framework should provide balance and breadth without such suffocation that innovation is stifled. The more that content, rather than outcome, is prescribed, the less spontaneous the development of new learning approaches will be, and the more teachers will see themselves as functionaries rather than creators. It could be argued that the 1987 Teachers' Pay and Conditions Act and the 1988 Education Reform Act have knocked recalcitrant unions on the head and established who is boss. The point having been made, more flexible curriculum and assess-ment structures, beyond even the Dearing compromise, are crucial to stimulate further growth. A good gardener always knows when to prune and feed.

So far, revised structures have not resolved the problem of differen-tiation which runs through every curriculum document of the last quarter of a century and, in truth, was at the heart of the tripartite and comprehensive restructurings of secondary education. George (1992: vii) defines differentiation as: 'every child's right to go as far and as fast as they can along every dimension of the school curriculum without any brakes being put on them'.

Differentiation is about quality rather than equality. Although George's theme is the needs of the gifted and talented, he points out that almost all children are gifted or talented in some way. For him differentiation is indivisible. If a school has the skill and determination to differentiate for one group it will probably do it for all. The National Commission found that when specific attention was given to the needs of very able pupils there was often an enhancement of the quality of teaching and learning and a raising of the expectations and standards of all pupils. George worries that his book may not change the minds of critics who feel that social education for the gifted is unfair, undemocratic or élitist, but, since he wrote his book, the political tide may well have turned on this issue.

But the difficulty with differentiation lies with the delivery. George confesses that

> Creating conditions to achieve it is a difficult task and differentiation for all . . . is an illusive goal. The word keeps surfacing because the detailed practice to produce it is so hard to sustain and the solutions to the problem are very challenging . . . The word differentiation has become a live issue because schools experience difficulty in coping effectively with the wide range of pupils that come through their doors.
>
> (George 1992: 102)

The National Commission thinks that modularity will help but warns of the 'double whammy' facing teachers, namely that fixed-pace whole-class teaching leaves many pupils unsatisfied and that self-paced work can result in low productivity. While the National Commission points to the superior grades achieved by GCSE Geography pupils using a flexible learning approach, and of 11–13 pupils using the Cognitive Acceleration through Science Education project, both based as much on higher level thinking skills as on content, Hargreaves (1994) is not convinced that this alone provides the solution, arguing that the very institutionalised routine and structure of large secondary schools impose their own limitations on the capacity to differentiate:

> The standard comprehensive school in the secondary sector is probably in decline. The trend should continue and not be reversed, even under a different government. The end of the comprehensive school does not mean the end of the comprehensive principle which can be realised through a variety of forms . . . The differentiation I have in mind is neither as trivial as the City Technology Colleges nor as

regressive as selection at eleven by intelligence testing. Institutional diversification is needed along two rather different lines. The first is curriculum specialisation . . . close to the 'magnet' schools developed in the United States in the early 1980's . . . The other form of diversification is specialisation along philosophical, ideological or religious lines . . . as has been the case in the independent sector for many years . . . It means many smaller schools before the age of 16, i.e. more 11–16 than 11–18 schools, to provide the necessary range of choice for parents.

(Hargreaves 1994: 17–18)

This is the only form of structural evolution not yet tried. It allays George's fears of élitism. It is reflected in the pragmatism of the Labour Party's 'Diversity and Excellence' education policy document of 1995 whose very title suggests a political paradigm shift.

But there is an inner contradiction in Hargreaves' thinking. There may not, in reality, be a great deal of difference between allocating places to children based on specialism preference and selection by intelligence testing. It is inconceivable, for example, that the language magnet school allocations will not be tipped in favour of those with a higher general language ability. Indeed, it could be argued that once the mixed-ability movement of the 1960s and 1970s was abandoned within comprehensive schools, when sorting pupils by banding and setting became the norm, then selection was bound to come back on the agenda. Hargreaves recognises this. He admits that magnet schools will attract high calibre staff and more resources in their specialism, and will, thereby, leave a remnant of 'sink schools'. But, he says, they exist anyway. This seems to side-step the most fundamental of the problems facing British (and American) education, the educational deprivation of many inner city areas. A fatalistic acceptance that the poor will always be with us does not solve the problem. We will return to this issue later.

Whether the content of the National Curriculum as we understand it will suffice for long into the twenty-first century is a moot point. It may signify the end of the old factory industrial era rather than a preparation for the new high-tech post-industrial era.

Beare and Slaughter (1993) have a broader curriculum vision which poses a fundamental question about the moral purpose of education in a world of growing environmental hazard and social dislocation. They warn that the changes of the next one hundred years are likely to exceed those of the last one thousand years in impact, speed, scope and importance and that education traditionally tends to reflect the past rather than concentrate on future issues. These they identify as an extended life-span, the ethical dilemmas created by medical and technological advances, man-made global environmental changes, the implications of nanotechnology, possible new waves of epidemics and terrorism and the decline of the sovereign state in a world economy of insecure job tenure:

> within the present context ... of compulsive technological dynamism, competitive individualism and a radical loss of meaning and purpose ... schools are put in an impossible position. They stand at the crucial interface between past and present, charged both with the conservation of culture and with its radical renewal.
>
> (Beare and Slaughter 1993: 15)

In this context conventional patterns of schooling will, they argue, become obsolescent. Education in generic skills in the post-industrial society will have to become integrated with the economy to service the shift to technological innovation. Yet, they argue, the danger lurks that economic efficiency will eradicate those qualities, unmeasurable immediately in cash terms, such as a child's self-esteem or a love of the arts, and that the continued compartmentalisation of knowledge will inhibit the holistic view of the world and its problems. They foresee a continuing tug-of-war between social/economic requirements and individual and cultural ones.

Beare and Slaughter make the telling argument that, in a world of increasingly unpredictable economic and social change, marked by the decline of the one-company career, and of the family, church and village as socially cohesive influences, only the school will survive as an institution of cultural transformation to which all will, for some years, be attached. To influence the shaping of events in this rapidly changing world (shades here of Hargreaves' citizenship) Beare and Slaughter argue for a curriculum infused with problem-solving futures scenarios using techniques of planning, forecasting, war-gaming and scenario analysis.

> The goal is not to make students into futurists but rather to help them understand what their options are. In so doing they can introduce into the present a wide range of choices – for example, in energy, transport, lifestyles and relationships ... It is our observation that when low-level human motives such as fear, greed, and hostility become associated with powerful technologies, the result is indeed a long-running disaster ... When a right relationship is re-established between people, culture and technology, a new world of options emerges.
>
> (Beare and Slaughter 1993: 129)

So, while technology dominates the world economy, the school curriculum should place great emphasis on the human effects of this revolution so that students become reactive, and moral shapers of events rather than passive spectators. This new definition of spiritual and moral growth beyond the dry confines of statutorily defined Religious

Education or the tortuous attempts to define Christian worship, is picked up by Hargreaves (1994) although his solution is not so far-reaching:

> Many parents, in their natural concern for the moral development and welfare of their children, will continue to support religious education ... Yet there are times when government should beware of responding directly to parental wishes, and instead look beyond them to the more deep-seated needs of the young within a rapidly changing society ... Moral education will in the future need to be more closely linked to civic education if it is to provide a common core of values.
>
> (Hargreaves 1994: 32)

Beare and Slaughter certainly provide a visionary view of the curriculum. Whether it would be seen as too socially critical or could be separated from political pressure group agendas is debatable. On the other hand the swings of public mood, from the welfare state corporateness of the 1950s through the individualism of the 1960s and 1970s to the economic liberalism of the 1980s and 1990s, may well bring us back to a form of social and cross-party concern for the environment and an expectation of schools that will make the propositions of Beare and Slaughter seem quite commonplace.

Yet their broad vision does not address the problem that Hargreaves ignores, those who remain in the 'sink schools'. They will more than likely be synonymous with the worst educated whose 90 per cent employment prospects in Britain in the 1970s have slumped to 70 per cent in the 1990s, with the prospect of a further fall into the next century. Robin Marris (1995) observed in *The Times* that Britain and America have one-third of these 'low-eds' engaged in washing cars, in committing crimes, or on invalidity or early retirement. They will also be synonymous with the 100,000 British 12–13 year olds who regularly truant and evolve into the permanently unemployed underclass.

The National Commission argues for preferential funding for disadvantaged areas and places great emphasis on encouraging innovation such as design studio business units within schools to work with pupils, alternative curriculum programmes (for which the National Curriculum, if it cannot motivate, must give way), or new types of schools or learning centres established on an experimental basis. This makes sense. Recent improvements in examination results have been more marked at the middle and upper levels. The gap between the educationally rich and poor has widened.

The evidence is mounting, especially from the United States, that concentration on quality day care and nursery provision elevates achievement. This returns to the belief of the National Commission (1993) that such provision enables children to enter school with a positive outlook based on developing self-esteem, commitment to learning, and a belief that, if they try, they can succeed. The effects of any new ventures in early years' education are, however, long term for secondary schools. In the meantime the success of alternative schools for habitual truants in some of our inner cities shows that the conventional school may be replaceable. There may, therefore, be a compelling case for some radical deschooling in crisis areas. Barber (1993) doubts that current national education policy is by itself likely to alleviate the huge educational difficulties facing deprived urban areas. While he does not discount the findings of effective school research, that some individual schools can 'buck the trends', he feels that high staff turnover and the volatility of the inner city environment can cause rapid regression. In such severely disadvantaged circumstances one may therefore question whether the school, concentrating on the educational basics in isolation, can ever win through without a broader vision of the school as the hub of a family welfare service. In the United States (Kentucky, San Diego, Minneapolis) there have been attempts to treat family needs holistically, with schools as a focus for unemployment, housing, welfare and health services. Thus, the urban school becomes the hub of comprehensive care and education services. All-year-round programmes would be offered to children from the age of three. Older children would be provided with before- and after-school care and all-day care during school holidays. However, some American experience has shown that students who have rejected the school also reject the other services that become associated with it. It is not a guaranteed cure for social alienation.

In the second half of the twentieth century each generation has made a fresh foray into structural reform, in 1944, 1964, and 1988. A pragmatist might say that current reforms need a generation to bed down before the next restructuring is considered. Thus the early twenty-first century will probably see some of the incremental refinements of the National Commission introduced, the consolidation of a 14–18 curriculum with the lines between academic and vocational blurred even further and, with both major political parties, despite their rhetoric, accepting that past structures have not worked well enough, 'magnet' and 'alternative' schools being the only structural alternative not yet tried. There can be no return to the looser curriculum structures of yesteryear. The only rationale for any government contemplating such a move would be teachers' success in implementing the National Curriculum, but that would merely demonstrate the need to continue it.

But there is also a compelling financial argument for a National Curriculum. The provision of pre-school education and smaller classes in Key Stage 1, for both of which the educational evidence is overwhelming, will need either new money or more effective use of old money. There appears to be cross-party acceptance that the post-war welfare state, whether in education, health or social services, is unaffordable in its traditional form. Secondary and higher education will have to accept that the luxury of options carries a high cost. The more common the curriculum core the more cost-effective is its delivery. The National Commission's vision for Key Stage 5 may, by reducing the plethora of current options, release some funds for redistribution, but will only scratch the surface of the funding problem.

Lofthouse (1994: 145) concludes that, given the contrasting views of stakeholders as to the purpose, and priorities, of education, we are left with the view that 'From the clash of interested parties the only certainty to emerge is the unresolved nature of the curriculum.' If so, government must continue to be the legislative umpire. In a democratic society there can be no alternative. But government will probably be increasingly forced to look for curricula that can be delivered effectively at minimal cost so that the educational needs of all age groups can be met.

The result need not be depressing. With the probable abandonment of further wholesale enforced reorganisations of schools and relatively little room for manoeuvre on the structure and content of the curriculum, there will, in the immediate future, be only the one task left on which to concentrate, namely not just how young people learn but how they 'learn how to learn', without which the skill is short-lived and non-transferable. After fifty years of expansion, reorganisation and arguing about resources and curriculum content, there is now just this one focus that has any validity. That is no bad thing.

Learning and teaching in the twenty-first century

Headteachers do not manage learning. They lead and manage the teachers who manage learning and the human and financial resource infrastructure that supports the process, and they do so in loosely-coupled institutions. That is why a well-led school with teachers who are committed to the learning process is vibrantly exciting, because there is significant freedom for good teachers to pursue the shared vision. Conversely a loosely-coupled school with disparate aims and inadequate teachers is an educational disaster area for its students.

Similarly, teachers do not manage learning in quite the direct way that management language suggests. The learning process is too complex and partially understood for that. What one intends to teach and what is learned do not necessarily follow each other in irrevocable sequence, except on the simplest mechanical level. The anecdotal evidence of teachers repeating a successful lesson with a different group and obtaining markedly different results is familiar. The individual psychological contracts which influence learners' attitudes are so diverse (see Handy 1993), and shaped by so many factors of which only some are within the teacher's control, that predicting outcomes, or even being aware of all of them, is a hazardous business. At one level the conceptual connections made by an Einstein are not capable of forecast and will probably defeat pre-determined assessment profiles. At another level the psychological baggage of an abused child may provide a major obstacle course for learning intentions to materialise.

It is a recognition of the complexity of learning, rather than a criticism of its professionals, to say that teaching has an element of randomness. Good teachers are expert at creating a variety of stimulating learning opportunities of which pupils, more or less take advantage. However, teachers know only something, but not enough, about their pupils' learning ways. The best available advice from OFSTED is to deploy a variety of teaching approaches. On the positive side it is true that these will provide pupils with the opportunity to learn a greater variety of skills. For example, the skills of group work can only be learned experientially. On the negative side it begs the question of each individual's naturally preferred learning method. The scatter-gun approach will still miss as often as it hits the target.

The reality is that people do have different preferred ways of learning. Gregorc (1982) identified two spectrums, of perception and of order. Our perception of information will vary from the concrete to the abstract. The concrete is rooted in the physical senses and is most comfortable dealing with the observable. The abstract is rooted in the intuitive, subjective and emotional and is most comfortable dealing with ideas and feelings. Our ordering of information too will vary on a spectrum from sequential to random. Sequential learners process information in a logical and linear fashion. The random learner absorbs and uses information in a non-sequential way and is a more holistic thinker. No one method of learning is more effective than another. However, different people have different preferences.

Gregorc calculated that the population is divided into four categories. 'Abstract sequential', 'abstract random' and 'concrete sequential' groupings each comprise about 27 per cent of the population, the other 19 per cent being 'concrete random'. Those who prefer a concrete random approach are often the most difficult to teach in a traditional class setting which they find restricting. They are frustrated by the environmental, personal and task restrictions that are placed on them. Those who prefer an abstract random approach are less comfortable with highly structured tasks and develop their own problem-solving approaches.

Lack of awareness of pupils' preferred methods may often lead the teacher to underestimate their ability or misinterpret poor performance as a learning or behavioural problem. When children start in a particular school they are often diagnosed for attainment but not for preferred learning style. If one therefore tries all approaches, without a learning style audit, there is a stronger chance that students will be appropriately targeted some of the time but an equally strong chance, given individuals' different learning methods, that each will be missed some of the time.

The potential for information technology to resolve some of these uncertainties holds a key to successful differentiation. In the commercial and professional world psychometric tests have been developed to a level of sophistication which enables a searching personality profile of any individual to be drawn and related to given aptitudes required for a job. A similar process could be used to identify pupils' preferred learning strategies and relate them to required learning tasks.

There is already evidence that the supportive computer program can greatly enhance the self-esteem of the slow learner. Its structured approach to learning, reinforcement of success and gentle correction of error, without humiliation, removes the threat from learning. It is not a long conceptual leap from this to a computer analysis of pupils' preferred learning styles and their relationship to different learning sequences. Teachers still tend to expect pupils to learn in the way they themselves have learned. Computers can apply the right method to the right pupil. This does not eliminate the need for pupils to use alternative ways of learning such as group work, which is an important employment and social skill, but could permit them to undertake individual learning in the most suitable style.

Computers too could resolve the thorny problem of progress which bedevils teachers and has been, from April 1996, the revised focus of OFSTED inspection. The huge chore of hand marking diagnostically, linking the next piece of work to the areas of development identified in the last piece, and repeating this process for each individual in the class, is a form of intensive mass production with imperfect quality controls that industry left behind years ago. Assessment could pass from teacher to machine, appropriate 'mixes' of pupils could be identified for collaborative group work, areas of the curriculum with which an individual pupil struggles could be identified and diagnostic treatment proposed. In terms of pupil progress this could be the most powerful usage of computers by teachers and a further tool in ensuring appropriate differentiation. To sound a note of caution, however, this would not lead to the total displacement of the teacher. Teaching has always been an essentially human relationship in which pupils model themselves on teachers. A teacher's role model as enthusiast, learner and mentor cannot be replicated by machine. The human balance must be preserved, especially in an age when television and computer games dominate too many lives to the detriment of social development, and in the end, like the film strip or transparency, may lose their cutting edge of novelty.

None the less, the traditional function of the teacher, as an expert distiller and disseminator of information, will change to a significant degree. What is the point of having hundreds of teachers seeking to explain the causes of the First World War, when the best teachers in the world can interact with students through the network and link them up to CD-ROM or other textual facilities in the best-resourced electronic libraries? The Open University, writ large, will descend into schools. Teachers of knowledge will metamorphose to tutors of students. The danger is that central government financial imperatives will find this an attractive option for reducing teacher numbers with the cost of the new technology being found by reduction in labour costs. In further and higher education, teacher–student ratios have already been radically altered in a harsher financial climate without technology as the main spur. That logic may well extend to all post-16 education and technology, as described above, could play a constructive role as an instrument of rationalisation. But, if the *in loco parentis* role of teachers in the mandatory years of education is to be meaningfully retained, then their mentoring and modelling role cannot be replaced by technology even though computers will make some aspects of learning and assessment more effective.

Wood (1993) speculates about the classroom of 2015. He is concerned about how such change will come about. While he is right to be concerned about the social and political will to encourage such change, we must, in the worst scenario, achieve it because other countries will take the lead. The National Commission estimates that the teacher of the twenty-first century:

> will be an authority and enthusiast in the knowledge, ideas, understanding and values presented to pupils ... an expert on effective learning with a knowledge of a range of classroom methods ... with the capacity to think deeply about educational aims and values and thereby critically about educational programmes ... willing to motivate and encourage each and every pupil, assessing progress and learning needs in their widest sense.
>
> (NCE 1993: 196–7)

The chances of achieving this are improved by high levels of structural unemployment which will attract better qualified recruits. Yet, for teachers to have the detailed knowledge and insight into the individual's learning processes, and to become experts in the applications of technology, our perceptions of teachers must change. Teachers too must alter their perceptions of themselves, an issue to which we return in the next section. Teachers' multi-faceted roles may divert them from the core task, expertise in learning strategies. There has already been a perceptible shift as statutory demands erode the time that might have been given to extra-curricular activities and as the number of stress-related retirements increases. The speed of future technological changes will demand constant re-training. Society will have to decide what it wants its teachers to excel at and what is peripheral to be provided by others. Will Handy's shamrock (1990: 169) become typical of the school organisation, with the core workers as highly specialised professionals in the application of technology to learning, and most other activities, not just services such as cleaning but whatever are considered to be non-core activities, such as sport and the creative arts, being contracted out? Or will the continued dissolution of pupils' social and family bonds work in the other direction, making the school's socialisation and moral mentoring roles even more vital in providing stability for young people? The evidence is strong that parents' choice of schools is influenced as much by the softer performance indicators relating to social strengths as by the academic. If that is so for parents who care it must, by default, be a pre-requisite of a school for children of neglectful parents. Many a teacher can tell the tale of the problem child in the community for whom school provides a relatively tranquil oasis where relationships with adults have some predictability. Technological advance cannot alter the human needs exemplified by Maslow (1970) where belonging and love, self-esteem and self-actualisation reign supreme. Whatever the technological imperatives for twenty-first century education, these higher order needs of children and teachers are interdependent. While the balance between teacher as information controller and teacher as tutor may shift, the human needs of children and teacher will remain constant.

But even in a static scenario the problem of the poor teacher remains. If that could be resolved overnight the quality of education nationally would make a quantum leap forward. In 1993 the National Commission on Education reported that 27 per cent of lessons in secondary schools were deemed poor, rising to 45 per cent of lessons for 8–11 year olds in disadvantaged areas. There is a desperate need for schools to put this aspect of their own house in order. The contractual basis of teachers and headteachers will need fundamental change. On the one hand, the ill-defined minimal criteria for what constitutes an adequate teacher, allied to the teacher's security of tenure, make proof of incompetence a long and arduous job and prolong children's damaged education in the process. On the other hand, the security of tenure of the headteacher, which is unlinked to performance outcomes except where OFSTED's 'failing school' status looms, can encourage management inertia when faced with the hard slog of proving incompetence. The two together encourage mutual acceptance of failure. The move to fixed-term renewable contracts for teachers, linked to performance expectations and performance pay, could be one answer. This does not have to be as threatening as it sounds. OFSTED inspections have shown that the overwhelming majority of teachers have nothing to fear. However the potential threat of increased instability in a profession, where perpetually high turnover in a school is detrimental to quality learning, is a potentially dangerous consequence. Moreover, the gain of speedily displacing the poor teacher may be more than offset by the fear engendered in that solid majority of dependable teachers whose will to innovate and take risks will be stifled by fear of failure.

While poor teachers are not necessarily created by poor managers, the damage they do is certainly exacerbated by poor management. The truth is that the onus lies ultimately with headteachers. OFSTED finds that headteachers are generally not strong on monitoring and evaluation, yet, without such in-built processes a school's staff development plan lacks focus or a framework against which to assess a teacher's progress. The issue of a cohesive staff development programme for good teachers, emerging from agreed vision, aims and objectives, is central to the improvement or sacking of poor teachers. For a poor teacher to work in a rudderless school provides excellent defence material for an astute union, even more so in a time of rapid change. An interesting industrial parallel is given by Sir John Harvey-Jones (1994: 117): 'the half life of an electronic engineer is now considered about three and a half years, which means that one half of everything being taught has been superseded or enhanced by new knowledge.'

What is the half life of a teacher, middle manager, senior manager or headteacher? Quite simply, headteachers who do not evolve good development programmes will never resolve the 'half-life' implications for their competent teachers and will provide a let-out for the incompetent minority who damage children's education. Yet headteachers also need better support systems so that the potentially lonely fight in the interests of the pupils has all the legal clout it can muster against the professional strength of the unions who are expert at defending to the last ditch the career of the bad teacher.

The learning school of the twenty-first century

We live currently in a reactive educational climate. In a market environment schools react to customers. The National Curriculum in its present form is still essentially reactive, tying teachers into a framework of public accountability which some would see as controlling and punitive in its original intent. Yet the restructuring which ERA introduced shares one common failing with all previous attempts in this last half century. It does not attempt to deal with the learning core. It holds to the view that if the right structural and environmental circumstances exist then the quality of learning will improve. It places great faith in the indirect influence of the market and centrally determined outcomes. Different times produce different nostrums, from selection to mixed ability, from monolithic comprehensive social engineering to free market customer response, from centralised financial planning to LMS, from local authority control to free-wheeling GM schools. But, as Fullan (1993) says:

> The hardest core to crack is the learning core – changes in instructional practices and in the culture of teaching toward greater collaborative relationships among students, teachers and other potential partners. Stated differently, *to restructure is not to reculture ...* Changing formal structures is not the same as changing norms, habits, skills and beliefs.
>
> (Fullan 1993: 49)

The provision of greater local self-control may raise the esteem of a school, make a headteacher more satisfied, increase capitation spending and enable some enhancement of the environment. There may even be new management approaches involving widespread participation to give teachers greater ownership of the budget-making and school planning processes.

But there is no evidence in England, North America or Australia that such restructuring persuades schools to pay more attention to issues of curriculum and learning styles. OFSTED limits itself to quality control rather than quality growth. Its reports are summative rather than diagnostic. The National Audit Office in its search for value for money in grant-maintained schools also gets the emphasis wrong. Financial and decision-making processes and their accompanying bureaucratic processes form the agenda. The NAO provides interesting breakdowns of unit costs under a legion of headings. Although there is no denying the potential use of these measures as tools, the NAO concentrates on everything but the core issue of learning. Its agenda is process efficiency rather than learning effectiveness, except in the most banal way, that one school's GCSE grades cost less to produce than those of another school. In such a climate schools may be becoming more efficient at doing the wrong things or, at best, not efficient enough at doing the right things. Learning processes are so complex that it is tempting to look at other more easily assessable processes. It is rather like the army being more concerned about whether soldiers can drill efficiently than fight effectively.

If truth were to be told, members of school senior management teams may fall into the same trap. The finite control that can be exercised over a budget or a timetable bestows a sense of pleasant satisfaction and mystique in an occupation where the pursuit of pupil learning goals can be so amorphous and exhausting. The transformation of headteachers (and some are very good at this) into fund-raising entrepreneurs may look exciting but will it improve learning in schools? The confusion of a satisfied senior manager with a pedagogically productive one becomes all too easy. And senior managers who do not make pupils' learning the hub of their existence will also be reluctant to monitor it, thus leaving its progress to the chance enthusiasms of those who are left in the classroom to get on with it.

For Fullan (1993) the obvious conclusion is that we cannot have students as continuous learners and effective collaborators without teachers sharing these same characteristics. Fullan refers to the four themes which emanate from the research of Nias *et al.* (1992) into successful curriculum development: teachers learning in a climate of support; the time needed for teachers to change their beliefs and practices during which tensions and disagreements have to be worked through; shared values and decision-making structures with commitment of time and development of leadership not just at headteacher level but through the teacher body; and the unpredictable and dynamic nature of the change process as factors beyond the control of the school continually present themselves. Fullan (1993) concludes that:

> Reculturing leads to restructuring more effectively than the reverse. There is no doubt a reciprocal relationship between structural and cultural change, but it is much more powerful when teachers and administrators begin working in new ways only to discover that school structures are ill-fitted to the new orientations and must be altered.
>
> (Fullan 1993: 68)

Transformational leaders, including the headteacher, rather than the single heroic headteacher leader, will be the change agents. The school as a collaborative learning organisation will be the only alternative influence on the curriculum of the next century to fill the vacuum inhabited at the moment by pages of statute law and government circulars.

But collaborative progress as a learning organisation is not easy. HMI and OFSTED concern for participative decision-making, evident in inspection reports over the years, is too simplistic. Fullan (1993) warns:

> Teachers must work in highly interactive and collaborative ways, avoiding the pitfalls of wasted collegiality . . . Collaboration is one of the most misunderstood concepts in the change business. It is not automatically a good thing. It does not mean consensus.
>
> (Fullan 1993: 81–2)

Senge (1993) too is critical of self-serving cosiness:

> Participative openness, the freedom to speak one's mind, is the most commonly recognised aspect of openness. This is because the philosophy of 'participative management', involving people more in decision-making, is widely espoused . . . Participative openness may lead to more 'buy-in' on certain decisions, but by itself will rarely

lead to better quality decisions because it does not influence the thinking behind people's positions . . . It focuses purely on the 'means' or process of interacting, not on the 'results' of that interaction . . . While participative openness leads to people speaking out, 'reflective openness' leads to people looking inward . . . to challenge our own thinking.

(Senge 1993: 277)

So how does a headteacher develop a reflective school? Fullan (1993) is clear about the initial problem:

We don't have a learning profession. Teachers and teacher educators do not know enough about subject matter, they don't know enough about how to teach, and they don't know enough about how to understand and influence the conditions around them. Above all, teacher education . . . is not geared towards continuous learning.

(Fullan 1993: 68)

Subject matter in schools may be less of an intrinsic weakness in England and Wales than in North America but the other areas of relative ignorance are certainly an issue. The teacher's classroom isolation has long been a matter of concern, although 'directed time' since 1987 and statutory appraisal have made a difference. But collaboration will tend to produce comfortable group-think or defensive balkanisation where teachers have not embarked on a continuous self-education programme and have, thereby, neglected the necessity of thinking for themselves. Only the capacity for independent reflection can develop the creative tension on which effective collaboration thrives and enables systems to change through the coalescing of emerging ideas.

Initial teacher training cannot be the sole repository of blame. This covers a very short time span compared with the thirty to forty years that teachers spend in schools. The real issue is what a school subsequently does to create a reflective culture.

- Is the headteacher seen to be a continuous learner? Are the purposes and outcomes of that learning experience shared with the staff?
- Are senior managers predominantly instructional leaders or have they been side-tracked into the function of chief executives rather than leading professionals? The answer to this conveys important symbolic messages to teachers.
- Do senior and middle managers encourage bottom-up appraisal of their function as managers of learning?
- Are middle managers experts and role models in managing learning in a variety of situations or are they power barons who control areas of resource with a financial but not a learning accountability?

- Are the use of 'directed time' and the allocation of staff development resources related to the outcomes of appraisal and of the monitoring and evaluation of pupil learning?
- Is monitoring and evaluation of the learning process dominated by senior management or shared by middle management, based on research about the outcomes of teaching and learning approaches, the better to inform subsequent planning?
- Are human resources allocated in such a way that their relevance to the learning process is clear for all to see? For example, are senior managers seen to have more adequate support staff services than teaching staff?
- Are financial resource allocations based on learning or political needs? For example, does the allocation of capitation according to agreed formulae sustain power structures rather than target learning needs?
- How do senior managers react to the teacher who has made a mistake or not achieved a target? Is it a matter for blame or for analysis? If the latter, is it self-analysis, shared analysis or imposed analysis from above?

Children's learning is rarely linear; nor is the learning of teachers. A school without an element of tension is probably not learning. To take pupils' *and* teachers' learning to a new plane will require uncertainty and an element of chaos as ideas are collaboratively sieved to produce a synthesis.

CONCLUSION

To try to pre-determine the curriculum of the twenty-first century is a chancy game. In the early days of the next millennium the content and structure will be an adaptation of the current position. It is also fairly safe to predict that technology will then play an increasing role and that society is unlikely to become more cohesive. Education's role will be to accommodate the needs and tensions of both while striving to maintain Britain's competitive position in a highly-skilled global economy. How that will be done is less easy to predict in detail. The real issue is whether schools will have the capacity to generate internal solutions and whether governments will permit sufficient flexibility to allow systems to emerge with a variety of types of schools and room for curriculum experiment, or will find the attractive accumulation of central control too tempting. In a new age, when the old mid-twentieth century assumptions of the welfare state cannot affordably be sustained, teachers can only influence the agenda if, by developing proactive learning organisations, they secure a position of respect and authority on the issue of pupil learning. This might offset the inadequate quality of much current educational research, criticised by Hargreaves (1994), that encourages very expensive but untested legislative substitutes such as the first version of the National Curriculum. Was this really political arrogance or was it pent-up frustration at the apparently aimless inertia of a disunited profession? Hargreaves should have the last word:

> Sketching the future of schools is a hazardous business; it is easier to state predilections than to make predictions, to say what schools should be like than what they will be like. Later, when certain developments have flowered, we shall all with hindsight detect the historical seeds and explain why one germinated and another died. Our capacity to predict which among contemporary embryonic developments are likely to flourish over the next two decades is limited, probably because the 'drivers' and the 'barriers' of educational change are too little understood.
>
> (Hargreaves 1994: 52–3)

> It is important to reflect on the concepts that are central to this chapter and the competencies necessary to utilise them. To enable you to do this and to form an action plan, we suggest that it would be of assistance to make an enlarged photocopy of the three pages in Appendix A.

REFERENCES

Barber, M. (1993) 'Raising standards in deprived urban areas', in *Briefings for the Paul Hamlyn Foundation National Commission on Education*, London: Heinemann.

Beare, H. and Slaughter, R. (1993) *Education for the Twenty-First Century*, London: Routledge.

Chapman, J. (ed.) (1990) *School-Based Decision-Making and Management*, London: Falmer.

Dimmock, C. (ed.) (1993) *School-Based Management and School Effectiveness*, London: Routledge.

Fullan, M. (1993) *Change Forces: Probing the Depths of Educational Reform*, London: Falmer.

George, D. (1992) *The Challenge of the Very Able Child*, London: David George.

Gregorc, A. F. (1982) *Gregorc Style Delineator: Development, Technical and Administration Manual*, Columbia, CT: Gregorc Associates.

Handy, C. (1990) *The Age of Unreason*, London: Arrow.

Handy, C. (1993) *Understanding Organisations*, London: Penguin.

Hargreaves, D. (1994) *The Mosaic of Learning: Schools and Teachers for the New Century*, London: Demos.

Harvey-Jones, J. (1994) *All Together Now*, London: Heinemann.

Lofthouse, M. (1994) 'Managing the curriculum', in T. Bush and J. West-Burnham (eds) *The Principles of Educational Management*, London: Longman.

Marris, R. (3 Oct. 1995) 'Growth is the best way to reduce social dislocation: undereducated unemployed', *The Times*, p. 29.

Marshall, R. and Tucker, M. (1992) *Thinking for a Living: Education and the Wealth of Nations*, New York: Basic Books.

Maslow, A. H. (1970) *Motivation and Personality*, New York: Harper and Row.

Moon, B. (1991) 'The National Curriculum: origins and context', in T. Brighouse and B. Moon (eds) *Managing the National Curriculum: Some Critical Perspectives*, Harlow: Longman.

National Commission on Education (1993) *Learning to Succeed*, London: Heinemann.

Nias, J., Southworth, G. and Campbell, P. (1992) *Whole School Curriculum Development in the Primary School*, London: Falmer.

Reid, K., Hopkins, D. and Holly, P. (1987) *Towards the Effective School*, Oxford: Blackwell.

Rutter, M., Maughan, B., Mortimore, P. and Ouston, J. (1979) *Fifteen Thousand Hours: Secondary Schools and their Effects on Children*, London: Open Books.

Senge, P. (1993) *The Fifth Discipline: the Art and Practice of the Learning Organisation*, New York: Century Business.

Walford, G. (1993) 'Selection for secondary schooling', in *Briefings for the Paul Hamlyn Foundation National Commission on Education*, London: Heinemann.

Wood, D. (1993) 'The classroom of 2015', in *Briefings for the Paul Hamlyn Foundation National Commission on Education*, London: Heinemann.

13 Managing school finance

Peter Downes

There is a clear trend across the world for publicly funded schools to be given greater responsibility for the use of financial resources. This is usually linked with the concept of self-management or site-based autonomy, so that such schools move along the continuum of autonomy which was discussed in Chapter 3. After some introductory remarks, this chapter examines the implications of devolved finance and exposes two myths of school autonomy, those relating to the extent of autonomy and the nature of change. It then challenges the assumptions about school expenditure, encouraging a new and more strategic creativity. The chapter proceeds to discuss the stages in the budget cycle. The final section poses some possibilities for the future funding of education.

INTRODUCTION

Perceptions of financial autonomy depend heavily on previous experience and the educational context of the individual country. For example, French headteachers may well consider that they have financial autonomy when in practice they only control the budget for premises, routine administration and purchase of teaching materials. All teaching costs and the allocation of teachers are controlled by the Academie which itself follows a highly centralised national pattern. French headteachers feel relatively autonomous compared with their previous experience of a nationally directed education system. Heads of schools in England and Wales, having had 'control' over all site-based costs (including teaching and non-teaching staff, premises, materials, administration) since 1988 (or earlier, in the case of Local Financial Management pilot schemes) may conversely feel that they do *not* have financial autonomy because they are frustrated by their lack of control (unless they are in grant-maintained schools) over structural repairs and over aspects of the site.

We need therefore to be careful in talking about LMS and GMS when we are in an international context. Site-based management, Global budgeting, Lump Sum budgets, Bulk funding and Block grant budgets are similar concepts in different contexts but in significant points of detail they may differ. In all these situations, the overall trend is established: greater freedom to deploy resources is being granted to those directly responsible for the day-to-day management of schools and the knowledge, skills and competencies required to carry out this responsibility successfully are an essential element of preparation for a senior management post and for development within it. This chapter will use the term site-based management when referring to devolved financial management in the school context.

The broad arguments which justify the development of site-based management have been clearly laid out in Chapter 3 and need little further elaboration. Experienced practitioners of LMS and GMS in the English context speak of increased motivation through sense of ownership, more appropriate decisions based on intimate local knowledge of circumstances, greater incentive to make savings in routine running costs and a greater incentive to raise income for the school through the higher usage of the buildings outside school time. We have come a long way in the last twenty years, especially when we consider the letter written by the Head of Deacon's School, Peterborough, to the City Education Officer in Peterborough and recently unearthed by the Cambridgeshire Director of Education, John Ferguson:

> As the present system of providing stamps through your department seems to have broken down, I am writing to ask whether it would not be possible for us to buy stamps direct from the Post Office out of some cash float which you would give us. We could then record all stamps used in our postage book in the normal way.
>
> It seems ridiculous that we should have to send a boy down to your office whenever we need stamps, especially as yesterday nobody was available to issue stamps; and now we are told that it is very inconvenient for one of your officers to get out of his chair and go down to the City Treasurer for us to get the stamps when we need them.

THE OUTCOMES OF DEVOLVED FINANCE

It is all too easy to see site-based management as merely a method of shifting financial decision-making away from the Local Authority bureaucrats to those responsible within the school. The implications and outcomes are, however, far deeper. I would identify five outcomes in particular.

First, the decision to disburse funds to schools in direct proportion to the number of pupils being educated has sharpened the thinking of heads, governors and, to some extent, classroom teachers. They now

realise that, in order to offer a viable service, they have to attract sufficient pupils; in order to attract pupils, they have to deliver a satisfactory
quality of service. It is no longer valid to assume that schools can offer
a packaged experience which pupils and parents more or less accept
unquestioningly. Other chapters in this book look in more detail at
quality and marketing, at raising standards of teaching and learning; it
is the financial dimension which is the spur which pricks us into action.

The second outcome of LMS and GMS is that it has not only given
heads and governors the positive benefits referred to above but has also
transferred to them the difficult decisions in a time of shrinking
resources. Smyth (1993: 3) regards this as part of the 'cruel hoax' of self-
management: 'school self-management has come to mean no more than
an opportunity for schools to manage dwindling fiscal resources within
tightened centralist policies over curriculum, evaluation and standards.'

In difficult days in the past, it was always possible to blame 'them',
meaning the officers of the Local Education Authority (LEA). The head
could shelter behind the remoteness of those who had, say, reduced the
staffing levels. Even though it is now technically the governors who
make the decision to make teachers redundant, it is the head who bears
the full brunt of criticism and resentment. Passing on bad news and
taking the blame though one is not guilty is an unexpected competency
of headship today.

A third outcome of LMS and GMS, and one which the government
clearly did not intend to happen, is that more and more people are
becoming better informed about the national educational budget and
can understand the unconvincing basis on which it is constructed. For
the last few years, much of the literature on financial management has
focused on ways of achieving better value for money *within* schools.
Great ingenuity has been deployed to find better ways of controlling
premises costs, for example; the search for better discounts off purchases
is an unending quest; many tasks have been identified which were
formerly done by teachers which can be done more cheaply by non-
teaching staff. Governors facing under-resourcing in spite of all their
efforts to make savings have at last started to question the size of the
quantum. Until 1995, they were generally fobbed off with the allegation
that LEAs were being inefficient, or were holding on to too much money
at the centre, or were making the wrong priority decisions. The year
1995 will be seen by educational historians as that in which central
government's role in the funding of schools was exposed. Quite technical information about Standard Spending Assessments, Area Cost
Adjustments and sparsity factors, previously understood by a handful
of professionals, is now widely discussed, not only by heads and
deputies but also by governors and parents. No longer can central
government confuse the public into thinking that it is providing enough

money. Only a few years ago, it was possible for Kenneth Clarke as Secretary of State for Education to assert that 'we have increased expenditure *in real terms* by over 40 per cent since we came into office in 1979' and people tended to believe him. When Gillian Shephard tried to say the same thing (uplifted to 50+ per cent by then) in 1995, she was laughed at. We now understand more clearly that when the government talks of 'real improvement', it means relative to the Gross Domestic Product deflator, but the deflation figure for education spending is much higher, giving therefore a much lower 'real' increase in terms of volume of service to pupils.

> Only when we all agree on the reality of the indicators can we hope to have an intelligent and well-informed debate about national priorities. Until then, politicians will continue to put on their 'virtual reality' headsets and picture the world as they would like us to believe it to be, rather than what it really is.
>
> (Downes 1995: 8)

A fourth outcome of LMS and GMS in the English context is that it has tended to increase competition between schools to the point where the overall ethos of publicly funded education as a service to the nation's young people has been undermined. The effect of grant-maintained status has been particularly influential in this respect. Its impact on the former sense of partnership and collaboration has been patchy across the country: at best, LMS and GMS colleagues continue to work together to try to provide the best for all pupils in a given area; at worst, heads formerly working together in the same LEA do not even speak to each other, or, in extreme cases, do not allow their school teams to compete against each other!

A fifth outcome of the introduction of LMS and GMS, and one to which we will return at the end of the chapter as we look forward into the future, is that it has brought sharply into focus the whole question of who 'controls' education. The precise relationship between central government, local government, the professionals in school (head, deputies, teachers), the amateur watchdogs (governors) and the customers (parents and pupils) has been put under scrutiny more acutely than ever before. Tensions, not all of them destructive, have been created; guidelines and policies are being written with greater zeal than ever before and possible new structures are being debated.

School leaders and managers cannot be oblivious to the external pressures outlined above but they have, of course, to give their attention to the day-to-day management of financial resources. For this they need a range of skills and competencies which their predecessors did not require, especially if they are to give the strategic overview and vision which are implicit in the concept of leadership as defined in this book.

THE TWO MYTHS OF SCHOOL AUTONOMY

Before proceeding further to evaluate finance and the budgetary process, two myths of autonomous financial control and budgeting need to be examined.

The first myth which needs to be dispelled is the idea that state-funded schools are genuinely autonomous. The constraints and restrictions on schools are greater than ever: the curriculum is centrally defined, national testing is in place and is reported to the public, schools are inspected according to a national framework, contractual hours of directed work for teachers are nationally specified as are national pay scales, hours of attendance for pupils are strongly recommended. According to Weiler (1989), we currently have a situation where the rhetoric is that of decentralisation (self-managing schools), but the behaviour is decidedly that of centralisation (central setting of goals, targets, the devising of instruments of surveillance and the fixing of resourcing). Participation under these conditions is superficial and restricted to whatever the central authority chooses to allow.

Even at the most mundane level, increasingly severe regulations restrict the ability of the school managers to find inventive solutions to problems or to reduce costs: the number of pupils who can be crammed into a laboratory on health and safety grounds is tightly defined; all electrical appliances and plugs must be tested annually (Provisions and Use of Work Equipment Regulation 1992); buildings must be safe and be accessible to disabled pupils and staff (Workplace [Health and Safety and Welfare] Regulations 1992); maximum and minimum heating and lighting levels are laid down; pupils should not be used to re-arrange furniture in classrooms unless one is satisfied that they are not contravening the Manual Handling Operations Regulations 1992; the risk for office staff and pupils staring at VDUs should be assessed in accordance with the Health and Safety (Display Screen Equipment) Regulations 1992; compulsory competitive tendering regulations set up a framework of constraints which frustrate the efforts of a manager to make provision for a cost-effective co-ordinated maintenance service.

In addition to the legislative restrictions, the teaching profession has a long-standing concept of 'custom and practice': non-contact time is given more generously to those who get paid more for greater responsibility; newly qualified teachers (NQTs) have a lighter teaching timetable than more experienced teachers; interference by senior management into what happens within each classroom is kept to a minimum; there is an assumption that everybody is committed and hard-working (the professional ethic) and that differential payment related to performance is unthinkable. Some of these assumptions are being challenged in the changing environment which expects higher performance and is prepared to monitor more closely.

The second myth that needs to be tackled is the idea that change in schools, as far as the learning experience of pupils is concerned, can only be incremental. Within the business world it is possible and sometimes desirable to restructure a company rapidly and dramatically. This is because outside competitive pressures are such that the company would go bankrupt if it did not make such changes. Within schools, the purpose of the company is the development of young people who are engaged in a process of learning. The structure of that learning must be dynamic and changes must be made. The budgetary process, as currently structured, is a strong contributory factor to incremental change. The annual budget round, subject to transitory political pressures, makes it difficult to plan in detail with any confidence beyond one year ahead. Good leaders with the vision of the longer-term future will also have the management knowledge to forecast what the cost of the vision will be.

In the present state of affairs, so-called self-managing schools are, for reasons beyond their control, tightly constrained. Maychell (1994) found that the impact of LMS on schools' patterns of spending was rather less than might have been expected but that there were examples of increased expenditure on support staff, on resources for learning and on the environment but very little extra on non-contact time for teachers. Their autonomy is more apparent than real but even within the constraints, there is room for imagination and some flexibility. The next section examines some of the opportunities for flexibility at the school level.

CHALLENGING ASSUMPTIONS: THE NEW CREATIVITY

The most important aspect of school autonomy is the reconsideration of whether or not the available money is being used effectively. This is where there is scope for leadership, vision and lateral thinking. The senior managers' aim must be to get the job done most effectively at the lowest cost. In a large secondary school, it is not uncommon for a relatively highly paid deputy head, or a teacher with non-contact time and a responsibility allowance, to organise the daily cover for absent staff. Perhaps the task could be carried out just as well, and more cheaply, by a non-teacher, paid at a much lower salary, thus releasing the teacher to carry out the teaching role for which s/he was appointed, as well as being available as a form-tutor. The work of a Learning Support Team might be more effectively carried out by employing fewer teachers and more Learning Support assistants, normally paid at 40 per cent of a teacher's salary.

This kind of evaluation challenges routines and long-standing assumptions. Its effect in the secondary sector is to increase the contact ratio of the staff, that is, to reduce the time devoted to administration, which increases not only the teaching load but also preparation, marking, report-writing and parental contact. A judgement has to be made as to how far the contact ratio can be increased. It is arguable that a higher contact ratio, used to produce savings which are then fed back to the teaching staff by way of clerical, technical or administrative support, or by the purchase of better teaching equipment or materials, might actually produce better learning opportunities for the pupils. If the higher contact ratio is needed as a desperate measure to balance the budget without bringing in compensatory benefits, the changes will be less than welcome.

As the pace of technological change quickens, the dilemma posed above in relation to the apparent replacement of teachers by support staff for administrative purposes will apply with increasing urgency to the greater use of technology at the 'expense' of teachers in the classroom. At some point over the next few years, the expectation of class size units of thirty as the basis for the school's teaching will be replaced by a model where, for part of the week at least, the teacher will become a Learning Co-ordinator, probably of a group larger than thirty, with a considerable input of computers, CD-ROMs and Internet access, supported by classroom assistants and IT technicians. The costing of this mode of learning will be more sophisticated and this revolution will challenge our basic assumptions about pupil–teacher ratio as the touchstone for provision, seriously undermining the teacher unions' case for statutory class sizes.

THE BUDGET CYCLE

Effective school managers and leaders need to understand the budget cycle and to train their teams to understand it as well. Even after several years of decentralised funding, there are still teachers coming up with bright and expensive ideas in late June and expecting them to be implemented in September. The budget process is not to be seen as something which happens frenetically between late January and early April. It is an ongoing process which can be considered in four phases: audit, forecasting, implementation and evaluation.

The audit phase

In the *audit phase*, the management team seeks to acquire the best possible information about the costs of each part of the school's activities. There are five main headings which together account for 98 per cent of expenditure: the premises (heating, lighting, water, essential maintenance, redecoration); administration (telephones, equipment, stationery, examination entry fees, service contracts); non-teaching staff (secretaries, technicians, learning support assistants, accounts staff, caretaking); teaching staff (number of staff employed, responsibility points); and direct expenditure on books and materials for pupil use (traditionally called 'capitation' but now more usefully called 'learning resources'). The secret of successful budgetary audit is to disaggregate costs into sufficient detail to allow decisions to be made in the implementation phase. In relation to premises, for example, it will be useful to know the unit cost of redecorating a classroom. Under administration, it will be useful to know the cost of re-equipping a classroom with fifteen tables, thirty chairs, an overhead projector and a screen. The hourly rates of pay for non-teaching staff can be calculated so that a judgement can be made on how learning can be most effectively delivered. In understanding the budgetary audit of 'learning resources', the management team needs to be informed about the unit cost of sets of text-books, computers and disposable resources, ideally building up their understanding afresh each year as costs change, rather than simply taking last year's figures and tweaking them. Knight (1993) makes a useful distinction between 'money management' and 'cost management', indicating that the latter is harder than the former.

As teaching costs account for upwards of 70 per cent of the budget in most schools, it is here that the greatest care has to be taken at the audit phase and this must be linked with the curriculum planning discussions which will be taking place during the Autumn term. The detail will vary according to the size of the school: a small primary school will know the cost of a teacher (remembering to add on-costs to the basic salary) and they will be able to work out the implications of increasing the number of classes or, more likely, reducing the number of classes and increasing the amount of mixed-age teaching. In a secondary school, particularly a larger one, the calculation is slightly more complex. The audit needs to come up with a figure showing the cost of adding an extra teaching period to the curriculum plan or, similarly, the saving effected by reducing the curriculum plan by a period. The most reliable way to arrive at this figure is to start from the current year's teaching budget, subtract the salaries of head and deputies, subtract the cost of responsibility points and divide the resulting figure by the number of periods in the current timetable. This will produce a per lesson cost, as shown in the worked example in Table 13.1.

In the primary sector, a similar calculation based on the financial cost of teachers would not be helpful as the variation in teacher costs in a smaller establishment could be misleading. It might be more helpful to look at available teacher hours, and consider how these are being applied, especially in relation to enabling subject co-ordinators to support colleagues in specialist subject areas while children are present (as distinct from assisting with lesson preparation, production of materials

Table 13.1 Worked example of per lesson cost

Total teaching staff (108) costs	£2,459,053
less salaries of Heads and Deputies	£161,852
	£2,297,201
less cost of responsibility points	£409,476
	£1,887,725
divided by number of weekly taught periods in the curriculum (2117)	£891
plus on-costs @ 15.61%	£139
Full-year cost of a teaching period	£1,030

and so on which can be done when children are not there). A primary school of 340 with 15 teachers (including head and deputy) has 322.5 teacher hours available of which 279.5 are pre-committed by organising the school into 13 teaching groups at an average class size of 26. This leaves 43 hours (13 per cent) of the time available for leadership, management, curriculum support and administration. Increasing the basic class size to 28 would release a further 21.5 hours. If half of the 'remaining' hours are needed for leadership and management functions, 32.25 hours would be available for curriculum support, that is, 2.68 hours per teaching group per week.

It is during the audit phase that each heading of expenditure will be reviewed to see if a more economic price could be achieved. Could a better tariff be negotiated for the supply of gas? Has the water meter been checked for size and has the system been checked for leaks? Could books be bought more cheaply by going direct to the publisher rather than going through a wholesaler? Can a better service contract be negotiated for the reprographics equipment? Have there been any technological improvements to the telephone system which would reduce costs or improve efficiency? During the Autumn term, the management team will be working their way through this task.

Who is the management team? In the early days of devolved finance, it was not uncommon to find the finance post attached to a single person, sometimes the head or more usually a deputy 'with a grasp of figures'. It is now more common and more desirable to sub-divide this task among a number of colleagues, probably involving a senior member of the non-teaching staff (accountant, bursar) as well as deputies and other members of staff. Involvement at this level of detail, carefully targeted, brings in the ideas of a wider range of people, provides a good training experience and broadens the group of people in the school who understand the processes.

The forecasting phase

The *forecasting phase* follows, usually in January and early February. The forecasting process covers both the forecast of income and the forecast of expenditure. After the annual collation of pupils on roll (Form 7 in the UK), it will be possible to calculate what sum will be added to or removed from next year's budget as a result of discrepancies between the September forecast and the January actual. The September forecast of pupil numbers will be arrived at with help from the LEA or, in the case of GM schools, by experience of recent year opting patterns. Schools with Sixth Forms will probably have the outcomes of the GCSE mock exams and will be in the middle of the cycle of post-16 option evenings and parental consultation, out of which will emerge a fairly rough forecast of the Year 12 intake. Schools which admit from outside their own school at 16+ will have to forecast on the basis of applications received and the previous year's uptake pattern.

The estimating of income for primary schools suffers from increasing uncertainty as parental choice gradually works its way down from secondary to primary level, especially in urban areas. The LEA will be able to provide guideline figures but it is feared that these may become increasingly unreliable in areas where the introduction of nursery vouchers may actually take young children out of LEA-provided nursery schools feeding into infant schools and 'lose' them among a range of other providers. The most appropriate response at the school level would be to prepare best and worse case scenarios based on all the available information.

By this mixture of precedent, demography and guesswork, an agreed estimated roll is arrived at, on which the allocation of funds will be based. This can be converted to Age Weighted Pupil Units (AWPUs) and then the LEA will forecast the likely cash value of the AWPU. From this the provisional income figure should emerge, sometime in February depending on the efficiency of the LEA. GM schools usually receive their information later, which does not help the planning process.

Another important feature of forecasting is calculating incremental drift and turnover in teaching and non-teaching staff costs. In the case of non-teaching staff, incremental drift (i.e. moving up to the next point on the pay spine) has a relatively small effect since the salary steps are small and most employees reach a 'salary bar' quite quickly. In the case of teaching staff, the cost of incremental drift can be substantial, depending on the proportion of the staff who are not yet receiving the maximum points for qualifications and experience. Alongside forecasting this 'incremental drift', it is tempting fate to forecast turnover. This is the reduction in cost created by an older teacher leaving and being replaced by a younger one for the new academic year, that is, for the last seven months (September to March) of the financial year. Turnover can, of course, be negative: the appointment of older teachers to replace younger ones increases the costs to the school. It is essential to encourage staff who are planning to leave, for whatever reasons, to make their intentions known to the senior management team as early as possible. Early information can help to make the turnover forecasting more accurate but perhaps the soundest advice is to expect a nil turnover so that any turnover which actually emerges during the appointing season (usually April to July) can be regarded as contingency money. It is also important to have a shadow staffing plan so that a school relates its staffing decisions to a strategic framework, rather than making short-term decisions which have long-term implications.

Armed with information from the budgetary audit and the forecasting, the senior management team and governors can carry out detailed planning in late February and March. This is where the greatest demands are made on senior managers. Many experienced practitioners believe that, if there is going to be reasonable understanding and acceptance of the final budget, there should be an extensive consultative process so that the various governors' committees and the teaching and non-teaching staff can be fully aware of the implications of the budget. If one of the implications is that teachers have to be made redundant, the necessary statutory measures must be started early enough to give all those involved time to make appropriate representations. If this is mishandled or deadlines are missed, the governors could find themselves having to pay the Autumn term salary of a teacher they thought they were going to dismiss at the end of August.

The implementation phase

Much of the *implementation phase* of the budget is carried out from April to July. New appointments are made or people dismissed, as the case may be, orders for maintenance and re-decoration work are placed, teaching materials ordered, extra responsibility points allocated for new responsibilities being undertaken. The budget can be fine-tuned at this stage, provided that the governors have given the head adequate powers of virement. To have to call committee meetings to approve minor changes is a time-consuming and wasteful exercise. Much depends on the confidence that the governors have in the head and senior management team. During the teacher appointment season, turnover may produce a contingency sum but, in a context of tight budgets, a wise head will not overcommit the contingency until the actual September intake, and, in the case of primary schools, the January/Easter intake, materialises.

The budgetary evaluation phase

Budgetary evaluation operates at two levels. The first is an internal examination of resource use and the second is a comparison with patterns of resource use in other organisations.

School autonomy should challenge us to think afresh about the issues of economy, efficiency and effectiveness of resource use at all levels within a school. This is a challenge for curriculum managers and other middle managers within the school, not just for senior managers. In all parts of the school's activity, therefore, all activities need to be scrutinised with these questions in mind:

- Is this activity being carried out economically? (Could we purchase the service/resource from elsewhere at a lower cost? Are we getting the best discounts?)
- Is this activity being carried out efficiently? (Are highly-paid people carrying out a low skill activity?)
- Is this activity being effective in promoting learning? (This is the key question and one which challenges every teacher each hour of their working lives.)

A school which gives appropriate attention to these questions, not just once as a set-piece INSET day activity but as a regular part of its self-evaluation, is on the way to becoming a cost-effective organisation. It is one of the tasks of the senior manager to create a self-analytical approach at all levels within the school. For most teachers, the process is a daunting one. This is understandable; most are already burdened with increasing National Curriculum pressures, more demanding assessment procedures, increasing behavioural and social problems in their pupils, higher expectations as the influence of the 'market' increases. They are reluctant to take on the process of a critical cost-benefit analysis of their activities. The senior manager has to be sensitive to teachers' natural diffidence towards getting over-involved with what they perceive to be the task of management and yet, without the understanding and involvement of middle managers and of teachers at the everyday level of the classroom, little progress can be achieved.

There are a number of ways into this problem. The first is to set up a consultative committee structure so that information can be passed on and views received in an orderly way. Most schools have a staff consultative committee on finance and, in some cases, the Governors' finance committee co-opts teacher members to make sure that teachers' views are heard and seen to be heard. At the same time, the teachers on such a committee have the responsibility for passing on issues to the staff in general and for receiving opinions on priorities. Rather than setting up a special consultative structure for finance alone, another approach is to use the existing network of meetings and to make sure that they all have the appropriate information available so that all discussions can be undertaken in the light of the financial implications of the decisions they might be about to take.

Another way of spreading awareness down from the senior management team to the people who are going to live with the consequences of the financial decision-making process is to give a devolved budget to middle managers. For example, a middle manager could be given a budget to cover the repairs, maintenance, decoration and furnishing of the suite of rooms housing her/his tutor-groups. There is nothing like having to manage an actual budget, however small, to activate interest in financial management. In some schools, the middle managers not only have the autonomy to manage their learning resources budget but are also given the freedom to convert, at notional values, some staffing time into money for learning resources, or responsibility points into non-contact periods. Very few schools, even large ones, have gone all the way down the cost-centre track, that is, giving each department its entire budget as a share calculated on the basis of its curriculum input. The tedium of apportioning the fixed costs, and the accentuated problems of actual salaries compared with average inputs, has deterred even the most enthusiastic self-management evangelists.

The second level of budget evaluation is to look outside one's own school to compare expenditure percentages in schools of a similar size and character. This approach, known as 'benchmarking', is being encouraged by the DfEE as a way of pushing schools into examining their expenditure more critically. The work of the Audit Commission (1993) led the way in this work but the sample used was too small and the presentation too confused to be of any practical help. More recent work by McAleese (1995a, b) and by the DfEE (1995) has improved the debate and revealed some stark differences in expenditure patterns in schools of identical size.

THE FUTURE FUNDING OF EDUCATION

Most of what has been covered so far has been suggestions about ways in which financial management can be handled within the school on a year-to-year basis and, by implication, has indicated the competencies which will be required: distilling good information from crude data, seeing long-term implications of short-term decisions, communicating relevant and manageable issues to semi-interested colleagues, having the imagination to see effective ways of changing long-standing routines. The key role of school leaders, however, is to look farther ahead and it is in the sphere of finance that external political factors well beyond our control cause us to suffer from uncertainty and turbulence. Crystal-ball gazing is a skill which school leaders might well seek to develop. What might they see?

If the present structure of educational financing is to continue, there will be an uneasy tension between central and local government, annual anxiety about the level of funding with its effect on long-term strategic planning. Experienced staff may be made redundant and then a school may have to recruit less experienced and less well qualified staff when funding policies change. It is not surprising that there will often be an unwillingness to embark on costly long-term re-equipping of, say, the information technology aspects of a school for fear of being unable to complete the programme and meet the expectations raised.

Alternatively, we might see a changed policy which reforms the present structure of educational financing. The first reform would be to make the financial and academic year come into step. The annual pattern might look as follows: in late October, the School Teachers Review Body makes its recommendation on the level of teachers' pay, the essential building block for the coming year. The government then takes this into consideration when making its budget announcement which comes in late November, followed shortly by the announcement of its Revenue Support Grant allocations to local authorities. The local authorities can tell schools in February what their budget will be for the following financial year which starts in September. This gives schools adequate time to plan. The second reform would be to move away from a one-year funding pattern to a three-year programme but this would require such an overhaul of the national fiscal system that it seems unlikely. The third reform would be to move away from the long-standing anomaly of distributing money to schools on the basis of an average unit but charging schools the actual salaries of their teachers. This could be solved by creating a notional staffing agency within each LEA, leaving all schools free to appoint as they do now and to decide the number of teachers they wish to employ, but debiting each school on the basis of the average cost of all teachers in the LEA. The fourth reform would be to produce a national funding formula derived from a careful analysis of what funds are needed to provide a given level of service. Such an approach would have been considered impossible until recently but the improvement in technology and in the data available now makes this feasible. The Secondary Heads Association (SHA) has argued in *A Better Cake* (West *et al*. 1994) that such an approach would open up the funding process to proper public scrutiny, make clear the lines of accountability and ensure equitable but not identical funding for all schools. A national formula for the generation of the budget does not conflict with the basic principle of LMS because the application of the budget at local level would still remain the prerogative of the governors, head and senior managers. All the flexibility, vision and lateral thinking implied in the rest of this chapter would still be required. Some critics of this approach fear that this would have the effect of reducing local democratic decision-making and would put the responsibility for funding levels fully on to the shoulders of central government. There is no reason why central government could not provide the base funding for all schools and leave local government to top up provision on the basis of genuine local democratic responsiveness.

Another scenario is the possibility of taking education funding away from central government entirely and making it fully the responsibility of the local community, as already happens in many states in North America. This would require a change in the taxation system, possibly by replacing the council tax by a local income tax, with a lower level of national income tax. The difficulty we face in implementing this is that the units of local government, especially since Local Government reorganisation which has created more small unitary authorities, are too small to provide an equitable tax base. The variations in provision from area to area would become even more extreme than they already are and this would pose significant ethical problems. A system of regional government, or possibly regionally based Education and Training Boards with tax-raising powers, would be worth considering.

Yet another possibility is that the market-place could take over entirely and all parents would receive a voucher to be traded in at a school of their choice (subject to the limitations in selective schools), the voucher to be 'topped up' by a fee or levy charged by the school. Most schools would become 'fee-paying' and would operate autonomously, deciding their own entry criteria and charging for whatever level of service the parents are prepared to pay for. This scenario, broadly espoused by right wing pressure groups, is the ultimate nightmare for anybody who values equity and believes that education should offer opportunities for all pupils, not just those fortunate enough to be born to wealthy parents or to live in favoured circumstances.

The financing of schools brings us face to face with fundamental questions about the nature of democracy and the society in which we live. Is the public education service a public good or is it a marketable commodity, subject to the pressures and uncertainties of the commercial world, and demanding from its leaders a high level of entrepreneurial skill in order to allow their establishment to survive, let alone deliver a satisfactory level of service? Grace (1994) is unequivocal on this topic:

Education should be regarded as a public good because its free, universal and equal-access provision is fundamental to the generation of other public goods. It is essential for the effective operation of a democratic society and for the enhancement of civic intelligence and participation. It is a powerful source for the nurture of moral, social and community values and responsibilities, and for introducing all children to moral and ethical concepts. It represents, through the schooling system, a democratically provided public service for the enhancement of the intellectual and creative potential of all citizens-in-the-making, with a formal commitment that this enhancement process should not be related to the class, race or gender of the student or to his or her ability to pay for it. It is premised upon the social and public value of maximising the resources of talent in a population in conditions which establish a sense of fairness and of equal opportunity for all in that process.

(Grace 1994: 135)

Whatever happens, it is probable that school leaders of the future will have to live with all the constraints and pressures of inadequate funding and deploy imagination and energy to provide the level of service they see as a minimum. They will have to be ready to pursue value for money; they will have to explore avenues of sponsorship/partnership from local industry and commerce; they will have to be ever more imaginative in the use of school premises for fund-raising purposes; they will have to tap more decisively into direct support from parents; they will have to be in eternal pursuit of applying technology to make learning better and less expensive; they may need to seek private funding for building projects; they will initiate joint projects, for example with the authorities and organisations responsible for leisure services and arts development; they will have to weigh up the potential value of the torrent of new initiatives (such as earmarked funding for language colleges, centres of excellence in teacher development); they may need to negotiate franchising contracts with and from other providers, especially further education colleges. Skilful management of the external financial boundaries is now an important competence for school leaders. At the same time as being resourceful managers of the micro-budgets of their own establishments, they will have to be the pressure group leaders on the macro-political level if funding reforms are to come about.

It is important to reflect on the concepts that are central to this chapter and the competencies necessary to utilise them. To enable you to do this and to form an action plan, we suggest that it would be of assistance to make an enlarged photo-copy of the three pages in Appendix A.

REFERENCES

Audit Commission (1993) *Adding Up the Sums*, London: HMSO.

Department for Education and Employment (1995) *Benchmarking School Budgets: Sharing Good Practice*, London: HMSO.

Downes, P. (1995) 'Government spending claims are "unreal" ', *Managing Schools Today* 5(2): 6–8.

Grace, G. (1994) 'Education is a public good', in D. Bridges and T. H. McLaughlin (eds) *Education and the Market Place*, London: Falmer.

Knight, B. (1993) *Financial Management for School: the Thinking Manager's Guide*, Oxford: Heinemann.

McAleese, K. (1995a) 'The cost of contact', *Times Educational Supplement*, 10 November

McAleese, K. (1995b) *Managing the Margins*, Leicester: Secondary Heads Association.

Maychell, K. (1994) *Counting the Cost: the Impact of LMS on Schools' Patterns of Spending*, Slough: NFER.

Smyth, J. (ed.) (1993) *A Socially Critical View of the Self-Managing School*, London: Falmer.

Weiler, H. (1989) 'Why reforms fail', *Journal of Curriculum Studies* 21(4): 291–305.

West, A., West, R. and Pennell, A. (1994) *A Better Cake: Towards a Rational Approach for Financing Education*, a report commissioned by the Secondary Heads Association, London: Centre for Educational Research, London School of Economics and Political Science.

14   Marketing schools
Strategic perspectives

Brent Davies and Linda Ellison

The concept of marketing in education is not new nor has it been introduced because of the move to various forms of self-management and self-governance for schools in the UK and internationally. It is clear, however, that it has been given increased emphasis with the reform and restructuring of education that has taken place in various countries during the second half of the 1980s and throughout the 1990s. As a result, marketing has become a far more overt and prominent activity for school leadership and management.

It is important before we go much further to distinguish between *markets* as allocation systems in education and *marketing* as a means by which an individual school influences the system by relating to its particular community, most notably to the parents and students. It is possible to have a market allocation system that gives choice without schools being engaged in individual marketing as well as to have schools marketing themselves within a centralised bureaucratic allocation system. An understanding of these two concepts is necessary if school leaders are to have the correct focus.

MARKET ALLOCATION SYSTEMS

Market systems in education are based on similar concepts to those found in the private sector of the economy. In the private sector the provision of products or services is dependent on individual consumers expressing a series of preferences through the purchases that they make which, in turn, determines what businesses produce. It is the aggregation of the consumers' individual purchase decisions that is the driving force. Businesses will purchase materials, hire labour and organise production to meet the needs of those consumers. Le Grand *et al.* (1992) describe markets as:

> a form of economic organisation in which the majority of allocation
> decisions are made through the ostensibly uncoordinated actions of

large numbers of individuals and private firms. The co-ordination of activities ... comes about because each factor of production (land, labour and capital) and each commodity has a price to which diverse groups respond in a way that reconciles their separate actions.

(Le Grand *et al.* 1992: 21)

Support for markets can be seen in a definition by Thompson *et al.* (1991: 3): 'The pursuit of self-interest by individually motivated and welfare maximising individuals leads to the best outcome not just for them but for society as a whole.'

Critics of the market system would, however, argue that producers do not just respond to consumer demands but manipulate that demand by promoting particular consumer products at the expense of others thus, eventually, reducing consumer choice. With the collapse of the Soviet Empire, the market system has become the dominant economic form in the world. Its proponents argue that centralised planning through large bureaucratic agencies is unable to meet effectively and efficiently the needs of consumers in terms of quantity or quality of goods. The opposite of markets may not just be state control but rather concepts such as 'hierarchies' and 'planning'. Berger (1990) uses this distinction as follows:

By 'market' is usually meant an allocative and distributive mechanism, the counterpart of which is not the state but 'hierarchy' and 'planning'. Whereas the 'unit act' of markets is voluntary exchange, the 'unit act' of hierarchies is 'command'.

(Berger 1990: 104)

This distinction can be seen in the UK situation where LEA hierarchies and command cultures have been disrupted, especially in the secondary sector, by the growth of self-managing and self-governing schools.

The market philosophy, whereby individual companies or organisations provide products or services through the price mechanism, is one that has been applied to the privatisation of state-owned industries. The UK led the world in selling large numbers of previously state-owned industries to private owners and returning the provision of products or services to the price mechanism and away from centralised planning. This philosophy has been extended to those government activities which, while remaining state-owned, have introduced market forces in the form of prices and consumer preferences into the allocation mechanism.

In education, the market mechanism has been introduced with parental choice of schools being related to providing customers (parents and students) with 'market' information in the form of school indicators to make that choice. The most significant of these indicators are the results of the Standardised Attainment Tasks (SATs), linked at key age stages to the National Curriculum, and the results of GCSE and A level examinations. Both sets of examination results must be included in the school's prospectus and are published locally and nationally alongside those of other schools in the form of 'league tables' which include attendance figures. However, as Levačić (1995: 25) points out, because 'these are raw data which take no account of students' prior attainment and social background, they are misleading indicators of schools' relative effectiveness'. The enhancement of parental choice of school is allied to the funding mechanism for schools. All state schools have their funding determined by a formula which gives major importance to the Age Weighted Pupil Unit (AWPU) through which money is allocated according to the number of pupils, adjusted by the age of those pupils. If schools achieve more choices by consumers and increase their pupil roll, their funding increases, thus enhancing their ability to employ more teachers and to buy other educational resources. Alternatively, the failure to achieve pupil choices results in a declining pupil roll and funding with a consequent decrease in available resources. Therefore, although parents do not make direct payments to schools in this educational marketplace, their school choice decisions do turn very rapidly into financial allocations to schools such that a price and market effect can be seen to be operating. Thus, in theory, the market mechanism allocates school places through individual parents and pupils making choices between individual self-managing schools and those schools then receive resources according to the number of parental choices that they can accommodate. When schools make conscious attempts to influence that parental choice they engage in a number of activities that are called 'marketing'.

It is important to recognise that market allocation systems in education have severe critics. Notable among these is Smyth (1993) who, in his introduction to *A Socially Critical View of the Self-Managing School*, uses work by Codd (1993) to berate what he calls this 'brave new educational world' by denigrating market and other reforms as leading to a situation where

> schools are pitted against one another for resources and students;
> teachers are rewarded according to what they produce;
> students are assessed against nationally determined yardsticks.
>
> (Smyth 1993: 9)

Whilst it is clear that there is room for considerable debate as to whether centralised partnerships are better than competition between schools, it is difficult to understand the inherent evils of 'teachers being rewarded according to what they produce' or 'students are assessed against nationally determined yardsticks'!

A useful perspective on market systems might be to consider that market influences rather than market forces are operating in education and that concepts of quasi-markets may be more appropriate. Levačić (1995) raises doubts about whether market conditions exist in the state education sector:

> Given that state school places are rationed by administrative criteria and not by price, schools with desirable characteristics as perceived by parents and with insufficient places to meet demand are over-subscribed, since excess demand is not rationed by price as in a normal market.
>
> (Levačić 1995: 25)

She concludes, however:

> For all its deficiencies of structure and information, the school quasi-market has become more competitive through more open enrolment in the context of surplus places in many areas, and parents now have more information, particularly if they choose to seek it out.
>
> (Levačić 1995: 26)

It is clear that the use of market forces in education is an emotive issue between Left and Right on the political spectrum. This is complicated by the complexity of the reforms which include National Curriculum frameworks, standardised tests, four-yearly inspections of schools, self-management and governance of schools and compulsory teacher appraisal. It is not the purpose of this chapter to go further in the argument for and against the use of market forces in education but rather to acknowledge that schools, while they do not operate in a full or market environment, are subject to considerable market influences and that environment may have considerable impact on how the school is led and managed. Key among the management activities is the marketing function in the school.

MARKETING

Essentially we see marketing in education as *the means by which the school actively communicates and promotes its purpose, values and product to the pupils, parents, staff and wider community.*

Marketing in education involves a whole sub-series of activities such as building reflective and responsive cultures in schools, researching customer and societal needs and wants, defining the aims and values of the school, and developing effective methods of promoting the school. We have attempted an initial definition of marketing which seeks to move the concept away from merely selling the school. We can build on this by considering other definitions. Traditional business perspectives are typified by the Chartered Institute of Marketing definition, quoted in Pardey (1991: 11): 'identifying and satisfying customer needs at a profit'. This is based on the concept that organisations exist to make profit. Although this may not be easily transferred to an educational setting, there are some parallels because schools do have to remain financially viable.

Kotler and Armstrong (1990: 5) define marketing as 'A social and managerial process by which individuals and groups obtain what they need and want through creating and exchanging products and value with others.' This type of definition starts to move away from the simplistic ones traditionally found in the business world. It can be improved upon, for example by Brown (1987: 3) who believes that 'marketing is a complete approach to running a business through focusing all of the company's actions on to the customer.' This is supported by Drucker (1973: 4) who states that 'the aim of marketing is to know and understand the customer so well that the product or service fits him and sells itself.' The value of these definitions is that they seek to relate the internal organisation's processes to meeting the customers' needs, an approach which is very useful as it has direct parallels with education and the school sector. Our definition of marketing as 'the means by which the school actively communicates and promotes its purpose, values and product to the pupils, parents, staff and wider community' is one which follows this trend of relating internal operations to meeting customer needs.

Before examining our view of the marketing process itself, we would like to spend some time considering the nature of those individuals and groups who benefit from the educational process: the consumers, customers or clients. Where the term *consumer* is used, then for the core purposes of the school that clearly relates to the pupil. There are, however, occasional aspects of the school's work where someone else could be perceived as the consumer, for example at parents' evening or a staff training day. In the context of the pupil as the consumer, many people would see the person making the choice of school (or 'decision to buy') as the *customer*. This could be the pupil or the parent or a joint decision, depending on the age of the child. An extension of this definition could include the funders of the child's education such as an LEA. There remains confusion about the term *client*. Often this is used when referring to a range of stakeholders such as pupils, parents and also industry as a beneficiary from the skills and knowledge acquired by the pupil. It does not really matter which terminology is used by the school as long as there is an understanding that it is the beneficiary of the product and service who should be at the top of the organisational chart rather than those who offer the product and service.

We now move on to the communications with these individuals and groups. There is a classic saying that 'virtue brings its own reward'. This is not necessarily the case; virtue with a good marketing strategy is likely

Table 14.1 Stages of marketing a school

Stages	Tasks
Market research	Finding out about the school's environment, its competitors and its potential clients including what they want or need from the school
Analysing a school's products and services	Analysing a school's strengths and weaknesses in terms of its products, such as the curriculum, and its services, such as the culture and the support offered
Defining and aligning wants and needs	The difficult task of aligning parental and pupil 'wants' with pupil 'needs' and the ability of the school to provide them, thus defining the product and service of the school.
Promotional approaches	Analysing the methods of explaining and promoting the product and service
Deploying the marketing strategy	Carrying out the action plan for implementing the appropriate promotional approaches
Monitoring and evaluating: the product itself and the marketing process	Constantly monitoring and evaluating the quality of the educational product and service so that the reality matches the rhetoric of the marketing information
	Periodically determining whether the time, money and energy spent on marketing was used effectively

Source: Adapted from Davies and Ellison (in press)

to be much more effective. Having a high quality school is not enough; everybody needs to know about it as well. Davies and Ellison (in press) see marketing as operating through a number of stages, which have been adapted in Table 14.1.

Table 14.1 provides a good example of an action strategy but it must be set within a broader view of marketing and the school. The marketing process is often seen solely as being the school communicating with its external 'publics' or 'stakeholders'. For a strategic perspective it is necessary to pull out from the various marketing stages the strategic tasks that form the key leadership and management challenges for school leaders. It is crucial that senior managers in school operate a twin-track policy of designing a strategic marketing approach that deals not only with the external market but also with the internal culture and stakeholders of the school (the internal market). Indeed, it is unlikely that any long-term improvement can be achieved in a school's marketing strategy, and hence its image, unless the internal culture of the school lives up to the expectations of the external stakeholders. To bring about this positive strategic marketing culture we see three strategic tasks as being essential: creating a customer-focused culture, creating a strategic cause and creating a proactive staff.

Creating a customer-focused culture

Why do schools exist? To provide employment for teachers or education for children? Are these the same thing or are they in conflict? In a way this may be considered to be a simplistic question, but on a more fundamental level it draws on the central tenets of the Total Quality Management (TQM) movement. TQM puts customers and customer satisfaction at the centre of organisational activity (see, for example, West-Burnham 1992; Bowring-Carr and West-Burnham 1994). In the public sector, one of the frequent criticisms is of supplier or producer 'capture' whereby the needs and wishes of the individual consumer take second place to those of monopoly suppliers. Do schools, through entrance tests and requirements, choose children or do children choose schools? A valuable exercise for a staff training session is to ask the staff of a school to list its assets. Very often the list will include the buildings, the equipment, the reputation of the school and the quality of the staff. In reality, the only asset is the pupils themselves for without them there is no use for the buildings and equipment. Similarly, if the child is at the centre of the school then the child's learning must be at the centre of the school's activity. This is different from focusing on teaching and learning, where the first ingredient is the supplier, the teacher, with the child as learner being second. Children learn in a number of ways, one of which is through interaction with the teacher. In an average UK school a pupil attends for 190 days out of 365, approximately 52 per cent of the year. At most that child is taught for six hours each day, which is 25 per cent of the day. As a result, at best, only 13 per cent of a child's time (25 per cent of 52 per cent) is spent in lessons. With this realisation, how do we reconceptualise schools as the core of a child's learning experience that facilitates the other 87 per cent of the learning time, rather than conceiving schools as the 'fountains of all knowledge' and the only place where learning goes on? The shift in culture that we need to enhance in schools is the way in which we focus on the importance of the child and of the child's learning.

Creating a strategic cause

> One person with a belief is equal to a force of ninety-nine who only have an interest.

John Stuart Mill

Factors contributing to a school's culture include the way that children are valued and responded to, the way that the centrality of learning is expressed by the school and the way that teachers work together and share the same values. Only if the individuals in the school value each other, have a strong and focused purpose, celebrate success and reinforce the values of the school will that culture have a chance of being translated to the wider community. The best ambassadors of a school are the pupils and teachers when they meet the wider community because it is then that the reality of the quality of the school is translated to that community.

Kawasaki (1995) makes a very powerful argument for creating a strategic cause for organisations. He states that 'the starting point for evangelism is a cause – something you believe in and want others to believe in as much as you do' (1995: 90). He goes on to outline four key factors in a cause:

- A cause embodies a vision. A cause isn't a namby-pamby, me-too idea. It is a radically different way to radically change the world – or at least make a dent in the world. It represents someone's dream. It is a calling, not just a good idea.
- A cause seizes the high ground. It isn't negative, destructive, or neutral. Its intent is to make the world better . . .
- A cause redefines experiences. It creates new needs, sets standards . . . and changes how things are done. A cause has effects that are irreversible.
- A cause catalyses strong feelings.

(Kawasaki 1995: 91–2)

Pam Dettman, on taking on the leadership of an all girls' school in Australia, has put forward a radical feminist perspective about changing the culture, as she describes it, from a 'prissy little girl' culture with a dependency mind-set to one which 'creates the women leaders of tomorrow'. The cause, to make these pupils articulate, technologically-competent and proactive leaders, ready to claim their right place in society, is an equity one set in terms of achievement for women.

One of the strategic tasks of leaders in schools is to develop and sustain programmes whereby those who work in the school are clear about its aims and values and are able, by working together, to translate those into action.

Creating a proactive staff

While leaders and managers in school must create a responsive quality culture and a strategic cause, another significant aspect of their work is to oversee the mechanics of translating the cause to the wider community.

Those in a school must understand that they have the central responsibility for promoting a positive message about the aims and achievements of the school. While in industry 'customer care' courses are a standard feature, how many teachers have attended one before their first parents' evening? Of all the methods of marketing, the most powerful may still be the description of the school given by the teacher on a Friday evening in the local pub or the child's account of her/his experiences to parents. These have far greater force than glossy prospectuses. Marketing in depth is the only effective long-term strategy. Unless all the individuals in the school both recognise that and then promote it, the effects of marketing are very likely to be short lived.

The strategic marketing process

Having worked on these three organisational cultural perspectives, leaders in schools should then set the broad strategies for each of the key marketing activities. Using the strategic planning process as outlined in Chapter 7 (strategic analysis, strategic choice and strategic implementation) it is possible to allocate the stages of the marketing process (Table 14.1) as shown in Table 14.2.

Table 14.2 The strategic marketing process

Strategic analysis	Market research
	Analysing a school's products and services
Strategic choice	Defining and aligning 'wants' and 'needs'
	Promotional approaches
Strategic implementation	Deploying the marketing strategy
	Monitoring and evaluating: the product itself and the marketing process

Strategic analysis

Chapter 7 suggested various techniques and approaches for strategic analysis. In using those techniques in the marketing context the task is to define the school's environment and, subsequently, customer wants and needs in order, at a later stage, to match those with the product or service that the school proposes to offer. This is not to say that the school needs to repeat the strategic analysis process as part of its marketing, rather that the information gained can be used to meet marketing as well as other management needs. Marketing should not be seen as a bolt-on activity which takes place at a later stage just to ensure publicity.

For clarity, we recommend dividing the analysis into two areas: market research, which examines the external variables, and the analysis of the school's products and services, which examines the internal variables. In both cases, there is a need for a systematic and logical process so that valid information is gathered. There should be a consistency of approach from year to year so that trends, for example in pupil numbers coming from a particular area or in perceptions of the teaching quality, can be identified.

Market research

The key factors relevant here are the school's environment, the nature of the market and the nature of the competition.

An evaluation of local and national trends (in terms of economic, legislative, societal and educational trends) and the way that they impact on the school provides the strategic backcloth for understanding the school's operating environment.

The second factor to consider is the nature of the market. It is important to recognise that there is no such thing as 'the' customer; they are not all alike. A range of demographic factors can be found such as variations in geographical location, race, gender, size of family, educational experience of parents and siblings, previous school, parents' employment patterns and occupation, income, attitudes and beliefs, age and character. This results in many different potential customers who have differing interests, needs and wants. Such differences will affect the expectations of the school, the actual product and service to be offered and the way in which marketing messages are put across. The differences can be used to understand changes in attitudes and to categorise the market into segments so that the school can, through its educational activities and through its marketing strategy, focus on the particular needs of the different groups. Knowledge of the size of each segment can help to determine the nature of demand for the school and can provide a picture of the potential customers, rather than actual ones. Especially significant for a school is information about how and why various schools are chosen, the 'lost customers' and the areas where the school is not active. This can guide future developments.

In terms of the school's competitive relationship with other schools, the third key factor, there needs to be an identification of the competitor schools and the newly emerging competition, their viability and market shares, their image and their actual performance. This will inform discussion about the advantages and disadvantages of the school in relation to the other providers of education.

A more strategic question which brings together information from the three areas outlined here is 'what will customers expect of a school in five years' time and how will our school and our potential competitors seek to meet those expectations?'

Analysing a school's products and services

Assessing the school's products and services through an examination of the internal operational variables is a parallel activity with assessing the school's market, the external factors.

The traditional Business School view of marketing as being about the four P's of product, price, place and promotion is applicable to education, but with limitations. The school's product and its future developments, which could be viewed as both the educational process and the output, and in particular its product in relation to those of other schools, is a valuable frame of reference. Direct price comparisons can be made between independent schools but in the state sector the concept of opportunity cost may be more valuable. Here the cost of a student attending one school instead of another, for example in terms of parents' time spent driving or transport costs, may be a major considera tion. Place is important in terms of location, and the quality of buildings and facilities are significant choice discriminators. The style and appropriateness of promotional activities can also influence choice.

While these factors can be considered by senior managers or by a working group, it is important to share the customer's viewpoint in a more credible way by asking the various groups for their opinions. This might be considered as a fifth 'P' – 'ask the people' – and it will provide a source of information to be used when communicating with prospec- tive customers. Our research (Davies and Ellison 1995) demonstrates how the differing perceptions of pupils, parents and teachers provide invaluable evidence for school management about the school's product and service. The project involves a survey of a sample of pupils and parents (usually one-third in each year group) and all of the staff. Thirty questions are grouped into categories and then randomised before being given as a questionnaire to the stakeholders. The categories are:

For pupils and parents	*For teachers*
Quality of teaching and learning	Communications in the school
Satisfaction with staff	Quality of the working environment for the staff
Communications	
Standards of student behaviour	Professional environment in the school
Quality of school facilities	
General factors and overall satisfaction	Quality of education supplied by the school
Equal opportunities for students (or, for parents, the role of the governors in the school)	Professional support offered to teachers
	Role of the governing body
	General satisfaction with the school

The results are tabulated for each of the categories in each of the pupil, parent and staff questionnaires. Any additional comments made by the clients are summarised so as to preserve anonymity. An example of the results obtained is given in Table 14.3.

Table 14.3 Sample parent response in the 'quality of teaching and learning' category

	Yes	No	Not sure
1 Do you feel that the school is offering the right type of education for your child?	88	3	9
4 Do you feel that your child is sufficiently challenged by the school to encourage maximum learning and development?	53	28	19
11 Do you feel that the number of students in your child's classes is appropriate?	67	22	11
18 Do you feel that your child is set the right type of homework?	58.5	34.5	7
15 Do you feel that your child is set the right amount of homework?	62	32	6
Average for this section	65.7	23.9	10.4

Source: Davies and Ellison 1995

The surveys provide access to representative information rather than the partial information which schools often obtain from vociferous parents or pupils either at the supportive or critical ends of the spectrum. The current pupils and their parents are undoubtedly the most significant influencers of 'decisions to buy' and an accurate up-to-date view of their perceptions is important. The staff questionnaire enables the senior managers to have a more honest view of the staff's perceptions than almost any other method because there are always going to be problems with anonymity. When assisting schools with this work, we have often received and analysed the staff questionnaire ourselves to assure confidentiality.

Results in different categories need to be interpreted very carefully. For example, in one school, the parents' 'yes' response on the adequacy of communications from the governors was 39 per cent. This caused concern amongst the governors and senior management team. However, it may be considered that far more senior management attention needs to be given to a 69 per cent 'yes' response from the parents about satisfaction with the way that students' work is assessed. It must be emphasised that the results show perceptions and may not be related to actual pupil needs. For example, a 'yes' rate of 67 per cent shows some dissatisfaction with class size. This could indicate a need to communicate more clearly, through the marketing strategy, about teaching and learning styles or about the existence of additional help in the classroom.

With this example and in all the areas, it is very important that the results are seen as generating areas for consideration and not as definitive statements of fact. The information should be triangulated with other sources in the school to build up a list of key issues to inform both development and marketing. The process of carrying out such a survey needs careful handling. While it often shows a lot of support for the school, there can be sensitive issues raised or individuals who are not ready to see such an instrument used. Once the survey has been initiated, the respondents will expect to see the results. The climate must be right for such a venture.

Kawasaki (1995: 76) provides a useful model which links an organisation's ability to provide with the customer's interpretation of the value of those products or services. This may be seen in the graph in Figure 14.1 which has been adapted to an educational setting.

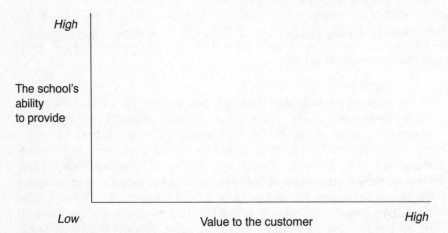

Figure 14.1 Model linking school's ability to provide products or services with the customer's evaluation of these

Source: Adapted from Kawasaki 1995

The model can be used to analyse the information which has been gathered as follows:

1 Determine the most important features of the school's 'product' and service.
2 Position all the features on the graph.
3 Study the position of the features. Those that are high and to the right are the key ones that can be promoted fairly easily as the school can

demonstrate effectiveness and the customer is keen to accept the feature. Those which are high and to the left may need special consideration in the marketing strategy if the customer is to change her/his attitude to their value. Those features which appear elsewhere need consideration through other management arenas in the school.

Linking our research to the process in the graph demonstrates the importance of systematically finding out clients' opinions and not just relying on assumptions or opinions and of linking into the internal product analysis (e.g. through a SWOT analysis). Such information from key participants can then be used to inform the marketing strategy and the development of the educational product and service.

Strategic choice

Having engaged in a process of researching the environment, the clients' wants and needs and the perceptions of the current products and services that the school offers, the next stage is to choose the key areas for the school's future activities and then to promote them. This is a process that is articulated in the school development plan. Once this framework is established the promotion or communication of the school's key strengths and activities can take place.

Defining and aligning 'wants' and 'needs'

The strategic choice process highlights a fundamental problem in marketing in the education sector, that of the difference between 'wants' and 'needs'. In a business setting, the aim of marketing would be to supply consumer wants at a profit. In education, the professional judgement of the educator may determine that the child needs certain types of help or support while the customer or consumer, the parent or the child, may want something completely different. For example, while the teacher may diagnose that the child needs remedial support with language, the parent may harbour unrealistic wants in terms of that child becoming a brain surgeon. One of the significant strategic differences in marketing in education as opposed to in the business sector is the way in which schools make choices that reconcile those differences or adopt management strategies to educate parents as they articulate their wants.

Promotional approaches

Promotional approaches should be a planned and sustained way of establishing and maintaining the reputation and image of the school with its stakeholders. Leaders of the marketing process can utilise one

Table 14.4 The promotional mix

Approach	Examples	Audience	Purpose
Advertising (for pupils, staff, events)	Prospectuses, brochures, flyers, press advertising and advertorials	Mass	To inform, persuade, remind, condition
Personal selling	Tour of the school, word of mouth, often by parent or pupil	Individuals, groups	To condition, inform, remind
Promotional events	Open days, roadshows, events e.g. plays, sports day, vouchers	Interested groups	Goodwill, to motivate, inform, 'spur the sale'
Publicity (no cost)	Press releases, media mentions, use of premises by the community	Mass	To inform, educate

of a number of approaches (which we have expanded on elsewhere, for example in Davies and Ellison 1991) from the promotional mix that is briefly summarised in Table 14.4.

It is worthwhile considering not only which approaches are currently used by the school and are most appropriate but also which approaches the competitors use. The approaches should be examined in terms of the internal as well as the external markets. The internal market of existing pupils, parents, teachers and governors all need to have their view of the school enhanced and developed with up-to-date information and positive communication. If this does not happen then any external marketing will flounder when those outside the school meet the groups that make up the internal market and the external projection does not meet the internal reality. This is one of the key strategic mistakes that schools make, which results in marketing being superficial in that it presents an image to the outside world that is not shared or recognised by the internal world of the school. The significant order is to concentrate first on the internal market and then, later, on the external market.

The use of the promotional approaches has to be set within an implementation strategy which will be considered next.

Strategic implementation

The implementation phase consists of two elements: deployment, and monitoring and evaluation.

Deploying the marketing strategy

This comprises a number of staged activities:

- Establishing and building an effective marketing team.
- Clarifying and prioritising marketing aims and then setting out in a written plan the objectives and responsible person for each activity.
- Implementing the promotional approaches that best achieve the aims and objectives.

Monitoring and evaluating: the product itself and the marketing process

In an industrial context, marketing and production are closely linked. Similarly, pupil achievement, 'the product of the school' and the marketing strategy are linked. In the monitoring and evaluation of the product, the focus is to encourage constant reference back to the quality of teaching and learning and to pupils' outcomes so that the reality of the 'product' relates to the concepts being promoted. Strategies for review could also examine the relative performance of the school's 'products' and their lifecycles (see Chapter 7). This information is significant in informing the future marketing strategy as the approaches chosen will depend on an activity's lifecycle position. A focus on marketing should not be at the expense of management time spent on planning improvement to the quality and outcomes of the learning process.

A significant part of the evaluation process considers the effectiveness of the marketing strategy, the involvement (and preparation) of the various parties and the impact of the different approaches used. There can be a cost benefit analysis which pays special attention to the opportunity costs of various promotional activities. An interesting approach is to audit the marketing activities from the viewpoint of the customer.

CONCLUSION

Strategic marketing is a process of asking why schools should engage in the marketing process, what should be marketed, and when and how that marketing should take place. Too often schools rush into the 'how' part of the process and forget to define the purpose of marketing as part of the strategic development of the organisation. The strategic leadership perspective in this chapter has, we hope, helped to redress the balance.

It is important to reflect on the concepts that are central to this chapter and the competencies necessary to utilise them. To enable you to do this and to form an action plan, we suggest that it would be of assistance to make an enlarged photo-copy of the three pages in Appendix A.

REFERENCES

Berger, J. (1990) 'Markets and state in advanced capitalist societies', in A. Martinelli and N. J. Smelser (eds) *Economy and Society: Overviews in Economic Sociology*, London: Sage.

Bowring-Carr, C. and West-Burnham, J. (1994) *Managing Quality in Schools: a Training Manual*, Harlow: Longman.

Brown, R. (1987) *Marketing for the Small Firm*, London: Cassell.

Codd, J. A. (1993) 'Managerialism, market liberalism and the move to self-managing schools in New Zealand', in J. Smyth (ed.) *A Socially Critical View of the Self-Managing School*, London: Falmer.

Davies, B. and Ellison, L. (1991) *Marketing the Secondary School*, Harlow: Longman.

Davies, B. and Ellison, L. (1995) 'Improving the quality of schools: ask the clients', *School Organisation* 15(1): 5–12.

Davies, B. and Ellison, L. (in press) *Marketing the School*, London: Pitman.

Drucker, P. (1973) *Management Tasks, Responsibilities and Practice*, London: Harper and Row.

Kawasaki, G. (1995) *How to Drive your Competition Crazy*, New York: Hyperion.

Kotler, P. and Armstrong, G. (1990) *Marketing: An Introduction* (2nd edn), Englewood Cliffs, NJ: Prentice-Hall.

Le Grand, J., Propper, C. and Robinson, R. (1992) *The Economics of Social Problems* (3rd edn), London: Macmillan.

Levačić, R. (1995) *Local Management of Schools: Analysis and Practice*, Buckingham: Open University Press.

Pardey, D. (1991) *Marketing for Schools*, London: Kogan Page.

Smyth, J. (ed.) (1993) *A Socially Critical View of the Self-Managing School*, London: Falmer.

Thompson, G., Francis, J., Levacic, R. and Mitchell, J. (eds) (1991) *Markets, Hierarchies and Networks: The Co-ordination of Social Life*, London: Sage.

West-Burnham, J. (1992) *Managing Quality in Schools*, Harlow: Longman.

15   Information management

John Warwick

A few years ago, managing information technology could be left almost entirely to the school's IT manager. Today this is no longer true – and tomorrow it will be even less true. Whilst the new communication and information technologies have transformed manufacturing industries and business offices, so present and future developments will impact on the service industries and none more so than education. Information technology has a habit of reworking the status quo beyond all recognition. It was a British Home Secretary who said that the telephone would never catch on in England: 'it may be very useful in America, but here we've got too many messenger boys.' Education leaders and managers are likely to place their establishments at a severe disadvantage unless they understand the strategic impact of information technology, actively support it and take a creative lead in its use in the school. Effective educational leaders and managers are extending their existing skills and knowledge to encompass technological competence in the use of IT as a management tool. Information is a key corporate resource which requires just as much consideration and management as employees, finances and school organisation.

In the business of education, information is much more than just a resource. At the heart of learning is the creation of new personal information and meaning. Information is the lifeblood of educational growth. Wheatley (1992) has suggested that information is the creative energy of the universe.

> For a system to remain alive, for the universe to move forward, information must be continually generated. If there is nothing new, or if the information that exists merely confirms what is, then the result will be death. Isolated systems wind down and decay, victims of the laws of entropy. The fuel of life is new information – novelty – ordered in new structures. We need to have information throughout our systems, disturbing the peace, imbuing everything that it touches with new life. We need, therefore, to develop new approaches to

information – not management but encouragement, not control but genesis. How do we create more of the wonderful life source?

(Wheatley 1992: 104)

This is a challenging viewpoint for many senior managers of schools who can feel overwhelmed by the demands of government, not only in the amount of data being demanded by the centre but also by the legislative drive for schools to make more information available to parents in order that they can be better informed of the performance of their child and of the institution as a whole. Along with greater delegation and increased self-management comes the need for greater accountability, which is translated into the desire to measure progress against a range of performance indicators and to publish the results. The initial concern of schools, when financial delegation was being introduced, was whether or not they could cope with the business processes and their response resulted in considerable growth in the use of financial software in schools. Throughout this period, management concerns focused on their ability to establish appropriate systems for co-ordination and control. Inevitably, this concern became reflected in the nature of the management information systems in schools which were data-driven and were generally seen as administrative tools for the use of the school office and the systems manager. It was not long before schools realised that the real challenge was not at the business and operational level but was in developing strategic approaches to exploit their relative freedom to create world class schools.

Greater self-management has also lead to a change in the culture of schools. The fact that income is directly related to the number of students recruited and retained means that parents and students are perceived as customers whose needs must be ascertained and met. Just as car manufacturers have moved from Henry Ford's edict that the customer 'can have any colour as long as it is black' to the production of a range of products and options to meet the needs of different customers, so the challenge for the teaching profession is to produce learning programmes that are responsive to the individual needs of learners. Such an approach requires extensive needs analysis and the recording of progression. More data is generated and information must be readily available to a wider network of people. Information thus becomes a strategic resource to be managed at a corporate level.

Whilst the concept is simple, the process of managing information efficiently, effectively and economically presents many challenges; there are many types of data and information, and communication is complex because it always takes place within a cultural context so that the meaning given to the message received can always be different to that intended. Seniors managers often complain of the paradox: on the one hand having too much information to deal with yet on the other not having the right information with which to make decisions. Indeed, the lack of sufficient management information is frequently at the root of most problems in schools, be this at the level of governance or of the teacher in the classroom.

ORGANISATIONAL STRUCTURE AND INFORMATION FLOW

The manner in which information flows and is managed is determined by the nature of the organisation and its inherent management style. Firstly, it is important to make the distinction between data and information. Data is merely a collection of facts and figures, whilst information is processed data with the potential to describe something which one did not previously know. This leads to the essence of a management information system which is the processing of data into information that is then communicated to a user. Data incurs a cost, brought about by its collection, storage, processing and retrieval. Information, effectively used to inform decision-making and decision-taking, has a value. The challenge is to ensure that the value is greater than the cost. For example, there is a cost in collecting attendance data. The class teacher or form tutor can turn this data into information by looking at the pattern of absences of particular individuals. The head of key stage or year can aggregate the data from each class and compare attendance, noting any particular variance. The headteacher can aggregate the data even further to compare attendance by year group, or to compare with previous years or other establishments and then, possibly, to predict annual figures. However, if the data is merely collected and stored to be used only for future reference its value is small. Another example could be a school that undertakes a survey of parents, finds an area of concern but decides to ignore the results. There is clearly a cost involved and new information has been provided, but it is of little value since no action is to be taken.

The attendance example also highlights the fact that there are different information needs within an organisation. According to Beer's cybernetic model (Beer 1966: 424) the management process consists of five levels: (1) Operational; (2) Co-ordinating; (3) Control; (4) Planning; and (5) Policy. Within schools it is possible to see these five levels at work: (1) within the classroom; (2) at meetings, working parties and in pigeon holes; (3) at middle management; (4) at senior or strategic management and (5) at governor level. Data flows between these levels, exhibiting all the characteristics of a utility resource such as water; it can be owned, stored, wasted, retrieved, traded, channelled, blocked, inconsistent, of questionable quality or in short supply. Data may be stored in many

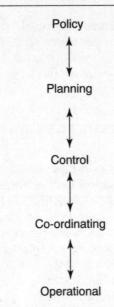

Figure 15.1 The five levels of management processes

different locations, which can be called nodes, with access to the node guarded by a gatekeeper.

In a school exhibiting the characteristics of a linear organisation as shown in Figure 15.1, information flows in very narrow, well defined channels. Policies are formulated by the governors who interface with the external world, plans are made and targets set by the senior or strategic team, which are then communicated down through the system to be re-interpreted as they pass through each node and gatekeeper. Those working at the operational level attempt to implement the plans and reach any targets given to them and at the end of the process the results may or may not be fed back up the system. In some organisations strategic managers never learn whether the target has been hit, whilst others do learn and readjust plans for next time. However, the information base on which planning, monitoring and evaluation takes place is weak because data is either blocked, channelled or re-processed as it moves up the system, whilst those working at the operational level are not informed about school-wide issues. The greater the number of nodes in an establishment the more likely it is that the data will be inconsistent, incompatible and inaccessible.

Monitoring and evaluation are essential to good management and linear organisations are likely to have in place some form of quality control in the form of a feedback loop as seen in Figure 15.2. The school has some *inputs* – these are the 'givens' – which the school can do little about such as

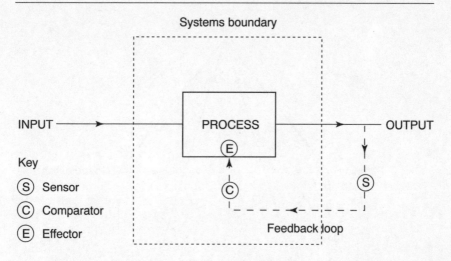

Figure 15.2 The feedback loop in a linear organisation

students' prior learning or the level of financial resourcing. As a result of the educational *process*, the student achieves some outcomes or *output* in relation to academic, civic, personal, social and vocational development. The purpose of the feedback loop is to measure the current state of the outputs through some form of sensor (S) and this information is carried back to a control mechanism called a comparator (C) which compares the state of the output against a standard or target. If there is a discrepancy then some change is made to the process by an effector (E). In education systems, the sensor is frequently outside the systems boundary, for example OFSTED inspections, public examination performance, league tables and national curriculum testing; in other words the output is measured once the process is complete. In addition, the lack of data or an inefficient data flow means that the feedback loop might take over a year to complete, which is unfortunate for students passing through the system, as they have only one chance and alterations as a result of feedback may come too late for them. This model can be applied to all levels of an organisation, from the whole school to a teacher in the classroom, although the feedback loop tends to be shorter at the lower levels of the organisation as the units tend to be smaller, such as the individual lesson.

Cultural forces and the search for an improvement in the quality of education are leading to new forms of school organisation, based more on the concept of networks. A school exhibiting the characteristics of a network organisation is shown in Figure 15.3, which links policy (at the top) with other management processes.

Removing organisational layers creates the opportunity to form networks of data flows. Whilst policies are still formulated by members

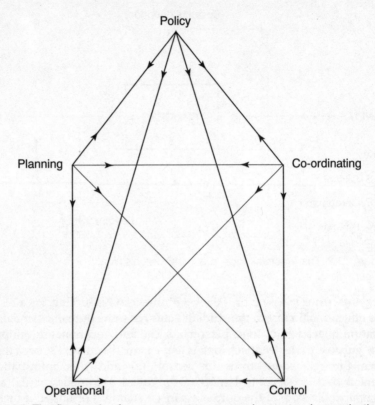

Figure 15.3 The five levels of management processes in a network organisation

of the governing body, who also interface with external networks, and strategic plans are formulated by a senior or strategic management team, the tactical planning, control, co-ordinating and operational functions are brought together to be the responsibility of other teams. In network organisations far more people have access to information, providing the opportunity for the democratisation of decision-making and for greater authorship of the decisions that are made. This, in turn, raises awareness of the need to collect many different types of data on school performance in order to provide the information that will enable the organisation to see whether its plans are being implemented and its targets achieved. Greater access to information and more widespread monitoring means that plans can be adjusted more frequently to ensure that the target is hit. It is rather like an aeroplane that submits a flight plan but constantly monitors where it is in relation to a number of indicators so that plans can be adjusted if it is blown off course by unexpected events. Here the role of the leader is more akin to that of a coach seeking to encourage people to play well and to present the best

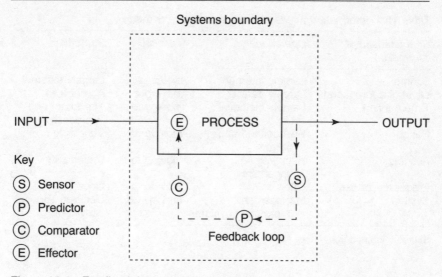

Figure 15.4   Feedback in a network organisation

of their ideas and achievements. In such organisations data is integrated, the number of data nodes is considerably reduced, as are the number of gatekeepers, thus increasing access. An integrated computerised management information system is in operation ensuring data is consistent and compatible. Terminals are linked through a local area network (LAN) supported by a systems manager. However, the systems manager is not the gatekeeper and the network can be accessed by a large number of staff, known as end users.

Network organisations also have a feedback loop but theirs is much more in the form of quality assurance (as compared to quality control in Figure 15.2) because the sensor (S) is inside the systems boundary and the process can be affected prior to any output. There is constant monitoring, with data passing around the loop at a much faster rate. In addition, the loop has an additional component, as seen in Figure 15.4, called the predictor (P). The predictor uses data about the current system together with a predictive model to estimate the future state of the system (rather than simply the present) which is then fed to the comparator as before.

Beer's cybernetic model (see p. 223) naturally gives rise to four levels of management information: (1) inquiry response; (2) operational planning and control; (3) tactical planning; and (4) strategic and policy planning. The type of information required at each of these levels differs significantly as shown in Table 15.1 (overleaf).

Because the management functions are clearly delineated in linear organisations, the different type of management information required is

Table 15.1 Information needs and management processes

Characteristic of information	Operational	Tactical	Strategic
Source	Largely internal	*moving to*	Largely external
Level of aggregation	Largely detailed	*moving to*	Aggregated
Time horizon	Largely historical	*moving to*	The future and predictive
Range	Well defined and narrow	*moving to*	Very wide
Accuracy	High with no uncertainty	*moving to*	Uncertainty
Frequency of use	Often	*moving to*	Occasional
System	Management information systems	*moving to*	Decision support systems

Source: Adapted from Lucey 1991: 116

easier to identify. In network organisations, awareness is needed of the particular function that a team is currently undertaking in order to ensure that it has the right type of information for the task in hand.

Table 15.1 provides the basis for measuring the effectiveness of an information system; it should provide the right information (*what* is needed to do the task) to the right people (those *who* have to do the task) at the right time (*when* it is needed) in the right way (*how* the information is presented) and in the right place (*where* decisions have to be made) to achieve the school's vision and purpose (*why* the information is needed in the first place).

MANAGEMENT STYLE AND INFORMATION FLOW

So far we have looked at the relationship between the structure of organisations and information flows. A further dimension is the relationship between management style and the way that information is managed. In the mid-1980s the US Department of Defense selection process for choosing contractors to write systems emphasised price and time scales as the critical choice factors. The Department was constantly disappointed as one contractor after another ran over budget and over time. This dissatisfaction led to the production of a Capability Maturity Model (Paulk 1993: 174) which allowed the positioning of organisations by their style of management and by the ways in which this is reflected in their management of information.

The model has five levels and 80 per cent of the contractors were deemed to be at *Level One*, called the initial level. This represents a process which is unstable and disorganised, in terms of both quality assurance and development practices. For example, the management of change is weak and there is little senior management exposure or understanding of the problems. Quality manuals may exist, but they are usually unopened and processes are being continually re-invented. There are a large number of information nodes, information flows having been built up in an *ad hoc* manner with many gatekeepers guarding information.

A further 10 per cent of organisations were at *Level Two*, described as the repeatable state. Here, the organisation has a number of stable processes with a repeatable level of control. Organisations at this level produce plans which are usually adhered to until a spanner is thrown in the works when a customer (either internal or external) requests a major change to requirements midway through a project. The new systems and information flows, which have had a great deal of investment, are likely to be only partially implemented. These systems and information flows are still not understood by senior managers and are deemed to have 'failed' and this leads to imminent regression to Level One.

Only 6 per cent of contractors were deemed to be at *Level Three*, described as being in the defined state. At Level Three, the processes have been defined to help consistent implementation and to act as a basis for making continuous progress. For example, a school faced with a crisis continues to use the defined processes which have been established to handle such circumstances. *Level Four* constitutes the managed level and, in the survey, represented about 3 per cent of contractors. Here the organisation purposefully gathers process data to understand, control and improve each process. It uses measurement to quantify the quality of the work and senior managers are able to understand the results of these measurements and to use them in support of their strategic objectives. The highest level contained only 1 per cent of contractors. Organisations at *Level Five* are said to be optimising; measurement is an integral part of the process and is used continually to improve and optimise the process. Much of the measurement data is collected automatically and processed into information that readily informs senior managers through an executive information system. A particular feature of such systems is their reporting of exceptions to the normal at all stages in the system and their ability to support senior management in the decision-making process.

The world-wide cultural pressure for more effective educational systems, with increased democratisation in decision-making, a focus on customer needs and monitoring performance at all levels, reflects the need to create educational systems which operate at *Level Five* of the capability model. Such a move inevitably results in an explosion of data and hence cost. For the resulting information to be of value, it needs to meet the criteria set out in Table 15.1 and, in particular, it is essential to be able to move large amounts of data quickly and accurately. There can, for example, be considerable income implications for sending in wrong or late data to government agencies. The ability to manage information at a corporate level is now dependent on the technology and, in particular, the establishment of open integrated systems. In a closed system there is a single source of input, the data is processed in some way to produce an output which does not feed into any other system. A stand-alone computer program such as a word processor is such an example. In an open system, the results can be fed into another system, after validation to ensure compatibility between the output of one system and the input of another. In both open and closed systems users within the organisation can find themselves duplicating input and working on different databases because one is not up to date and has not had recent changes implemented.

Difficulties in keeping data accurate and up-to-date can be overcome through the establishment of either an information pool or an integrated system. In the former, one or more sources of data are placed in a pool which can be accessed by other systems. The data is updated at intervals, usually termly or annually. Although some data within schools is not volatile, even small changes can have severe implications because there are so many users of the data. In an integrated system, the data is entered or edited only once and is immediately sent round the system to refresh other modules, the data is clean and immediately available. Such a system has significant management implications requiring clear procedures and agreement on data structures, data ownership (whose job is it to keep different data clean?), access and security.

THE IMPACT OF INFORMATION TECHNOLOGY ON SCHOOL MANAGEMENT

The Massachusetts Institute of Technology (MIT) Management in the 1990s Research Programme was set up to examine future managerial issues with particular reference to the anticipated advances in Information Technology. Two of the findings are particularly pertinent to education:

> Various forms of integration are at the heart of many of the necessary changes. It is not just a matter of combining databases or using a common database across all the departments of an organisation. It covers the wider issues of achieving close and effective working relationships between various parts of an organisation, for example in terms of structure, working relationships, common or inter-linked processes and shared information.

New forms and styles of organisation will make extensive use of electronic integration: workers will have terminals and workstations that are linked together, making people informed and flexible in their approach to tasks. Team working across internal and external organisational boundaries will be common, assisted by IT.

(International Computers Ltd 1992: 8)

Developments in communication and information technology are beginning not only to provide new management tools but also to have a profound impact on how schools operate and the nature and arena of learning. Whilst on the one hand it is important for technology to remain the tool rather than the driving force, it is also important to recognise that the technology does enable things to be done in different ways and so it can change behaviour and perceptions of what is possible. The challenge for senior education leaders and managers is to create a symbiotic relationship between the change forces impacting on people, structure, organisation and technology. Many curriculum innovations involving technology have 'failed' to succeed because the new technology is applied to an old curriculum. Whilst technology needs to support the learning objectives of the curriculum, so these objectives may need to change to exploit the potential offered by the technology. In History, for example, vast amounts of original source material could become available. The teacher could simply use these resources in the same way as textbooks are used or a strategic shift could be made so that the emphasis is not on learning facts about history but about being an historian. At the same time this would develop the essential information skills required by autonomous individuals within society.

Essentially, IT has been used as a tool to support the enquiry response, operational and control aspects of teaching and learning rather than the strategic aspects. Management is no different; organisations that implement computerised management information systems without making appropriate changes to their organisational structure and management style are likely to have a poor return on their investment. In the early 1990s the British government invested considerable sums to set up NERIS, the National Educational Resource Information Service. The concept was to make available, through computers linked to telephone lines, data of direct benefit to teachers and education managers such as information on the National Curriculum, teaching notes and classroom resources. The data was centrally stored and could be pulled down on to the school's computer or printed. The data was also made available on CD-ROM. When Government funding was withdrawn, and institutions had to pay for the data, the service collapsed. Various reasons were put forward, including the fact that the quality of material varied and it was just not worth the effort and paper to find the nuggets of gold;

others suggested that it was an idea before its time and that teachers had not made the cultural shift to access information in this way and hence did not change their behaviour.

Whatever the reason, the failure of NERIS provides important lessons at a time when communication networks, such as the Internet, are being developed. The experience shows that education is a specialist market and that users will not change their behaviour until it becomes more efficient, effective and economic to use such systems. Supplying the educational market with information over and above that of simply advertising products is far from commercially attractive, simply because the market is limited to one country with specialist needs. At a time of global communication, forces will be at work to create international curriculum development. In addition, schools will not use such new developments if costs are high and, even more worrying, are open-ended. Governments may well need to put pressure on commercial companies to ensure not only that schools, libraries and museums are connected to the new information grids but also that their use is free. On networks, such as the Internet, charges are made at the local tele-phone rate; in parts of America and Australasia local calls are free and many cable companies in the UK are offering a completely free service to schools.

The rapid increase of computing power will continue, the cost of memory will continue to fall whilst the relative cost of developing and maintaining software will increase. The power of the information grid in the mid-1990s is equivalent to a footpath compared to the concept of a superhighway. In recent years there has been not only the diversifi-cation of telecommunication services such as facsimile, video conferencing, electronic mail, on line shopping, and pagers but also the convergence of communications and computing into Information Technology. IT markets were initially separate, so telecommunications, computing, consumer electronics, broadcasting and the video industry were seen as very separate developments. Today they have converged into one entity.

The fundamental reason why this has been made possible is digiti-sation. Whilst the forms of communication were initially different, most of the communications technology was based on the analogue system. An input is transformed into an electrical pulse which is sent through either the atmosphere or copper wire to be received and decoded by a receiver. The problem is that such electrical pulses can be subject to all sorts of interference as they move from the transmitter to the receiver. It is impossible to guarantee that the output is the same as that of the input. The fundamental breakthrough was the introduction of digital communication, as exemplified in the change from the vinyl record to the compact disc (CD). Digitisation enables a piece of text, sound, still or video image to be broken down into small blocks, each represented by a series of 1s and 0s called bits. This string of digits can be sent through the information grid at the speed of light by means of fibre optics, with checking digits to ensure that the correct code is received. Because the code received is exactly the same as that transmitted, the system becomes reliable, fast, accurate and secure. Narrowband information grids, such as telephones and modems, can transfer data at the rate of 28,800 (28.8K) bits per second. Analogue transmissions take up the full band width, but digitisation allows the data to be compressed so that up to five signals can be transferred along the band. The United Kingdom, along with many countries, is developing a wider, intermediate band called an integrated services digital network (ISDN). This can transfer data at between 64 and 144 Kbits per second and will meet much of the short-term demand to support facilities such as electronic mail and the information grid, the Internet. However, the future lies in broadband fibre optics, capable of carrying an incredible number of signals at speeds of 2,000K (2M) bits per second and upwards. Such speed is essential if dynamic images are to be transmitted. A full screen picture takes up 50M bits, but very sophisticated picture compression techniques are being developed so that only the moving part of the image is updated.

Broadband transmission using fibre optics has been called the super-highway and will be the means by which most data will flow through world-wide information grids. Such networks began to appear in the mid-1990s, particularly in the academic community. By 1995 over sixty UK universities were connected by fibre optics on a closed information grid known as SuperJanet. At the same time, many schools were learning of the power of electronic data interchange (EDI) through the use of software developed by companies such as SIMS which enabled government returns, examination entries and results to be transmitted through narrowband networks.

CONVERGENCE: THE BREAKING DOWN OF BARRIERS

Convergence started when computers began to be connected across telephone wires and games became available on television. Convergence continued with the introduction into the market in the mid-1990s of multimedia systems which enabled text, sound, stills and video to be stored on one CD disk and accessed through a personal computer. Today the overlap is so great that the market and services are seen as one. The personal computer can be used to send and receive messages, pull down information from vast data banks, listen to music or watch television. What is more, each of these applications can be running at the same time. We are experiencing the breaking down of geographical and chronological barriers, two major gatekeepers to information nodes. One area where the chronological barrier has been removed is schools' television. Initially, when television programmes for schools were introduced, it was necessary to build the school timetable around the broadcasts. Then came video recording, which enabled the broadcast to be played back at a convenient time, usually to a group of students. However, each institution had to keep an extensive library of video tapes in order to service the organisation. Increasingly, we are moving to the position where the programme can be pulled down to individual computers, at school, in the home, or anywhere at a time to suit each user. Television broadcasts become no different to listening to a CD-ROM, they can be paused, they can be jumped forward or back, they can be pre-programmed or turned off ready to resume at a convenient time. Eventually, all such programmes can be made interactive, user response can determine not only what the end of a play might be but also what learning programmes will be followed. It is the potential of interaction between the learner and the programmes, at a time and place convenient to the learner, that will have a most profound effect on educational institutions.

Geographical barriers are being broken by the advent of the information grid which gives the ability to link into a vast communications network. In the United Kingdom, cable franchises and the telecommunications industry are being required to link educational establishments and libraries into this network free of charge. The growth in the size and speed of the information grid will be massive. One illustration of the breakdown of geographical barriers is the way in which schools from different continents now communicate with each other at both student and staff level. Another example is the advent of the mobile telephone. Once seen as pure science fiction and then as a plaything of the rich, mobile telephones are a growing part of daily life. Schools quickly saw their value when any trips or activities were taking place 'off-site' but now we have the ability to connect mobile telephones to laptop computers so that the many functions that can now be undertaken on a personal computer, including video conferencing, can be implemented from anywhere in the world. Whilst the resource implications of providing each student with a laptop computer and communication facilities may hinder progress, the rapid growth of personal computers in the home and the convergence of services, driven by entertainment, means that many students and their parents will have access to the information grid and the day is not far away when every school has its own electronic bulletin board, including current information such as this week's homework.

Whilst the technology makes all this possible, a major concern of schools will be the availability of resources in terms of both being able to purchase services on the information grid and having the hardware in the first place. The growth of personal computers (PCs), and particularly laptop computers, reflected the desire for users to have processing power. One scenario is that this trend will continue and such machines will become more powerful but will not dramatically drop in price. In such a scenario, data is pulled down and processed on the user's system. An alternative scenario is that, once the superhighway is established, end users will not need high powered machines; they can simply act as terminals connected to more powerful processors. Just as we will be renting broadcasts that come into our homes so we can rent software and processing power. If the use of the information grid were made free to schools, and possibly to pupils, then the school's central computer system could be accessed with relatively cheap hardware. The advent of the personal organiser is a reflection of this trend. It is possible to see a future in which teachers and pupils have educational organisers which can undertake small scale local processing but which also have communication facilities to allow interaction with the learning centre's system.

THE STRATEGIC IMPACT OF INFORMATION TECHNOLOGY ON SCHOOLS

The breakdown of chronological and geographical barriers through the increased power of communication and information technology will have a strategic impact on schools and on the whole area of learning resources. Learners will have a far greater choice; they will be able to log on to a variety of databases and learning services offered by information providers throughout the world. The gap between entertainment and education program(me)s will diminish; terms such as 'edutainment' and 'infotainment' are already entering the English language. For some, such developments will be seen as a threat, to be opposed and belittled, whilst others will seek ways to exploit such developments for the benefit of learners. Students may well find themselves working with partners with whom they have never before come into contact. Greater choice and more individualised learning program(me)s inevitably give rise to increased data, each individual learning program(me) has to be designed and the experience tracked and reported upon. Effective learning systems will be those operating at Level Five of the capability model, with progress being monitored, often automatically, and with exception reporting to the teacher or tutor. One possible scenario is that of the tutor designing, with the student, a programme of study for the following term, consisting of a mixture of classroom-based lessons, lectures, field trips, independent research, exercises from books and a set of learning modules on the computer. These are fed into a curriculum management module and the student is automatically booked on to such programs and is supplied with an individual learning plan giving programmes of study, dates, times and targets for the term. As the programme of study proceeds, results and outcomes are fed into the module which makes decisions for a revised programme for the rest of the term. Tutors and parents automatically receive reports on progress together with 'exception reports', probably through electronic means. Although classroom teaching and lecturing will still have an important role, the teacher becomes more of a coach than the provider of information, best summed up as a move from the sage on the stage to the guide on the side. The beginnings of such a trend can be seen in developments such as the Open Integrated Learning Systems (OILS; NCET 1995: 2). In such systems students are presented with tasks that are challenging but not threatening; as one student reported, 'computers don't humiliate you when you make a mistake.' As in computer games, the software responds to the level of response of the student, continually adjusting to explain and to set challenges that provide opportunities for success and self-esteem. Progress is automatically recorded and common errors, either by individuals or classes as a whole, are brought to the attention of the tutor. Early research (NCET 1995: 12) has shown greater productivity of learning in certain areas of the curriculum. Such computer learning systems are not seen as the appropriate tool for the whole of the curriculum; other resources will still be needed, however it is very likely that learning programmes will, in the future, be managed with the aid of a computer. Education leaders and managers are certainly going to be faced with some difficult strategic decisions in relation to the most effective use of resources, human and otherwise. These decisions will need to be based on good and reliable information.

As educational organisations seek to move to Level Five of the capability model, so management and executive software will be developed to service the need. Integrated databases will be developed, such as that provided by SIMS in the United Kingdom (SIMS 1996) or OASIS in Australia, with the potential of being able to hold an extensive range of both hard data, such as names, examination performance, and attendance, and soft data such as opinions, attitudes and levels of satisfaction. As schools begin to take on a greater strategic role, so they will be interested in comparing their data with other similar institutions through benchmarking. For example, examination performance, attendance, financial expenditure, staff absences, parents' satisfaction can all be compared to see whether the school is an 'exception'. Being such is not necessarily wrong, as long as the underlying causes can be explained in terms of the school's values, vision and strategy. Such a need, combined with the establishment of more sophisticated information grids, is likely to see the establishment of large databases against which the profile of the institution can be compared. Whilst, initially, this will be through the user interrogating the database, inevitably management software will be developed which will automatically monitor both the institutional database to report on exceptions (for example, if attendance rates suddenly change or if a class has been covered by more than six teachers in the term) and larger databases to report on significant differences between the institution and other, similar, organisations. A key skill for managers will be to identify the information that is likely to be of importance to them. IT systems can be used to generate so much data that we end with a situation where we have a thousand pieces of data looking for five good questions! Additionally, much of this data is likely to be presented in tabular or graphical form, and whilst the software will be able to indicate significant differences, the statistical awareness and level of numeracy amongst educational managers will need to be high. These functions, although of importance to managers, are still at the reporting and operational level. However, the move from management information systems to executive information systems signals a change of focus from the data to the processes of leadership and management. Consequently, in the future, sitting above any integrated database will be a decision support system for leaders and managers, a system that will assist them in making decisions and a system that can automatically take decisions.

The actual decision-making process in an organisation will be dependent on a number of factors including culture, organisational structure and the particular function under consideration. However, all such processes commence with a source that generates data, leading to prediction and inference, which when set against the values, vision and strategy of the organisation results in a choice leading to action. At one level, an integrated database is a *decision support system*; it can generate data to inform the individual(s) who will make the inference and hence the decision. The data that is collected to inform such decision-making is dependent on the constructs of the decision-makers, who may well decide that some information is irrelevant whilst some other is absolutely crucial. Other decision-makers may choose different constructs. The point at which the information system stops and the decision-making begins is on a continuum that ranges from decisions being made with no background data to decisions being automatically taken by the computer. Along from the use of databases to inform decision-makers is the *predictive decision-making process*. Here the decision-maker models the data through, for example, a spreadsheet or a specific modelling program. Curriculum and financial planning are examples where the decision-maker can test 'what if' type questions and radical alternatives can be tested. The user can change the variables in the model in order to find the preferred decision. Further along the continuum is a situation where the IT system actually *makes decisions based on criteria established by the manager*. For example, in an Open Integrated Learning System, the computer program(me) may recommend the next phase in the programme of study, having made such a decision based on the input of results, knowledge of what program(me)s are available and the criteria to be used in making a selection. In this case the user still has to confirm the decision or make alternatives. Such software already exists in, for example, recommending who is to cover a particular teacher's lesson when absent. At the far end of the continuum is where the computer system actually *takes the decision without any reference to the user* and sets the system in motion. Such systems will need to operate a very sophisticated feed forward system and represent what are known as 'knowledge-based' or 'expert' systems. Sitting on top of the decision support system will be a language system that will enable easy communication between managers and the computer system through the use of 'a natural language' so that managers will be able to type in questions such as: 'Tell me who is teaching George Smith tomorrow' and the computer will produce the list of names.

THE CHALLENGE FOR EDUCATIONAL LEADERS AND MANAGERS

There are many specific management strategies and approaches that educational leaders and managers can take in order to move to Level Five of the capability model and to place themselves in a position to exploit the new communication and information technologies as they become available. Whilst new technology will challenge the status quo, it remains a tool to be used to achieve the vision and goals of the institution. The challenge which senior managers have is to establish the values which underpin the operation of the new learning centres and hence their form of organisation and operation. Once the vision exists and strategies are developed to reach such a vision, then leaders and managers are in a position to identify and communicate the decision-making processes within the organisation, the flow of information and the communications structure. In such a systems approach, individuals, teachers and the institution as a whole will know their key areas of responsibility, they will negotiate targets and know for what they are accountable. They will know what decisions they have to make and to whom such decisions are to be reported. Consequently, they will know what data they need and will be able to complete a data audit using questions generated from Table 15.1. This is a very different systems approach to the normal design of management information systems, which ask what data can be captured, stored, organised and retrieved rather than what information is needed. Such an approach focuses on the people in the system and their interaction. If users are involved in the analysis, design and implementation of information systems which are relevant to their own work then, although the result may be less technically efficient, it is more manageable because users are committed to the system when it is operational, thus leading to greater effectiveness.

The establishment of targets leads to a range of questions such as: how are these to be monitored and by whom? what data is required? where will it come from? Internal processes, where conformity is needed, will also need to be made explicit and probably documented. Many of these processes will identify standards which need to be adhered to; once more, non-conformity will need to be measured and put into the feedback loop to be communicated to those who can effect change. Communicating information effectively and efficiently will remain a major issue over the next few years for both internal and external communications. The successful communication of information is crucial but not always straightforward; communication occurs both formally and informally. A communications audit, similar in scope to the decision-making audit, should help to determine the answers to a number of important questions built around Table 15.1, such as: what is being communicated? why is it being communicated? when and how frequently is it being communicated? to whom is it being communicated? how much information is being communicated and how much should be communicated? how important is the information? what does the recipient do with it once the information has arrived? From such an audit it should be possible to develop an information communications strategy which identifies the customers, the required information, the IT opportunities and the appropriate medium for communicating the information in question.

Once an organisation is clear about how it wishes to manage information and communications then it is in a position to identify the data and decision support systems that can be supplied through an IT solution. An audit of current methods for storing, retrieving and processing data and whether such data is fully exploited through an integrated system will provide a measure of the gap that has to be closed. Many leaders and managers are genuinely surprised at the range of data that can be stored on a management information system specifically designed for education and at the amount of information currently available to them. The problem is that systems managers do not know what information is needed by leaders and other managers whilst these others do not know what information is available. Dedicated educational systems can hold related data concerning background information on students, staff, curriculum plans, assessments, organisation, timetable and financial details, development plans, schedules, diaries, examinations, attendance, individualised learning plans, student profiles, Special Educational Needs data and library management. In addition, those working at a strategic level will be concerned with 'soft' data, that concerned with opinion and attitude. Knowing what the various stakeholders feel is important and measuring perceptions as to how well the institution is meeting its more intangible objectives are important pieces of information to the educational leaders and policy makers.

But to know how to exploit the technology will require some technological competence on the part of educational leaders and managers. At present most pupils leaving primary school are likely to have had more experience of using a computer than many headteachers. Keeping informed of new technological developments at a strategic level will be one of the key tasks of future leaders and managers. World class learning centres in the future will not just happen; someone has to have a vision of what is possible. What is clear is that the power of information technology will not be an inhibiting factor; it will be our ability to be creative and to create a new vision of what is possible. The problem will not be the technology but our ambition.

> It is important to reflect on the concepts that are central to this chapter and the competencies necessary to utilise them. To enable you to do this and to form an action plan, we suggest that it would be of assistance to make an enlarged photocopy of the three pages in Appendix A.

REFERENCES

Beer, M. (1966) *Decision and Control*, New York: Wiley.

International Computers Ltd (1992) *A Window on the Future*, London: ICL.

Lucey, T. (1991) *Management Information Systems*, London: DP Publications.

National Council for Educational Technology (1995) *Open Integrated Learning Systems*, London: NCET.

Paulk, M. C. (1993) *Capability Maturity Model for Software Version 1.1*, Pittsburgh: Carnegie Mellon University.

SIMS (1996) http//www.SIMS.co.uk

Wheatley, M.J. (1992) *Leadership and the New Science*, San Francisco: Berrett-Koehler.

Part III

Envisaging the future

16 Global trends and expectations for the further reform of schools

Brian J. Caldwell

The first part of the chapter utilises the concept of megatrends (see Naisbitt 1982; Naisbitt and Aburdene 1990; Aburdene and Naisbitt 1992; Naisbitt 1995). It extends and updates the work on megatrends in school education by Caldwell and Spinks (1992). The second part sets out expectations for the further reform of schools, with each a manifestation of megatrends in a short to medium term view of a likely and preferred future for leadership and management in schools. Essentially, it suggests that the future is already with us and can be discerned in an extrapolation of what is occurring now.

UPDATING MEGATRENDS IN SCHOOL EDUCATION

The scope of reform in school education around the world may be described in terms of megatrends. A megatrend is a major societal change which is consistent in direction, international in scope and enduring in effect. The concept was devised by John Naisbitt (Naisbitt 1982).

Some trends in school education have been under way in so many nations for such a length of time and with sufficient strength that they may be viewed as megatrends. In *Leading the Self-Managing School*, published ten years after Naisbitt in 1992, Caldwell and Spinks described ten megatrends on the basis of developments which were unfolding around the world. Writing in the future tense they proposed the following:

1 There will be a powerful but sharply focused role for central authorities, especially in respect to formulating goals, setting priorities, and building frameworks for accountability.

2 National and global considerations will become increasingly important, especially in respect to curriculum and an education system that is responsive to national needs within a global economy.

3 Within centrally determined frameworks, government (public) schools will become largely self-managing, and distinctions between government and non-government (private) schools will narrow.

4 There will be unparalleled concern for the provision of a quality education for each individual.

5 There will be a dispersion of the educative function, with telecommunications and computer technology ensuring that much learning that currently occurs in schools or in institutions of higher education will occur at home and in the workplace.

6 The basics of education will be expanded to include problem-solving, creativity and a capacity for life-long learning and re-learning.

7 There will be an expanded role for the arts and spirituality, defined broadly in each instance; there will be a high level of 'connectedness' in the curriculum.

8 Women will claim their place among the ranks of leaders in education, including those at the most senior levels.

9 The parent and community role in education will be claimed or reclaimed.

10 There will be unparalleled concern for service by those who are required or have the opportunity to support the work of schools.

(Caldwell and Spinks 1992: 7–8)

In most instances, momentum continues to build. Local management of schools with programmes shaped by centrally-determined curriculum and standards frameworks, is now common. National, state or system-wide tests, often with public release of results to enable school-by-school comparisons, are increasingly evident. Centralised structures, while arguably more powerful, are none the less leaner after down sizing, being now more a strategic core to steer the system, with curriculum and student services retained so long as service is valued, efficient and effective. The use of state-of-the-art information technology, while predicted, is still breathtaking. It is now almost a cliché to expect schools to encourage life-long learning, for individual satisfaction through productive work, albeit from job-to-job rather than through stable life-time employment. Increasingly, there is acceptance that all students must achieve a standard in literacy; the consequences of failure – for the individual, for later years of schooling and for society as a whole – are too costly.

These megatrends should now be updated. While progress has been made in some settings, the rate at which women are assuming leadership may be too slow at this point to warrant classification as a megatrend. The case for women in leadership is, of course, as strong as ever. In addition to merit and equity, there is a convincing argument that the leadership style of women tends to be more suited to the kind of organisation that is emerging at the end of the decade than that to which men have tended to be socialised. As Naisbitt and Aburdene have expressed it:

> The dominant principle of organisation has shifted, from management in order to control an enterprise to leadership in order to bring out the best in people and to respond quickly to change. This is not the 'leadership' individuals and groups so often call for when they want a father figure to take care of all their problems. It is a democratic yet demanding leadership that respects people and encourages self-management, autonomous teams, and entrepreneurial units.
>
> (Naisbitt and Aburdene 1990: 218)

Women may hold an advantage over men 'since they need not "unlearn" old authoritarian behaviour' (Naisbitt and Aburdene 1990: 217; see also the meta-analysis of research on male and female leadership reported by Eagly *et al.* 1992).

The megatrend of 'connectedness' in the curriculum is similarly not strongly evident, especially in respect to arts and spirituality. Evidence for greater connectedness could be claimed in curriculum reform, which in many nations has been comprehensively and often contentiously planned over the spectrum of primary (elementary) and secondary education, with a significant place for the arts in most instances. On the other hand, there is evidence of marginalisation of some subjects, especially the arts, as a consequence of cuts in funding. Development in the arts is then dependent on the capacity of parents to pay for private tuition. At the same time, paradoxically, the arts are thriving in many nations to the point where together they are now among the leaders in the economy.

On the basis of the foregoing, the list of ten may be pruned to a list of eight if one is to sustain the concept of megatrend. However, there is powerful evidence for a megatrend not listed, namely, the crisis in the funding of public education. In most western countries at least, it seems that public funds for public schooling are declining as a percentage of gross domestic product or as a percentage of total public expenditure. Certainly, it seems, there is a growing shortfall of public funds compared to public need, especially if megatrends on quality education for all, information technology, and lifelong learning are to be resourced. From a political perspective, this trend may be explained in terms of demography: in many parts of western nations, the majority of voters no longer have children in schools; a decade or two ago, the majority of voters had children in schools. A higher priority than before is now claimed for health care, law enforcement, and public transport:

people want to remain healthy, safe and mobile. Even then, it may be claimed, the funding of these public services falls short of need or demand. From a fiscal perspective, this broader trend may be explained in terms of endemic voter resistance to increases in taxation to support public services that are becoming ever more expensive for a range of reasons, not the least of which is the cost of technology that is needed to meet community expectations.

It is clear that the nature of schooling and the nature of the resourcing of schooling must change in the years ahead. To use the terminology of Hammer and Champy (1993), success in the reengineering of schools is likely to depend on success in the reengineering of public finance. Suffice to offer at this point an additional megatrend to the list presented by Caldwell and Spinks:

11   Public education will experience a crisis in funding that will only be resolved with further reform in school education and the restructuring of public finance.

EXPECTATIONS FOR THE SHORTER TERM

Expectations for the further reform of school education in the short to medium term will likely be shaped by critiques of what has occurred thus far and in the broader implementation of what is emerging as 'best practice'. Expressed another way, these expectations may be discerned in current practice. The time-frame is likely to be in the order of five to ten years, to the early years of the new millennium.

A review of recent critiques is a helpful starting point, because these make clear that further reform is warranted and will be dramatic in scope. In the United States, the concept of 'reinventing government' (based on Osborne and Gaebler 1993) has shaped recent efforts to restructure the public sector and it was only a matter of time before there was a call for 'reinventing education'. Gerstner and his colleagues (1994) have presented such an argument with rare force and focus:

Unlike businesses that are periodically forced to respond to new technologies, new demands from their markets, or the obsolescence of their products, no external forces have demanded that schools change. Schools have been able to ignore the revolutionary possibilities of technology, to keep the same hierarchical organisational structure, to preserve traditional rules governing the numbers of students in each class and type of school, and to stick with the traditional curriculum and teaching styles used throughout this century. The schools have not gotten worse, they have simply not changed for the better.

(Gerstner et al. 1994: 11)

In Britain, the effectiveness of recent major reforms has been questioned by David Hargreaves in his monograph *The Mosaic of Learning: Schools and Teachers for the New Century* (Hargreaves 1994). He considers that 'all these revolutions have largely failed' (1994: 2). In Australia, the case for refocusing the reform effort was presented by Dean Ashenden, in a report commissioned by the National Industry Education Forum (Ashenden 1994a,b).

> The present raft of reforms will make little or no headway on ... fundamental problems. National goals for schooling, the development of national curriculum profiles, decentralisation of the big school systems, softening of zoning for government schools and other measures address the right problems, but cannot overcome them.
>
> The greatest single weakness in these reforms is that they stop at the classroom door. The classroom is the student's workplace. It is, in essence, a nineteenth-century workplace – much more humane and interesting but recognisably the same place. It is an inefficient and inequitable producer of the old basics and simply incompatible with the new.

> (Ashenden 1994b: 13)

Taken together, these are formidable critiques. They support Drucker's view that 'no other institution faces challenges as radical as those that will transform the school' (Drucker 1993: 209). What has occurred to date may, in large part, be necessary, but not sufficient.

Eight expectations

1 *Expect the main features of recent structural reform to provide a framework for leadership and management*

Recent structural reforms that have seen local management within a centrally-determined framework of curriculum, standards and accountability are likely to be the norm in most nations where this book is read, with variations that reflect constitutional arrangements, historical traditions, cultural values, prevailing ideology and the rhetoric of the times. Continuity and stability within this framework is likely, allowing critical reforms in learning and teaching to take centre stage.

There have, of course, been powerful criticisms of this framework. From an international perspective, critics (see views summarised in Caldwell 1994; illustrated in Smyth 1993) have pointed to the naive faith shown in some nations in the market mechanism as an arbiter of quality in schooling, and the fact that curriculum and accountability frameworks have constrained decision-making at the school level. Researchers (see, for example, Fullan 1993; Malen *et al.* 1990) have pointed to the absence of evidence that local management has led *in direct cause-and-effect fashion* to improvement in learning outcomes for students. Others have pointed to the cuts in public funding for schools that have occurred in some places at the same time that local management has been implemented, noting that some schools have been 'winners' and others 'losers' in the resourcing of schools (see, for example, the views of principals reported in Bullock and Thomas 1994). In general, however, local management has been received well after experience in the new arrangements, despite opposition or scepticism at the outset and shortcomings in implementation along the way. Any reading of opinion in all the nations where significant change has occurred to date suggests that most schools would not wish to return to previous arrangements.

The situation in Britain is of great interest in this regard. The Labour Party initially opposed almost every feature of school reform by the Conservative Governments of Margaret Thatcher and John Major. Community acceptance of local management has been such that this aspect of reform will be continued, if not extended, by a Labour Government. With some changes to the funding advantage they enjoy, even grant-maintained schools should be secure.

As far as the centrally-determined framework in Britain is concerned, there is now broad acceptance of the national curriculum which, after a disastrous introduction, has now taken the form of a curriculum and standards framework. Even the system of tests and league tables of school-by-school comparisons seems secure, with a 'value added' component in the league tables a likely advance.

The point of the British analysis is that experience in the new structural arrangements has led to a high level of community acceptance that has been translated into political consensus on its major features. The issue in Britain, as in other nations, is the size of the school education budget in relation to need, and securing a quantum in the allocation of scarce resources when powerful claims are also being made by other departments and agencies in the public sector, at a time when the electorate is resistant to increases in taxation and a majority of voters no longer have children in school.

2   *While a period of consolidation in the main features of the framework is likely, expect further action on some unresolved matters*

Even though the structural arrangements are likely to achieve a measure of stability in the years ahead, there are important issues to be resolved, with resources and middle levels of governance or management at the fore.

One area where further work must be done is the allocation of resources to schools ('how the cake is cut'). One of the outcomes of local management has been the revelation, for the first time in most instances, of how resources have been allocated in the past. It is astonishing that it was only in the mid-1990s, more than one hundred years after the establishment of systems of public education, that such information has become available. The basis for funding primary and secondary schools has been questioned as a result, with the search under way for a closer match between stages of schooling and resources allocated to schools. Similarly for students with special education needs; matching resources to validly diagnosed need, with accountability for outcomes, is a high priority. Promising work is in progress, including 'activity led funding' in Britain (West *et al.* 1994) and matching resources to student learning need in the school global budget in Victoria, Australia (Education Committee 1995). Experience in Edmonton, Canada demonstrates that it is possible to develop an approach to cutting the cake that satisfies all interests. In each of these settings, the size of the cake remains an issue but the solution is a matter for the longer term; it is seemingly intractable in the short term.

Another issue is the manner in which schools will be supported. What central, regional and district arrangements are the most appropriate? This issue is not settled, with the role of the local education authority in Britain, the school district in Canada and the United States, and regional and district arrangements in Australia likely to undergo further change.

3   *Expect that advances in technology will energise the next stage of school reform*

The scale of the reform agenda is daunting if one appraises the readiness of schools to adopt new learning technologies; the views of critics are devastating. Gerstner *et al.* (1994) and Dixon (1994) start with the failure of schools to keep pace with change:

> Despite the invention of a staggering array of new information tools that store and communicate knowledge, and that entertain, challenge and extend the power of their users, schools transmit information as they have since Gutenberg. ... There is, to be sure, in some schools the promise of higher technology; a faint sense that things can and should be different. But this is the exception rather than the norm.
>
> (Gerstner *et al.* 1994: 12)

> Worldwide, school is a pufferbelly locomotive chugging incongruously through a high-tech landscape.
>
> (Dixon 1994: 362)

Seymour Papert, inventor of Logo, comments on the manner in which we have thus far limited the power of the computer in the classroom:

When there were few computers in the school, the administrator was content to leave them in the classrooms of teachers who showed greatest enthusiasm ... But as the number grew ... it made more sense to put the computers together in one room – misleadingly named 'computer lab' – under the control of a specialised computer teacher. Now all the children could come together and study computers for an hour a week. By an inexorable logic the next step was to introduce a curriculum for the computer ... Instead of cutting across and so challenging the very idea of subject boundaries, the computer now defined a new subject; instead of changing the emphasis from impersonal curriculum to excited live exploration by students, the computer was now used to reinforce the School's ways.

(Papert 1993: 39)

Some schools are now embracing the new technologies in the manner envisaged by Papert. The school as a workplace for teachers and students is indeed being re-invented. Advanced interactive multi-media learning programs are now being used or trialled in many school systems. Thousands of schools around the world have access to the Internet and are communicating daily with schools in scores of nations.

4   Expect that schools will be challenged to adopt a new organisational image

Hargreaves (1994: 54) called for schools to be better equipped with the new interactive technologies in his vision of schools for the twenty-first century but argued that schools as currently constructed are obsolete:

Schools must be constructed on the basis of a new institutional model before the technologies will be admitted and allowed to develop to their full potential. Factories are disappearing; modern businesses look very unlike the nineteenth-century heavy-industry factory ... We are glad to see the end of the traditional factory; why should we expect the school modelled on it to be welcome to children?

(Hargreaves 1994: 43–44)

More fundamentally, however, Hargreaves proposes a shift in the image of school, from the factory to the hospital. From the nineteenth century, we constructed our schools to resemble factories of that era, with students progressing from grade to grade, from room to room, as in a production line. Principles of school management were based on those in industry. Our schools have changed little: classrooms for students, teachers with limited administrative support, a small number of para-professionals and, with few exceptions, only modest advances in technology. Compare this with the modern hospital, with its astonishing array of technology, individual rooms, elective surgery, and complex professional and para-professional staffing structure.

The opening lines of Seymour Papert's *The Children's Machine* invite the same shift in thinking. He asks the reader to imagine time travellers from an earlier century, including a group of surgeons and a group of teachers, eager to see what changes have occurred in their professions over the last century. For the visitors to the hospital,

> they would in almost all cases be unable to figure out what the surgeon was trying to accomplish or what was the purpose of the many strange devices . . . the surgical staff were employing.

for the visitors to the school,

> they would fully see the point of most of what was being attempted and could quite easily take over the class.

Papert concludes that:

> In the wake of the startling growth of science and technology in our recent past, some areas of human activity have undergone megachange . . . School is a notable example of an area that has not.
> (Papert 1993: 1–2)

Not all will warm to Hargreaves' image of the school as hospital. It may be better than school as factory but it is not right. Some, such as Sam Stringfield of Johns Hopkins University, have called for schools to be high-reliability or 'no defects' organisations, much like the airline industry, where failures are taken very seriously. The crash of a plane results in protracted and expensive inquiries; we are only now starting to take seriously the 'crash' of a school.

Clearly, of course, we need a new image of school as school, but it is crucial that we reject the factory image and, even playfully, try others.

5   *Expect the need to accommodate a different view of teaching as 'the job'*

If we were to 'start again' with our design of schools as buildings and as places of work for students and teachers, they would look very different to those today. Gerstner *et al.*'s (1994) concept of 'reinventing education' or a derivative of Hammer and Champy's (1993) concept of 'reengineering' may well apply.

Further change energised by advances in technology, a new organisational image, and facilities that are more welcoming to students and teachers will be major elements in a reengineered school. Another element is likely to be the 'job' of teaching. Hargreaves calls for changes in schools for the twenty-first century which should:

- Have a core of full-time, highly trained professional teachers, on five-year renewable contracts, supported by a range of assistant teachers and part-time teachers who also work in other fields.

- Contract out substantial parts of their teaching functions, so that secondary pupils spend less of their time in school.
- Be permeable to their community, to business and the world of working adults, so that the boundaries between school and the outside world weaken.

(Hargreaves 1994: 53–4)

More fundamental is the manner in which all work and the concept of a 'job' is changing. These changes are described by William Bridges in *Jobshift* (Bridges 1995). He argues that *'the job* is not going to be part of tomorrow's economic reality' (Bridges 1995: x). He is referring here to the concept of a person working full-time and long-term for a particular organisation. Arguing from a view that 'the job is a social artefact', he contends that:

> The job concept emerged in the eighteenth and nineteenth centuries to package the work that needed doing in the growing factories and bureaucracies of the industrialising nations. Before people had jobs, they worked just as hard but on shifting clusters of tasks, in a variety of locations, on a schedule set by the sun, the weather and the needs of the day. The modern job was a startling new idea ... Now the world of work is changing again. The very conditions (mass production and the large organisation) that created jobs two hundred years ago are disappearing.

(Bridges 1995: viii–ix)

Bridges writes almost exclusively about jobs in business, but the very forces he identifies as shaping change in that field are impacting education, and the chief among these is technology. The kinds of changes he describes for business, which are advocated to some extent by Hargreaves for schools, are already evident in education. Why should we expect that education will or should be buffered against such change, particularly when it may be the means by which a range of specialist professional and para-professional support can enhance the processes of learning and teaching?

Bridges suggests that yesterday's organisation located every person vertically in a hierarchy and horizontally in a functional unit, with a formal job description and a career path up the hierarchy with corresponding increases in power and reward (Bridges 1995: 50–1). He extends Charles Handy's view of tomorrow's organisation as a three-leaf shamrock. For Handy (1990: 169), one leaf is the core of professional, technical and managerial staff; another is made up of external contractors who provide specialist support; the third consists of 'contingent' workers, who are temporary or part-time people who come and go as needed. Bridges suggests that the leaves are more permeable or transient than presented by Handy (Bridges 1995: 156–8).

These developments are, of course, already evident in education, but we have tended to view them as dysfunctional and an aberration rather than extensive, fundamental and inevitable change in the sense described by Bridges. None the less, many professionals in education are already accommodating this new (old) concept of 'job' and are finding themselves a rewarding and satisfying niche in a re-shaped profession.

6 *Expect that new reward schemes will be required for those who work in schools*

An immediate implication is the need to re-structure the traditional reward scheme for those who work in schools. Certainly, a scheme that reflects the hierarchical organisational model must be changed to reflect flatter structures and weaker bureaucracies. The pay of a full-time 'continuing' professional core may be mostly salary, but a component may be based on performance. Fee-for-service arrangements are likely to suit some specialist personnel who work across sites. For the longer term, Bridges suggests that:

> Whether by means of pay for skills, fee for service, share of the earnings, or some still-to-be-discovered form of compensation, the organisation of the future is going to find that salaries are as counterproductive as jobs. It is a truism that you get what you pay for, and with organisations needing to get new levels of effort and new degrees of flexibility from their workers, new kinds of compensation are going to be common place.

> (Bridges 1995: 166)

Another view of the importance of rewards may be derived from Lawler's prescription for high performance in decentralised organisations (Lawler 1986, 1992). He proposes four dimensions: structures and powers, knowledge and skill, information, and rewards. It is apparent that matters related to structures and powers have already been addressed but the others are not well-developed. Essentially, Lawler challenges us to devise a system of rewards that is consistent with the new structures and focuses on performance. Expressed another way, governments have been pre-occupied with changes in structure and power, but high performance in the self-managing school will not be achieved without new systems of rewards for those who work in schools, in addition to new levels of knowledge and skill.

Career structures that reflect levels of professional competence should replace those based exclusively on positions in an organisational hierarchy. A focus on performance does not imply yesterday's discredited merit-pay schemes, but a form of 'gain-sharing' that rewards the contribution an employee makes to school success, whether that be for a particular school improvement project or sustained long-term gains in a single subject or across the curriculum. Moreover, such a scheme is more likely now than in the past to reward the efforts of a team, since our experience in education and in other fields points to the importance of the team in the achievement of high performance.

7   Expect a shift in the concept of self-management, from the institution to the individual

Implied in the foregoing is the re-capturing of the original concept of self-management, because it referred to the self-management of one's own work and development. However, Bridges proposed a shift in this concept:

> The old concept was 'taking care of yourself' while you followed the leader. The new self-management is 'acting toward the business at hand (learning and the support of learning in the case of the school) as if you had an ownership stake in it'.
>
> (Bridges 1995: 167)

This does not mean, however, that teachers will return to what many perceive as a golden age of autonomy, given the balance of centralisation and decentralisation that is evident in recent reforms. What will be the scope for the exercise of professional judgement by the self-managing teacher? It will have few limits if we take seriously the mission to provide the very best of learning opportunities for every student. Leading a team of professionals and para-professionals using state-of-the art technologies and knowledge about learning will call for a level of professional skill that can be compared with that of a skilled surgeon.

Research on recent reforms (see Bullock and Thomas 1994, and Levačić 1995 for Britain; Cooperative Research Project 1995 for Australia) reveals an increase in workload for those employed in schools. While this may diminish as implementation proceeds and the framework is stabilised, it is clear that new patterns of workplace practice and resourcing will be required. It is equally clear that solutions of the past that relied *exclusively* on more teachers and smaller classes are too narrow. The solutions of the future call for a rich range of professionals and para-professionals, new learning technologies, and school design that is welcoming to students and staff, all in a mix that will be uniquely determined at the school level.

There is a need for further research on these developments, but the point is that work in school and personal self-management, constrained by curriculum and standards frameworks as demanding as those that face the skilled professional in the medical field, provides almost unlimited scope for the exercise of professional judgement and the achievement of high standards of professional practice.

8   *Expect an expanded role for educational leaders at the school level*

The evidence is 'on the cards' that the role of educational leader will be larger and richer in the years ahead. This will mean more than knowing about the curriculum, modelling fine teaching, and 'running a tight ship' in problem-solving and trouble-shooting in the school's teaching programme. It will mean knowing about major developments in learning and teaching that yield measurable improvements in outcomes for students. Leaders in primary schools, for example, should be familiar with Robert Slavin's 'Success for All' programme in early literacy, be able to build a team that can plan a school-wide strategy in early literacy, and be able to guide the school council or governing body in setting priorities for the allocation of resources. Leaders in secondary schools, for example, should be familiar with reforms such as those described in the Carnegie Report *Turning Points* at the level of the middle school, where there have been improved outcomes for students with the adoption of high-performing teams of teachers creating educational communities for young adolescents. These initiatives, along with many others in the United States, are described in the Ninety-fourth Yearbook of the National Society for the Study of Education (Oakes and Quartz 1995).

Another indication that a proper concern with educational management must be balanced by a capacity for educational leadership is provided by writers with outstanding international reputations in the area of school finance, who make clear that a deep understanding of research and practice on learning and teaching is required for the effective and efficient allocation of resources at the school level (see Hanuschek *et al*. 1994; Odden 1995). In large measure, their books are devoted to descriptions of cutting edge practice and research findings on outcomes for students.

Synthesis

Expectations for school reform in the short to medium term may now be summarised. These define the milieu for school leadership and management to the early years of the twenty-first century. Structural arrangements that have been constructed in recent years will be stabilised, essentially local management within a centrally-determined formulation of curriculum, standards and accountabilities. Unresolved matters will be addressed, especially determining how resources should be allocated among schools and what should be the roles of middle levels of governance and management in school systems. The crisis of funding for public schooling may prove intractable in the shorter term. Throughout this period, critiques of shortcomings and instances of best practice in current arrangements will take hold, especially in the use of technology; the design of buildings; and the creation of a more flexible workforce, with a range of professionals and para-professionals to complement the teacher. Educational leadership will be enhanced, because the provision of a quality education for all will demand that leaders have state-of-the-art knowledge about what works and why. At the very least they must be able to lead high performing teams of professionals who will design and deliver programmes based on knowledge along these lines that will be acquired by others. New reward schemes and a capacity for life-long learning will be the *sine qua non* of the new professional in school education.

REFERENCES

Aburdene, P. and Naisbitt, J. (1992) *Megatrends for Women*, New York: Villard Books.

Ashenden, D. (1994a) *Australian Schooling: Two Futures*, paper commissioned by the National Industry Education Forum, Australia, October.

Ashenden, D. (1994b) 'Better schools begin with better classroom reform', *The Australian*, 19 October, p. 13.

Bridges, W. (1995) *Jobshift: How to Prosper in a Workplace Without Jobs*, London: Nicholas Brearley.

Bullock, A. and Thomas, H. (1994) *The Impact of Local Management on Schools: Final Report*, Birmingham: University of Birmingham.

Caldwell, B. J. (1994) 'School-based management', in T. Husen and N. Postlethwaite (eds) *International Encyclopedia of Education* 9: 5302–8, London: Pergamon.

Caldwell, B. J. and Spinks, J. M. (1992) *Leading the Self-Managing School*, London: Falmer.

Cooperative Research Project (1995) *Taking Stock*, Report of the Cooperative Research Project (Directorate of School Education, Victorian Association of State Secondary Principals, Victorian Primary Principals Association, the University of Melbourne; Fay Thomas, Chair) on 'Leading Victoria's Schools of the Future', Directorate of School Education.

Dixon, R. G. D. (1994) 'Future schools: how to get there from here', *Phi Delta Kappan* 75(5): 360–5.

Drucker, P. F. (1993) *Post-Capitalist Society*, New York: Harper Business.

Eagly, A. H., Karau, S. J. and Johnson, B. T. (1992) 'Gender and leadership style among school principals: a meta-analysis', *Educational Administration Quarterly* 28(1): 76-102.

Education Committee (1995) *The School Global Budget in Victoria: Matching Resources to Student Learning Needs*, Interim Report of the Education Committee (Brian Caldwell, Chair), Directorate of School Education.

Fullan, M. G. (1993) 'Coordinating school and district development in restructuring', in J. Murphy and P. Hallinger (eds) *Restructuring Schooling: Learning from Ongoing Efforts*, Newberry Park, CA: Corwin Press, pp. 143–64.

Gerstner, L. V., Semerad, R. D., Doyle, D. P. and Johnston, W. B. (1994) *Reinventing Education: America's Public Schools*, New York: Dutton.

Hammer, M. and Champy, J. (1993) *Reengineering the Corporation: A Manifesto for Business Revolution*, London: Nicholas Brearley.

Handy, C. (1990) *The Age of Unreason*, London: Arrow.

Hanuschek, E. A. *et al.* (1994) *Making Schools Work: Improving Performance and Controlling Costs*, Washington, DC: Brookings Institution.

Hargreaves, D. (1994) *The Mosaic of Learning: Schools and Teachers for the New Century*, London: Demos.

Lawler, E. E. (1986) *High Involvement Management*, San Francisco: Jossey-Bass.

Lawler, E. E. (1992) *The Ultimate Advantage*, San Francisco: Jossey-Bass.

Levačić, R. (1995) *Local Management of Schools: Analysis and Practice*, Buckingham: Open University Press.

Malen, B., Ogawa, R. and Kranz, J. (1990) 'What do we know about school-based management? A case study of the literature: a call for research', in W.H. Clune and J. F. White (eds) *Choice and Control in American Schools*, Philadelphia, PA: Falmer, pp. 289–342.

Naisbitt, J. (1982) *Megatrends*, London: Futura.

Naisbitt, J. (1995) *Megatrends: Asia*, London: Nicholas Brearley.

Naisbitt, J. and Aburdene, P. (1990) *Megatrends 2000*, London: Pan.

Oakes, J. and Quartz, K. H. (eds) (1995) *Creating New Educational Communities*, Ninety-Fourth Yearbook of the National Society for the Study of Education, Chicago: University of Chicago Press.

Odden, A. (1995) *Educational Leadership for America's Schools*, New York: McGraw-Hill, Inc.

Osborne, D. and Gaebler, T. (1993) *Reinventing Government*, London: Macmillan.

Papert, S. (1980) *Mindstorms: Children, Computers and Powerful Ideas*, New York: Basic Books.

Papert, S. (1993) *The Children's Machine: Rethinking School in the Age of the Computer*, New York: Basic Books.

Smyth, J. (ed.) (1993) *A Socially-Critical View of the Self-Managing School*, London: Falmer.

West, A., West, R. and Pennell, A. (1994) *A Better Cake: Towards a Rational Approach for Financing Education*, a report commissioned by the Secondary Heads Association, London: Centre for Educational Research, London School of Economics and Political Science.

17 Thinking in time
A gestalt for schools of the new millennium

Brian J. Caldwell

How is it that some leaders are enervated by the dramatic transformation that is occurring in school education around the world, and look forward to every day with a sense of adventure, while others are traumatised, surviving on nostalgia or the false hope that all will be well again if they wait it out?

This chapter is centred on the competency of 'thinking in time', adapting a concept coined by Richard E. Neustadt and Ernest R. May in *Thinking in Time: The Uses of History for Decision-Makers* (Neustadt and May 1986). The approach calls for decision makers to think in 'streams of time' by looking at the present as part of an unbroken continuum between past and future. In the adaptation presented in this chapter, the reader is invited to see the future as part of an unbroken continuum from past to present to future. A similar approach is encouraged by Richard Luecke in his book *Scuttle Your Ships Before Advancing: And Other Lessons from History on Leadership and Change for Today's Managers* (Luecke 1994).

The first part of this chapter draws from publications of prominent authors who describe broader societal trends and imperatives that have major implications for school education in the longer term. The second part returns to the concept of 'thinking in time', adapting to leadership and management in schools a more expansive version of the work of Neustadt and May (1986) and Luecke (1994).

SEMINAL READING FOR THE LONGER TERM

Just as expectations for the short- and medium-term may be discerned in current practice, so may the outlines of the longer term be sensed in broader societal movements that are now underway, and that will start or continue to have their impact in schools over the next decade. In this section some directions that may be considered seminal are reviewed. These are drawn from four books that appeared in mid-decade. These are illustrative rather than exhaustive but are sufficient for the purpose at hand. Those selected are Peter Drucker's (1995) *Managing in a Time of Great Change*, Bill Gates' (1995) *The Road Ahead*, Kenichi Ohmae's (1995) *The End of the Nation State* and John Naisbitt's (1995) *Megatrends: Asia*.

'A century of social transformations'

Peter Drucker was born in Vienna in 1909 and educated in Austria and England. He has worked in the United States since 1937, first as an economist and management consultant and then as a distinguished professor. He has been Clarke Professor of Social Science at Claremont Graduate School in California since 1971. His books now span more than fifty years (he has recently been publishing one book each year), and there are few who can match the length, breadth and depth of his understanding of leadership and management in the context of broad societal movements over the course of the twentieth century. He is a model of the capacity to be highlighted in the concluding section of this chapter.

In *Post-Capitalist Society* Drucker described the scale of societal transformation and the challenges that face the school:

Every few hundred years in Western history there occurs a sharp transformation ... Within a few short decades, society rearranges itself – its worldview; its basic values; its social and political structures; its arts, its key institutions. Fifty years later, there is a new world ... We are currently living through such a transformation.

(Drucker 1993: 1)

According to Drucker, knowledge as a resource lies at the heart of such transformations over the last three centuries. Until the Industrial Revolution knowledge had been seen as applying to *being*. It then became a resource for *doing*. Following the Industrial Revolution, until about World War Two, knowledge was applied to *improving the doing*. These transformations characterised a capitalist society in which the factors of production were capital and labour. Since World War Two, however, knowledge has been applied to *knowledge itself* so that 'knowledge is fast becoming the sole factor of production, sidelining both capital and labour' (Drucker 1993: 19–20). It is now a post-capitalist society. The implications for schools, writes Drucker, are profound:

As knowledge becomes the resource of post-capitalist society, the social position of the school as 'producer' and 'distributive channel' of knowledge, and its monopoly, are both bound to be challenged. And some of the competitors are bound to succeed ... Indeed, no other institution faces challenges as radical as those that will transform the school.

(Drucker 1993: 209)

Drucker expanded his view of the scale of transformation, and the impact on and implications for schools, in *Managing in a Time of Great Change* (Drucker 1995). This is recommended reading for all school leaders, especially Chapter 21 'A century of social transformations'.

The nature of work over more than a century is traced, from an era when agriculture and domestic service were the dominant fields, through the early twentieth century when the blue-collar or industrial worker gained ascendancy, to the late twentieth century and the rise of the knowledge worker, a term coined in the 1950s by Drucker to describe those whose work requires a great deal of formal education, a capacity to acquire and apply theoretical and analytical knowledge, a different approach and a different mindset and, above all, 'a habit of continuous learning'. The union was important for the industrial worker, since this was the era when the bosses owned the chief factors of production: labour and capital. Now, observes Drucker, for the first time since the Industrial Revolution, the largest single group of workers – the knowledge workers – will own the chief factor of production, knowledge itself. When the expanse of this change is appreciated, it is more than a social change: 'It is a change in the *human condition*' (Drucker 1995: 203).

Many of the seemingly intractable social problems are connected to the difficulties of transition and the condition of some groups in society. In the United States, for example, the plight of urban blacks has been accentuated because most remain in blue-collar, unionised, mass production work, which are now the jobs that are rapidly disappearing.

Drucker (1995) spells out the opportunities and the threats to school education in a more optimistic manner than was evident in *Post-Capitalist Society*. It is, indeed, a knowledge society that is emerging, but:

> Paradoxically, this may not necessarily mean that the school as we know it will become more important. For in the knowledge society clearly more and more knowledge, and especially advanced knowledge, will be acquired well past the age of formal schooling, and increasingly, perhaps, in and through educational processes that do not centre on the traditional school – for example, systematic continuing education offered at the place of employment. But at the same time, there is very little doubt that the performance of schools and the basic values of the schools will increasingly become of concern to society as a whole, rather than be considered 'professional' matters that can safely be left to the 'educator'.
>
> (Drucker 1995: 204–5)

Drucker contends that we will redefine what it means to be an 'educated person', who will likely be somebody 'who has learned how to learn and who throughout his or her lifetime continues learning, and especially learning in and through formal education' (Drucker 1995: 205).

He warns against sterile credentialism, an over-valuing of immediately usable knowledge, and an under-rating of fundamentals and wisdom itself. Drucker reinforces the view that knowledge workers work in teams and should have access to organisations, even if they are not employees of organisations. These organisations will be more like symphony orchestras than hierarchies of superiors and subordinates, and management will be an artistic endeavour:

> Management, in most business schools, is still taught as a bundle of techniques ... to be sure, management, like any other work, has its own tools and its own techniques ... [but the] ... essence of management is to make knowledge productive. Management, in other words, is a social function. And in its practice, management is truly a 'liberal art'.
>
> (Drucker 1995: 219)

Drucker highlights the importance of the social sector in the light of the high mobility of the knowledge society and the decline of the family and the church; people no longer have 'roots'. He has little confidence in the welfare state, with its huge welfare bureaucracy:

> in every developed country, society is becoming sicker rather than healthier, and social problems are multiplying. Government has a big role to play in social tasks – the role of policy maker, of standard setter, and, to a substantial extent, the role of paymaster. But as the agency to run social services, it has proven itself almost totally incompetent.
>
> (Drucker 1995: 221)

The solution does not lie with the employing organisation in the style of the modern Japanese corporation because, increasingly, knowledge workers will not have lifetime or even extended security with a single organisation. It is 'neither "the government" nor "the employing organisation". It is a separate and new *social sector*' (Drucker 1995: 223), with the task of the social sector being 'to create human health'. There are thus three sectors in the knowledge society: a public sector, a private sector and a social sector.

Drucker is unambivalent in his view that school and education lie at society's centre, but the context presents a challenge to the traditional view of schooling. Schools and education will increasingly involve partnership of the three sectors and, with new arrangements in this partnership, they are bound to remain political issues. It is no wonder, then, that three of Drucker's six priority tasks for society in the twenty-first century involve knowledge and education:

- We will have to think through *education* – its purpose, its value, its content. We will have to learn to define the *quality* of education and the *productivity* of education, to measure both and manage both (p. 236).

- We need systematic work on the *quality of knowledge* and the *productivity of knowledge* – neither even defined so far. On those two, the performance capacity, and perhaps even the survival of any organisation in the knowledge society, will increasingly come to depend (pp. 236–7).
- We need to develop an *economic theory* appropriate to the primacy of the world economy in which knowledge has become the key economic resource and the dominant – and perhaps even the only – source of comparative advantage (p. 237).

Matters related to the quality and productivity of knowledge have, of course, been part of the reform agenda and have been contentious in most settings, but Drucker's analysis is convincing, and the stakes are high. Further developments are certain. Many educators who have been sceptical if not critical of efforts to tie curriculum and the work of schools to the needs of an international economy will be encouraged by the third item in the list of tasks set out above. It may be that the failure to develop an economic theory that takes account of knowledge as the key economic resource has helped to form the chasm between critics in education and policy makers and decision makers in other settings. Critics on the other side would counter that many educators, despite claims to the contrary, still see schools in the factory image as they hanker for solutions to current problems that reflect a bygone era. Drucker offers a means of bridging the chasm, but it will be a long-term endeavour.

The road ahead

A knowledge society is made possible in large part by the revolution in information technology. Advances in technology that will energise the next stage of school reform was one item in the agenda for the short- and medium-term. The books of Seymour Papert in 1980 (*Mindstorms*) and in 1993 (*The Children's Machine*) have proved helpful in describing the impact of personal computers on learning, with the latter cited in Chapter 16. Bill Gates' *The Road Ahead* (Gates 1995) serves the same purpose, written by one in a powerful and influential position. Gates was co-founder in 1975 of Microsoft Corporation and is now Chairman and Chief Executive. While some would view Chapter 10 'Education: the best investment' as advancing self-interest, there can be no doubt that his strategic intent with respect to schools must be understood and respected.

Reading this chapter leaves no doubt about the contribution of information technology to learning. It is immensely reassuring to those concerned about the future of schools – Gates assigns a central role as does Drucker – and fears that teachers and others will be devalued or replaced are laid to rest – 'technology will be pivotal in the future role of teachers' (Gates 1995: 185).

Gates describes in convincing fashion a range of approaches that will be commonplace in the new millennium: all classrooms on Internet; most students with computers at home and at school; teachers selecting and adapting presentations of the best teachers and incorporating the best supporting material on a topic-by-topic basis to create outstanding learning experiences for their students; use of digital whiteboards for learning in a range of topics, achieving an authority and visual detail that have not been possible hitherto, including the arts; customised individual learning in some subjects beyond any that can be created by a teacher, for either the learner experiencing difficulty or the learner who seeks challenge; and advanced simulations for problem-solving and creativity.

Case studies of schools in disadvantaged areas are presented as 'best practice' today that can be widely modelled in all schools in the future. Gates acknowledges that more fundamental problems must be addressed before technology can be effective:

> All this information, however, is not going to solve the serious problems facing many public schools today: budget cuts, violence, drugs, high dropout rates, dangerous neighborhoods, teachers more concerned about survival than education. Offering new technology won't suffice. Society will also have to fix the fundamental problems.
>
> (Gates 1995: 197)

Gates provides examples of partnerships between public and private sectors in wiring schools for the Internet and meeting the operational costs associated with its use, citing in particular the involvement of Pacific Bell, TCI and Viacom in offering free cables and free service in the neighbourhoods they serve in the United States. Leveraged contracts for free service in schools as development for profit proceeds in the wider community would appear to be a promising contribution in any nation to solving the problem of resourcing schools for the information age.

While generally constructive and optimistic, Gates draws attention to the low base in some settings, along the same lines as earlier critiques (see Gerstner *et al*. 1994). He asserts that 'Preschoolers familiar with cellular telephones, pagers, and personal computers [still] enter kindergartens where chalkboards and overhead projectors represent state of the art' (Gates 1995: 186). However the vision prevails of liberated and empowered teachers and learners, the former freed from having to prepare 'in-depth interesting material for twenty-five students, six hours a day, 180 days a year' through their access to the best teaching and the best support media; the latter engaged in customised learning with instant access to the most up-to-date information, at home, at school, or in the work place.

Knowledge is 'transnational'

The revolution in information technology makes possible a feature of the knowledge society described so concisely by Drucker:

> Knowledge as the key resource is fundamentally different from any of the traditional key resources, that is, from land and labour, and even from capital. It is not tied to any country. It is transnational. It is portable. It can be created anywhere, fast and cheaply.
>
> (Drucker 1995: 227)

The concept of the global economy has been energised by this revolution as much as by any other factor. The work of Kenichi Ohmae in *The Borderless World* (Ohmae 1990) and *The End of the Nation State* (Ohmae 1995) is important in understanding the longer-term future of school education and expectations for its leadership and management in the twenty-first century. In his most recent work, Ohmae provides further evidence that the nation state in the future will be a social and cultural phenomenon, with governments steering activity in the public, private and social sectors in a manner which is consistent with societal and cultural expectations, but the significant decisions of commerce will transcend national boundaries.

Ohmae provides an illustration of 'the new melting pot' in education, choosing Keio University's experimental Fujisawa campus in Japan:

> Because [all students] are on-line, they can offer real-time reactions and contributions to the curriculum, to the structure of their own programs of study, to the content of their courses, and to the quality of their instructors. If they need information to supplement a text they are reading or a report they are writing, they can track it down through the Internet. If they want to consult an expert anywhere in the world, they can reach him or her the same way ... They have stopped being passive consumers of an educational experience defined, shaped, and evaluated by the Ministry of Education. The technology has allowed them, in a most non-Japanese fashion, to become definers and shapers and evaluators – and questioners – themselves.
>
> (Ohmae 1995: 36)

The implications for schools are profound, given the centrality of their role in the knowledge society. Schools must foster knowledge and understanding of a world that knows no boundaries in commerce, yet must be respectful of societal and cultural values in its conduct. More important, however, schools must foster learning that is as empowering as that at Keio University.

'The most momentous global development of the 1990s'

The citizens of many nations will, however, enjoy an advantage through awareness of the critical role played by schools. Both Drucker and Ohmae highlight the phenomenon which is the focus of John Naisbitt's *Megatrends: Asia* (Naisbitt 1995). Naisbitt describes eight megatrends centred on Asia: from nation states to networks, from export-led to consumer-driven, from western influence to the Asian way, from government-driven to market-driven, from villages to super cities, from labour intensive to high technology, from male dominance to the emergence of women, from west to east. The two central themes are:

> Fifty years from now, it will be clear that the most momentous global development of the 1990s and the early part of the twenty-first century was the modernisation of Asia ... Asia was once the centre of the world, and now the centre is again returning to Asia.
>
> (Naisbitt 1995: xii–xiii).

Apart from knowledge of the phenomenon, the implications for educational leadership and management lie in learning about Asia and the Asian way, and appreciating that nations in Asia are placing a very high priority on school education. Given Drucker's view that knowledge provides the basis for comparative advantage in an increasingly competitive world economy (Drucker 1995: 237), educational initiatives in Asia across all sectors are striking. So too is the role played by the private sector, as illustrated in South Korea, now an economic powerhouse. For example, Samsung, Hyundai, Kia Motors and Pohang Iron & Steel have all built their own high schools. Naisbitt observes that 'For Asia to prosper, the infrastructure must be developed even as educational needs are identified and filled. It isn't either/or. It's both' (Naisbitt 1995: 181). The dramatic increase in participation rates of women in education is a key factor in the emergence of women in all fields, including leadership and management, a trend that runs counter to western stereotypes. Clearly, there is no room for complacency in the west as far as school education is concerned.

A gestalt for the new millennium

If broader societal change is as indicated in this seminal reading, is it possible to describe the nature of schooling beyond the short to medium term? What will be the condition of school education in the new millennium? It is neither possible nor appropriate to attempt to predict with precision, although alternative visions may be offered, each with a scenario for getting from here to there. It is possible, however, to offer a gestalt – a perceived organised whole that is more than the sum of its parts (Concise Oxford Dictionary) – without the detail. The detail will be clearer as the years advance, as opportunities are sensed and seized, and new factors come in to play.

There is now such consistency in views about the scale of social transformation that claims that it is all a conspiracy of the so-called 'new right' appear vacuous. Planning for the future on the basis of such claims may lead to dysfunction in professional practice.

In the view of this writer, there should and will be a settlement of these issues, with the emergence of an economic theory that accommodates knowledge as the key economic resource, one of Drucker's priority tasks for the twenty-first century (Drucker 1995: 237), and a discourse on teacher professionalism that sits comfortably with the social transformations of which Drucker writes.

The shapes in the gestalt may be represented in the following:

- The expectations for further school reform in the short to medium term set out in Chapter 16 are likely to be realised.
- There will be tight linkages between the requirements of global and regional economies, and new strategic alliances between the corporate sector, school education and national, state, regional and local governments in respect to life-long learning.
- Aspects of these strategic alliances will see students at what is now the upper end of secondary school undertake much of their learning in the workplace.
- The emergence of a private service sector will accelerate the movement to schools of the integrated service or full-service model that brings together at a school site a range of resources in the fields of education, health and welfare to assist the staff of a school to meet the needs of all students, especially those with special education needs or with disabilities and impairments (see Dryfoos 1994 for an account of the model).
- The crisis in funding for school education will be addressed in large measure through the aforementioned strategic alliances, with a much expanded role for the corporate sector; the full-service school model, with integration of services from a range of departments, organisations, agencies and individuals, not just those employed by the school authority; and abandonment of the factory model of schooling to allow flexible personnel arrangements and state-of-the-art technology resourced in part by leveraged contributions from industry.

- Further advances in technology may dramatically alter the shape of the gestalt in ways that cannot be perceived at this time.

THINKING IN TIME

The key competency encouraged in this chapter may be described as 'thinking in time', adapting a concept coined by Neustadt and May (1986) in *Thinking in Time: The Uses of History for Decision-Makers*. Based on their successful courses at the Kennedy School of Government at Harvard University, Neustadt and May invite decision makers to think in 'streams of time' by looking at the present as part of an unbroken continuum between past and future. In this chapter, the reader is invited to see the future as part of an unbroken continuum from past to present to future.

To some extent the competency is a requirement for strategic leadership, defined in operational terms by Caldwell and Spinks (1992) as:

- Keeping abreast of trends and issues, threats and opportunities in the school environment and in society at large, nationally and internationally; discerning the 'megatrends' and anticipating their impact on education generally and on the school in particular.
- Sharing their knowledge with others in the school's community and encouraging other school leaders to do the same in their areas of interest.
- Establishing structures and processes which enable the school to set priorities and formulate strategies which take account of likely and/or preferred futures; being a key source of expertise as these occur.
- Ensuring that the attention of the school community is focused on matters of strategic importance.
- Monitoring the implementation of strategies as well as emerging strategic issues in the wider environment; facilitating an ongoing process of review.

(Caldwell and Spinks 1992: 92)

While these capacities are important for school leaders, they tend to deal with the present and future; they lack a historical perspective. Lessons from the past are often a useful guide in understanding the present and planning the future. In his intriguingly titled book *Scuttle Your Ships Before Advancing*, Richard Luecke (1994) recounts two episodes from history that illustrate the value of this approach.

The first occurred in August 1346 as England's King Edward III faced the superior forces of the French at Crécy. His front line consisted of yeoman archers who could deliver up to fifteen arrows per minute, hitting human targets at one hundred metres or formation targets at three hundred metres. On the other side, French knights on horse back were supported by Genoese mercenary crossbowmen who could fire two bolts per minute, each able to pierce heavy armour at great distance. The English were drawn in a circle around their supply carts; the French relied on the shock power of war horses at high speed.

The outcome was the loss of just 300 English. Up to 16,000 French perished under the barrage of English arrows 'that must have appeared like a dark swarm of hornets lofting into the sky, hanging there briefly before raining down with a thousand hissing voices' (Luecke 1994: 148).

Sixty-nine years later, in October 1415 at Agincourt, the same result was achieved by England's Henry V: some 6,000 French lives were lost to Henry's 150.

Luecke writes of these events under the title 'Revitalising enterprise through innovation', and concludes:

> In continuing the string of French disasters, Agincourt demonstrated the tenacity with which the nobility clung to the technologies and tactics that had accounted for past glories, even in the face of over-whelming evidence that their usefulness had long faded. Their stubborn resistance to change brings to mind the modern warning, 'When faced with a steam-rolling technology, you either become part of the technology or a part of the road.'
>
> (Luecke 1994: 153)

In a finer-grained analysis, Luecke suggests that the failure of the French to adopt massed archery was as much the resistance to a new culture as it was to new technology:

> Downgrading the central role of the knight in favour of peasant archers, and placing them at the front ranks as the English had done, would have altered social arrangements in feudal society, and the iron men of France would have none of it.
>
> (Luecke 1994: 150)

Is there a counterpart in the reform of school education in the modern era? The challenge at hand is to transform a system so that the rhetoric of a quality education for all is brought to realisation, and to achieve that outcome with scarce resources in arrangements that give more authority and responsibility to schools, directed and supported by a scaled-down bureaucracy that is energised by a powerful strategic core.

One is tempted to suggest that the traditional organisational arrange-ments are the counterparts of the French knights, with crossbowmen firing at regular intervals their deadly armour-piercing bolts ('a centralised system providing a standard and predictable service'), and that the innovative arrangements involve a new technology that has a rapid fire capacity to hit a host of fast-moving targets ('a decentralised

system with a capacity to respond to a multitude of student needs').
More appropriate, however, may be a modern counterpart to the French
reluctance to abandon a way of doing things that, tragically, proved
unsuccessful, with defeats that spanned more than half a century.

We have now had a decade or more of experience in some nations
of what is arguably the most sweeping change in school education since
the rise of the modern public school system. Despite evidence that the
old ways of doing things will no longer work or are no longer valued,
there are some who still cling to the hope of return to a 'golden age'
that was simple, stable, centralised and standardised.

While providing the inspiration for the use of the concept in this
chapter, Neustadt and May have a much narrower period in mind when
they call for 'thinking in time'. They propose that policy makers and
decision makers facing a particular issue should take account of its
history. They draw on accounts of events such as the Cuban missile
crisis in the 1960s and the hostage-taking in Iran in the 1970s to show
success and failure in utilisation and non-utilisation of the approach.
Rather than asking 'what's the problem?' one should ask 'what's the
story?' Timelines should be drawn and classic questions such as 'when',
'what', 'where', 'who', 'how' and 'why' should be posed to help to trace
and articulate the history of the issue. They give particular attention to
'placement', a technique that calls for analysis of the life experiences of
key actors to account for what actions they have taken in the past and
what actions they might take in the future. One might, for example,
apply the approach to account for the similarity of government policy
around the world in respect to the emergence of local management
within a centrally-determined framework. The rhetoric of reform and
the nuance in action may be explained and predicted in part by the life
experiences of the key actors, including ministers, union officials and
academics. This approach has value in the repertoire of school leaders
and managers, and is a useful analytical tool in training, but a more
expansive use of the concept is advocated here.

Combining all approaches is the competency of 'thinking in time' as
advocated here, including the deeper historical awareness illustrated by
Luecke, the more personal 'placement' advocated by Neustadt and May,
and trend analysis along the lines of Drucker, Gates, Ohmae and
Naisbitt. 'Thinking in time' should underpin the management techniques
of strategic planning and the formation of strategic intent. It should be
an overarching approach for leaders engaged in vision-building. In these
respects it may be considered a 'meta-competency' for school leaders
and managers in the twenty-first century. Being 'stranded in time' is a
condition that may result in an incapacity to cope or may impair what
might otherwise be a successful career as a leader and manager.

REFERENCES

Caldwell, B. J. and Spinks, J. M. (1992) *Leading the Self-Managing School*, London: Falmer.

Drucker, P. F. (1993) *Post-Capitalist Society*, New York: Harper Business.

Drucker, P. F. (1995) *Managing in a Time of Great Change*, Oxford: Butterworth-Heinemann.

Dryfoos, J. G. (1994) *Full-Service Schools: A Revolution in Health and Social Services for Children, Youth, and Families*, San Francisco: Jossey-Bass.

Gates, B. (1995) *The Road Ahead*, New York: Penguin.

Gerstner, L. V., Semerad, R. D., Doyle, D. P. and Johnston, W. B. (1994) *Reinventing Education: America's Public Schools*, New York: Dutton.

Luecke, R. A. (1994) *Scuttle Your Ships Before Advancing: And Other Lessons from History on Leadership and Change for Today's Managers*, New York: Oxford University Press.

Naisbitt, J. (1995), *Megatrends: Asia*, London: Nicholas Brearley.

Neustadt, R. E. and May, E. R. (1986) *Thinking in Time: The Uses of History for Decision-Makers*, New York: Free Press.

Ohmae, K. (1990) *The Borderless World: Power and Strategy in the Interlinked Economy*, London: Fontana.

Ohmae, K. (1995) *The End of the Nation State: The Rise of Regional Economies*, London: HarperCollins.

Papert, S. (1980) *Mindstorms: Children, Computers and Powerful Ideas*, New York: Basic Books.

Papert, S. (1993) *The Children's Machine: Rethinking School in the Age of the Computer*, New York: Basic Books.

Competency development profiles

Stage 1: Identify the concepts and competencies in the chapter

	CONCEPT AREAS					
COMPETENCIES						

***Stage 2*: Evaluate your personal knowledge and competencies and that of your colleagues**

1 What have I learned about my own skills, knowledge development and competencies in this area?

2 What have I learned about my colleagues' knowledge and competencies in this area?

Stage 3: Devise an action plan to facilitate appropriate development

From the matrix in Stage 1, list the **concept areas** in which you feel you need
to develop further/deeper understanding:

1. ....

2. ....

3. ....

4. ....

5. ....

From the matrix in Stage 1, list the **competencies** which you have identified
as needing further development:

1. ....

2. ....

3. ....

Outline the strategies you will employ to implement a programme of
development of the above concepts and competencies:

1. ....

2. ....

3. ....

4. ....

5. ....

Contributors

AUTHORS AND CO-EDITORS

Brent Davies Brent is Professor and Director of the International Educational Leadership and Management Centre at Lincoln University campus. Brent taught in the secondary school sector in London for ten years before moving into higher education. He is a member of the National Council of the British Educational Management and Administration Society and chair of their International Committee. His specialist interests are devolved school management, school finance and reengineering in education. He is a Visiting Professor at the University of Southern California (USC) where, as co-director with Professor Brian Caldwell (University of Melbourne) and Professor David Marsh (USC), he runs an annual International Principals' Institute. Brent has lectured and published widely, producing seven books, including titles on school development planning, marketing schools, and financial and resource management in schools, and over fifty articles and conference papers on many aspects of self-managing schools in Australia, the UK and the United States of America.

Linda Ellison Linda is a Principal Lecturer in Education Management at Leeds Metropolitan University. She has been teaching education management in higher education for ten years and currently leads a masters programme for educational leaders. She has written many books including *Education Management for the 1990s, Managing the Effective Primary School, Marketing the Secondary School*, and *School Development Planning*. She has a number of research projects in this area and has published widely in academic and professional journals. She has worked with school principals in a variety of countries including the UK, Hong Kong, Australia, New Zealand and the United States of America. Linda is an assessor with the National Educational Assessment Centre, a leading organisation in the UK for the assessment of competencies at middle and senior management level. She is a member of the National

Council of BEMAS (British Educational Management and Administration Society) and of its International Committee and is currently the National Honorary Secretary.

CONTRIBUTORS

Michael Billingham   Mike is currently a Fellow at Lincoln University campus and a core tutor on the International Educational Leadership and Management MBA. He has had thirteen years of headship experience, first in a large mixed comprehensive in Hertfordshire and then in an inner city boys' comprehensive school in central London. Prior to that he had taught extensively in secondary modern, grammar and comprehensive schools and a sixth form college. He has been Visiting Headmaster Fellow at St Catherine's College, Cambridge and was seconded to Hertfordshire County Council in 1989 to investigate the training implications of Local Management of Schools. He was a member of the Steering Committee of the Eastern Region Teacher Education Consortium from 1991 to 1994. His particular interest is in school effectiveness and improvement.

Brian J. Caldwell   Brian is Professor of Education and Head of the Department of Education Policy and Management at the University of Melbourne and is a Visiting Professor at Lincoln University campus. Brian has co-authored or co-edited ten books and about 100 chapters, articles, commentaries, monographs, research reports, occasional papers and learning resources. He is co-author of two books which have been best-sellers for their respective publishers: *The Self-Managing School* with Jim Spinks in 1988 (Falmer) and *Creating an Excellent School* with Hedley Beare and Ross Millikan in 1989 (Routledge). He has given about 250 invited addresses and refereed conference papers in all Australian states and twelve other nations, and has served as consultant on about 200 occasions, including over twenty international projects and consultancies. His international experience has included work in, Burma (Myanmar), Canada, Hong Kong, Kenya, Laos, Mauritius, New Zealand, Pakistan, Papua New Guinea, the UK and the United States of America, with assignments for OECD, UNESCO, World Bank and Asia Development Bank.

Peter Downes   Peter is Head of Hinchingbrooke School, Huntingdon, Cambridgeshire, a comprehensive school of nearly 1,900 pupils and one of the first schools in the country to pilot Local Financial Management (LFM) from 1982. In 1988 he was editor of one of the earliest books on local management, published by Blackwell. Before going to Hinchingbrooke, he had previously been Head of Henry Box School in

Witney, Oxfordshire and had taught foreign languages at Banbury School and Manchester Grammar School. At that time he had a national reputation as a French textbook writer and as an advocate for the reform of modern language teaching and testing. He has been greatly in demand as a speaker and writer on the financing of schools. In 1994/5 he was President of the Secondary Heads Association, during which time he also travelled extensively, lecturing on school financial management in the USA and in Australia.

Viv Garrett Viv is a Senior Lecturer in Education Management at Sheffield Hallam University. She entered the world of higher education in 1990 after working in the school sector for over twenty years. She made the choice between furthering her career into headship or taking a step into the unknown challenges of university teaching and research. It is a choice that she has never regretted, hence her interest in managing change! She currently co-ordinates Sheffield Hallam's award-bearing programmes in Education Management and, with her colleagues in the Centre for Education Management and Administration (CEMA), is involved in the design and delivery of management development programmes for schools and colleges. She is also interested in education overseas and has considerable international experience, having taught, researched and undertaken consultancies in Europe, Asia and the Far East.

Guilbert Hentschke Gib is Dean of the University of Southern California School of Education and a Professor of Educational Policy and Administration. His most recent research work focuses on education policy, school governance, higher education administration and management, urban teacher education reform and school performance of youth from low-income families. Gib teaches graduate courses in comparative international education policy, higher education financial management and California education policy. He currently serves on the boards of the National Center for Education and the Economy, Los Angeles Educational Alliance for Restructuring Now (LEARN), the Galaxy Institute for Education, WestEd (formerly Southwest Regional Laboratory or SWRL), Policy Analysis for California Education (PACE) and on the executive committee of the Los Angeles Annenberg Metropolitan Project (LAAMP). He is a Visiting Professor at Lincoln University campus.

Max Sawatzki Max is a senior educational management consultant specialising in organisational restructuring, organisation development, performance improvement and the use of technology in optimising organisational performance. Max was a teacher, principal, inspector, and senior bureaucrat with experience in a number of education systems within Australia and overseas. His most recent position was that of Deputy Secretary of the Australian Capital Territory Department of Education and Training. In 1991 he was made a Fellow of the Australian Council for Educational Administration, in recognition of his contribution to leadership and management in Australian education. Since 1993 Max has been heavily involved in leadership and management training for school leaders. He is a Visiting Fellow at Lincoln University campus and he is also a visiting lecturer at the University of Melbourne and the University of Southern California.

Alan Trotter   Alan has thirty years' experience in education: teaching in comprehensive and grammar schools; managing and teaching adult education in Sweden and Norway; training FE lecturers in the UK; managing staff development in the Polytechnic sector and directing in-service BEd courses. He has carried out management and education consultancy for the UN. For the last eight years he has been an independent consultant and an associate with the Coverdale organisation working on management development programmes in industry. In the last five years he has published *Better Self-Management* (Longman, 1993), has worked on Education Management MBA programmes and has helped staff at various schools to develop management skills and teams.

Tony Tuckwell   Tony graduated in Modern History and trained as a teacher at Oxford University. His teaching career started in Portsmouth in 1966 where he spent thirteen years, mostly at St John's College, Southsea as Head of Department and in senior management with curriculum responsibilities. He worked for five years as Deputy Head of Sale Boys Grammar School in Trafford where he observed all sides of educational management and politics as a union Branch Secretary. He was appointed Headmaster of King Edward VI Grammar School, Chelmsford in Essex in 1984 and led the school into Grant-Maintained status in 1992. Tony is an experienced assessor and centre director with the National Educational Assessment Centre and was one of the first students to gain an MBA (Education Management) which linked competency and content approaches to education management.

John Warwick   John is an Associate Director of SIMS Ltd, the United Kingdom's leading supplier of management information systems to the education services with over 21,000 users. John's particular responsibilities within SIMS encompass international sales and market analysis for new products and services. John taught in a number of secondary schools before moving to Bedfordshire as Inspector of Mathematics and Information Technology. He moved through the ranks of the service, and prior to joining SIMS, held the post of Assistant Chief Education Officer. His main area of interest is in the use of information technology as a management tool at all levels of the education system, particularly those aspects which involve the use of educational statistics and performance indicators. He has also worked with national governments, government agencies, local education authorities and schools throughout the United Kingdom and overseas.

John West-Burnham   John is Professor of Educational Leadership and Management at Lincoln University campus. He taught in secondary, further and adult education for fifteen years before moving into higher education. He has worked as an education officer responsible for management development and was director of the first distance learning MBA in Educational Management. He has published widely on topics relating to quality management in education and human resource management. John has provided training and consultancy to a wide range of schools and organisations in the UK, Australia and Africa. His research interests include managing quality in education, the relationship between management and learning and models of leadership.

Index